THE FRONTIER
IN THE FORMATIVE YEARS

THE
FRONTIER IN
THE FORMATIVE
YEARS
1783–1815

△

REGINALD HORSMAN
University of Wisconsin-Milwaukee

HISTORIES OF THE AMERICAN FRONTIER
Ray Allen Billington, General Editor
Howard R. Lamar, Coeditor

UNIVERSITY OF NEW MEXICO PRESS
Albuquerque

In memory of
John D. Barnhart

FOREWORD

No SINGLE PERIOD in the history of the American frontier more decisively influenced the course of the nation's westward expansion than that examined in this volume. Pioneers had been advancing steadily for almost a century and a half before the Revolution halted their progress, but they had moved only a few hundred miles from the Atlantic coast. In Pennsylvania, Virginia, and North Carolina a few venturesome pioneers had breached the Appalachian mountain barrier by 1783, to build their cabins along the rivers of eastern Tennessee and in the Blue Grass country of Kentucky, or to extend their trading routes into Ohio's wilderness. But the vast interior of the continent was still occupied only by Indian tribes and a few scattered French and Spanish villages, which were monuments to the decaying empires of those European powers. The heart of the nation was yet to be won.

The spectacular changes that led to the occupation of most of this vast hinterland during the next twenty years resulted from two allied forces. One was the pressure of population. For more than a century settlement had been confined to the coastal lowlands and Appalachian foothills, while soils lost fertility through repeated cropping and families multiplied more rapidly than opportunity. As the mountain barrier was conquered, Americans glimpsed a vision of the giant domain awaiting their conquest. The vast Mississippi Valley spelled opportunity unlimited for all; there fortunes could be amassed by the most humble, improved social status achieved by the most lowly. So they crowded through the mountain gaps in the next years, lured by the dream of self-betterment, to push the frontier westward at a pace unrivaled in the past.

As essential to the conquest of the interior as would-be settlers was the newborn paternalistic attitude of the national government. So long as a distant Parliament shaped the course of westward expansion, the pace would be slow; England's officials sought to curb the flow of farmers into the Mississippi Valley in the interest of fur traders, the Indians, and other European powers that shared the North American continent. No such restraints governed the statesmen and lawmakers who assumed control of the United States that emerged from the Revolution. They were in tune with the popular demand, the desire of settlers to surge westward, whatever the fate of Indians or alien peoples who stood in their path. This concept revolutionized governmental policy toward the West. Assured of popular support, wily diplomats capitalized on Europe's troubled situation to win concessions from England and Spain that opened much of the far Northwest and Southwest to pioneers. National officials first challenged, then crushed the Indians in such campaigns as that of Anthony Wayne at Fallen Timbers. Congress climaxed governmental generosity to the West by adopting the Ordinances of 1785 and 1787, which created the first workable land and governmental systems in the history of the frontier.

With European meddling removed, the Indians cowed, and pioneers assured that they would surrender neither their liberties nor their privileges by moving westward, a flood tide of population swept into the Mississippi Valley. Between the middle 1790s, when military and diplomatic triumphs assured safe passage to the newcomers, and the outbreak of the War of 1812, frontiersmen advanced westward in a steady stream, overrunning Kentucky and Tennessee, extending into the Southwest, peopling most of the Ohio country, and sending a thin line of settlements down the Ohio through Indiana and Illinois. By the time the outbreak of a new war with Britain temporarily slowed migration, the settled areas of the West filled a vast triangle, its base along the Appalachian Mountains, its apex at the junction of the Ohio and Mississippi rivers. Nor did the War of 1812 drive back the newcomers, for despite ignominious defeats at the hands of the British, American troops decisively crushed Indian resistance in both Northwest and Southwest, paving the way for a still more spectacular migration after the peace in 1815.

This is the story so ably told by Professor Reginald Horsman. British born, with his undergraduate degree from the University of Birmingham (England) and his graduate degree from Indiana University, Professor Horsman brings to the writing of this volume an unrivaled knowledge of the years preceding the War of 1812 as well as an unusual objectivity stemming from his international training. His many scholarly articles and his several books on the period—*The Causes of the War of 1812* (1962), *Matthew Elliott, British Indian Agent* (1964), *Expansion and American Indian Policy, 1783–1812* (1967), and *The War of 1812* (1969)—reveal a mastery of the diplomacy and governmental policy of the post-Revolutionary era that is unmatched. In this volume he has added a new dimension to his research. Immersing himself in the writings of the frontiersmen themselves and of the travelers who visited their settlements, he displays a familiarity with the day-by-day life of the settlers that is unique among students of the period.

The result is a revealing and original book. Professor Horsman has chosen to compress the better-known aspects of his story—the advance of the pioneers, the diplomatic and military events, the legislative record—into four compact chapters. The remainder of the book is a detailed analysis of the frontier social order in its formative stage, describing the emergence of local governmental systems, cultural progress, the structure of society, and the evolution of the economy. Professor Horsman has written, in other words, a penetrating case study of one of the most significant periods in the history of American westward expansion. His observations and conclusions can be applied to other eras, and serve as a guide to scholars who would seek to understand the nature of the frontier social order in its broadest sense.

The eighteen-volume series in which this book appears—the Holt, Rinehart and Winston *Histories of the American Frontier* series—is designed to provide both professional and general readers with authentic but readable accounts of all aspects of the history of American expansion. Each book in the series tells a complete story and may be read by itself; together they constitute the first collaborative multivolume history of the frontier to appear in print. The authors and editor hope that readers will become better versed in what Lord Bryce once called the most American part of American history, and hence better world neighbors in an era when we must understand ourselves if we are to understand the peoples of the nations with whom we are in daily contact.

The Huntington Library   Ray Allen Billington
October 1969

PREFACE

IN THIS BOOK I have attempted to depict the main features of the American frontier in the years from 1783 to 1815 while keeping within the general limits of the *Histories of the American Frontier* series. The difficulties of compression were many. Certain aspects of frontier history in these years—particularly expansion into western New York and the Old Northwest, and diplomatic entanglements in the Southwest—have received detailed treatment by historians, while others, notably the origins of the Northwest Ordinance, still need monographic treatment. Clearly, in this book the particular interests of many specialists have been slighted, or dealt with in very brief compass.

Although some analysis of international complications is essential to an understanding of these years, the particular emphasis of this book is on the actual settlers rather than the diplomatic entanglements produced by their advance. In the first four chapters I have surveyed the main areas over which the American pioneers were advancing, and then, with the exception of a final chapter on the War of 1812, have devoted the rest of the book to thematic chapters on particular aspects of frontier life and development.

An effort has been made in these pages to look not only at the outer edge of American settlement—the cutting edge of the frontier—but also at developments in those areas that had just passed out of this initial stage in the frontier advance. The farmers anxious to acquire permanent homes, who came in as the hunters and backwoodsmen moved on, are less well-known than the Daniel Boones, but they tamed the land and attempted to create a society patterned on that of the East.

A large proportion of the efforts of the American people in these crisis years from 1783 to 1815 was devoted to expansion over new lands. The basis was laid for advance across the whole continent. A framework of government was established for western territories; a system for the survey and sale of lands gave a degree of order to the westward movement; and the advance of population made it clear that adjacent nations would have to fight if they hoped to prevent the advance of the American people across the Mississippi Valley. The history of the westward advance is sometimes written as though it involved a domestic expansion of pioneers across an empty American continent. In reality, of course, most of the continent had still to be obtained from foreign powers in 1783, and the American continent was inhabited by a variety of Indian tribes. Although the leaders of the American government had qualms of conscience, the frontiersmen saw no inconsistency in expanding the area of freedom across the land of dead or dispossessed Indians.

It is common to stress the romantic elements of the frontier advance, but perhaps more noticeable in these years is the hardship and the tragedy: hardship for the countless pioneers and their families who painfully carved small clearings in the forest; tragedy for the Indian inhabitants of this rich land who were ruthlessly swept aside; and often tragedy for the pioneers themselves—a saga of women dying in childbirth far from doctors, of families on the lower Mississippi decimated by yellow fever, or of pioneers lying dead and mutilated in a burning cabin along the Cumberland. The foundations of an American nation stretching to the Pacific were laid in these years, but these foundations rested not so much on a Thomas Jefferson or a young John Quincy Adams dreaming of the settlement of a continent, as on the nameless farmers and their families who from Maine to Georgia struggled with the great American forest.

I would like to thank Ray Allen Billington for his suggestions and criticisms; he has been a conscientious and affable general editor.

Milwaukee, Wisconsin   Reginald Horsman
October 1969

CONTENTS

MAPS

Expansion and Diplomacy in the Southwest, 1783–1796

*I*n the spring of 1783 American messengers carried to the Indians of the trans-Appalachian West the news that a preliminary treaty of peace had been signed between the United States and Great Britain. To many frontiersmen the Revolution was more than a war for independence from England, it was also a struggle for survival against a British-Indian alliance. For the Indians the Revolution was merely one episode in their continual effort to save their villages, fields, and hunting grounds from the land-hungry pioneers. They took advantage of British aid to bring devastation and death to American frontier settlers, but they had been unable to sweep away the infant trans-Appalachian settlements. Even during the war pioneers were ready to look for new lands and new homes, and while armies battled in the East settlers were trudging west on the Wilderness Road to Kentucky.

The Treaty of Paris in September 1783 gave to the United States territory far beyond its actual settlements. On the north the new country was separated from the British North American colonies by a vague boundary that stretched from Maine through the Great Lakes to the Mississippi; beyond the Mississippi the land was owned by Spain. On the south a disputed line ran from the St. Marys River in Georgia to the Mississippi. The United States argued that this line should be the 31st parallel, but Spain claimed land far to the north of that boundary. Whatever the actual border, Spain had possession of a strip of territory westward from the Florida peninsula along the Gulf of Mexico to the Mississippi River; the new settlers of the trans-Appalachian West would have to ship their produce to market through Spanish territory. In both the Northwest and the Southwest Indian tribes resisting the American advance were in an excellent position to receive help from powers that desired to block American expansion. The pioneers soon discovered that the peace treaty did not suddenly transform conditions on the edges of American settlement.

Although American sovereignty extended to the Mississippi, much of the land was still in the possession of the Indians. Numerous tribes hunted and planted throughout the region and saw no reason why they should give up their homes to American farmers. The settlers thought of the Indians as mere savages engaged constantly in hunting or warfare, although in many ways their villages and agriculture were more elaborate than those of the first wave of frontiersmen who supplanted them. The Indians were to prove a grave embarrassment to the American government in these early years. Their resistance taxed American resources to the utmost, and even after military victory the government was loath to accept the inevitability of Indian disappearance in the face of advancing American farmers. The American government in its Indian relations maintained a strange combination of battles, bribery, and stricken conscience. The pioneers were less confused. They wanted the land and assumed that the Indians, like the game, would have to go.

In 1783 salients in Kentucky and Tennessee were the only major American settlements in the vast area beyond the Appalachians. Far to the north, posts at Detroit and Michilimackinac were still occupied by the British, and in the Illinois country Vincennes, Kaskaskia, and Cahokia were still French in character. Even to the east of the Appalachian barrier there were large areas of unoccupied land. Northern New England, northern and western New York, northern Pennsylvania, and much of Georgia awaited the settler.

In the years between the Revolution and the War of 1812 the people of the United States flooded into large areas of these rich unoccupied lands. The American population, which was still under 3,000,000 in 1780, had increased to over 8,000,000 by 1815; this growth provided a steady stream of landseekers.[1] For younger sons of farmers who wanted lands of their own, for those dissatisfied with the social or political system, or for those merely hoping for prosperity, the West presented an irresistible lure. Some went to speculate in lands, search out likely town sites, or become merchants, but most went to carve farms out of the wilderness by their own efforts. The West was their Beulah land; the way to it was beset with dangers, but they expected to find there a land of plenty.

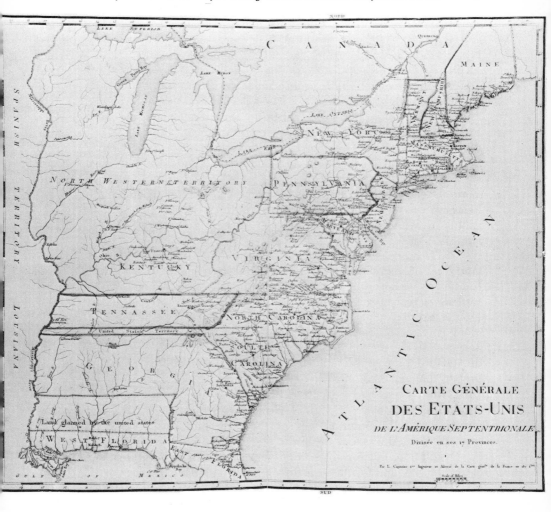

Map of the United States, by L. Capitaine, *ca.* 1796. (Courtesy of Kenneth M. Newman, The Old Print Shop, New York)

Of first interest to emigrants in the years immediately after 1783 were the outposts of settlement in what are now Kentucky and Tennessee; here a beginning had already been made. Pioneers from all over America journeyed to these areas in the 1780s and 1790s, but by far the greatest number came from the adjacent states of Virginia, Maryland, and North Carolina. In these South Atlantic states population pressure was increased by soil exhaustion in the oft-planted tobacco lands, and the plight of the small farmer was complicated by slavery. Some moved west thinking they would escape slave competition; others hoped they could recreate the system they had left and improve their own position in society. Expansion westward offered better lands, new opportunities, and the hope of a rise in status. It is not surprising that the population of some of the eastern counties of Maryland and Virginia declined in the years after 1790.[2]

Part of this southern exodus was deflected into the undeveloped western regions of Virginia, particularly into the area that is now the state of West Virginia. Especially attractive to the emigrants were the valleys of the Ohio, the Great and Little Kanawha, and the Big Sandy rivers. Settlers moved into these regions in the 1780s, in spite of Indian attacks, but expansion was slow until the late 1790s. Although a town had been laid out at the mouth of the Great Kanawha in the years immediately after the Revolution, Point Pleasant was still only "a small and indifferent village" of some twenty cabins in 1796, and in the same year Wheeling had no more than fifteen homes, all of wood.[3]

A far more powerful attraction to the emigrants of Virginia and Maryland, and of many another state on the eastern seaboard, was the region of Kentucky, which still in 1783 lay within the jurisdiction of Virginia. Its settlement had begun on the eve of the Revolution, and in the decade after 1783 it exerted a particular fascination on the American frontiersmen. To many it was that "new and beautiful country of *'canes and turkeys.'* " [4] The first section developed was the limestone region of Kentucky bluegrass in the central part of the state. This was a fertile rolling country, and the timber that covered most of it was broken by large tracts of open land. Often these tracts had cane 10 to 12 feet high, and there were also meadows rich with buffalo grass and clover.[5] The first settlers in Kentucky had plunged into this interior part of the state and had severed themselves from the settled areas of the East. They had suffered from Indian attack in the Revolution, but for all the difficulties and dangers the area had the lure of a promised land for the post-Revolutionary pioneers.

The main artery of travel to Kentucky in the years after 1783 was the Wilderness Road, following a trail blazed by Daniel Boone in 1775. This famous western route began north of Long Island on the Holston River, ran through Powell Valley to the Cumberland Gap and then across Kentucky to the bluegrass country. It offered a long arduous journey, and until the end of the eighteenth century it was suitable only for travel on foot or on horseback. Large parties gathered in eastern Tennessee and trekked together over the mountains. Some even came in winter. Women and children trudged through "ice and Snow passing large rivers and Creeks with out Shoe or Stocking, and barely as many raggs as covers their Nakedness, with out money or provisions except what the Wilderness affords." [6]

In many ways a more leisurely way of traveling to Kentucky was by boat down the Ohio River, but travelers were sometimes reluctant to use this route because of the danger of Indian attack. Settlers were vulnerable when they tied their boats up for the night, and even in the day the Indians used all possible tricks to lure them to shore; frequently the Indians resorted to the ruse of having a supposed escaped Indian captive shout and wave for help from a nearby bank. To lessen the danger, pioneers traveled in armed parties or made use of special passenger boats strengthened to protect them against attack. One such boat in 1790 was armored with 150 salt pans.[7]

The most popular time for emigrants to embark on the upper part of the Ohio was either in early spring or late fall. In both cases this gave the advantage of high water, in spring from the melting of the ice and in fall from the October rains. Another advantage of using the river in the fall was that the land journey to reach the Ohio could be undertaken on dry summer roads. The most convenient embarkation point for many southern pioneers was Brownsville (Redstone), some thirty miles south of Pittsburgh on the Monongahela. In low water, however, the Monongahela became nearly impassable and settlers left from Wheeling or the increasingly popular Pittsburgh, usually traveling on flatboats, or on simple rafts.

Neither the hardships of the Wilderness Road nor the dangers of the Ohio River could dissuade the settlers lured to Kentucky. Between 1783 and 1790 its population increased from an estimated 12,000 to 73,677, and every spring and fall boat after boat floated down the Ohio. To one observer

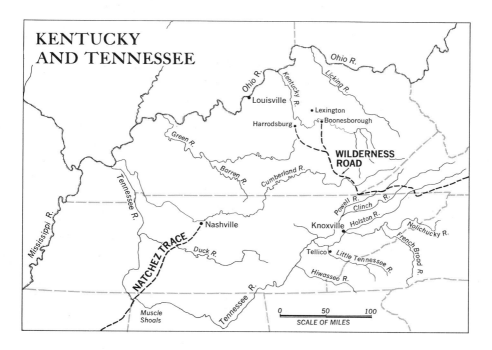

in 1785, it seemed "as if the old states would depopulate, and the inhabitants be transported to the new." [8]

The emigrants of these early years traveled through a rich wilderness. Immense flocks of turkeys, pheasants, and partridge darkened the skies, and buffalo were being killed along the Ohio until the 1790s. Deer, bear, and elk tempted the hunters, and there were innumerable squirrels, raccoons, and opossums as well as wolves and a host of other animals. On the upper Ohio in October 1785 on his way to negotiate with the Shawnee, Richard Butler dined on "fine roast buffalo beef, soup of buffalo beef and turkeys, fried turkeys, fried cat fish, fresh caught, roast ducks" and, unlike most travelers, he was able to enhance the meal with "good punch, madeira, claret, grog and toddy." [9]

Kentucky in the 1780s was a country of isolated agricultural settlements, with a few tiny villages providing centers for trade. It was a land of small clearings and log cabins "detached from each other by intervening forest, through which foot-paths, bridlepaths, and narrow, wagon roads, obstructed with stumps, wound their way." [10] The usual landing place for the traveler down the Ohio was Limestone, which remained a village of log cabins throughout these years. In 1785 a visitor commented that "every man walks with a rifle in his hand." The danger from the Indians became more acute after 1789, when general war broke out with the tribes northwest of the Ohio. Rangers (at the time called "spies") constantly scouted the land along the Ohio to warn of the approach of marauding bands, but Indians often crept through to raid a lonely cabin. Children were told "lie still and go to sleep, or the Shawnees will catch you." [11]

Kentucky towns remained small in spite of the increase in population. Limestone had only thirty or forty cabins as late as 1797, and was described as "a very dirty place." Louisville, in a prime location at the falls of the Ohio, consisted in 1784 of only a few huts, a jail, courthouse, and fort, although Kentucky's first historian John Filson, with all the abundant optimism of the westerner, said on leaving it in 1785 that "it is probably the foundation of one of the greatest Cities on earth." For all that, its unhealthy location and distance from the main lines of settlement restricted its growth. It was only a village in 1796.[12] The largest town in the state was Lexington, a junction for overland trade and travel, although situated a few miles from the navigable Kentucky River. It was first settled in 1779 and incorporated in 1782; by 1790 it had a population of over 800, and was becoming the trade center for a large hinterland. Kentucky continued to develop rapidly. It entered the Union in 1792, and by 1800 the population was 220,955, of which over 40,000 were slaves, most of them in the Bluegrass Region.[13]

This burst of expansion was the more remarkable because Kentucky settlers found it extremely difficult to secure a sound legal right to their lands; it was said in 1797 that "the uncertainty of titles to Kentucky lands is become quite a proverb." [14] From Revolutionary days Virginia had pur-

State House, Frankfort, Kentucky. *New York Magazine*, July 1796. (The New York Public Library)

sued a liberal policy in granting her Kentucky lands. She sold them cheaply in large quantities, granted them to her soldiers, and allowed pre-emption claims. As there was no organized prior survey, and settlers themselves located and marked out the lands they wanted, the confusion was considerable. After Kentucky became a state in 1792, she also granted lands on easy terms, and the individual settlers had great difficulty proving their titles against large-scale speculators. By 1800 many disillusioned Kentuckians were pushing northward across the Ohio.[15]

In less than twenty years after the Revolution, Kentucky was transformed from the beleaguered outpost of the war period, and pioneers were moving into most areas of the state. In 1797 the whole southern bank of the Ohio from Limestone to Louisville had "a civilised appearance."[16] Settlers even began to move after 1790 into what had been an unwanted area in southern Kentucky—"the barrens" between the Green and the Cumberland rivers. It remained, however, a very primitive area. After 1795 settlers began to move more rapidly into the valley of the Ohio above Louisville and into the valley of the Big Sandy River in eastern Kentucky. By 1800 only the extreme western part of the state, beyond the Tennessee,

John Filson, Kentucky's first historian. (Courtesy of the Filson Club, Louisville, Kentucky)

was still unopened.[17] What is perhaps most remarkable about Kentucky in these early years is that the fascination it held for pioneers persisted in spite of the constant Indian dangers and the many deaths. There is no clearer indication of the determination of the American pioneer to seek new lands and greater opportunity, and of the manner in which certain desirable spots caught his imagination, than the stream of pioneers who trudged over the Cumberland Gap or floated precariously down the Ohio in the twenty years after 1775.

Before the end of the Revolution settlements had been established in two widely separated areas of what is now the state of Tennessee but was then under the jurisdiction of North Carolina. As early as 1768 settlers began to move into the valley of the Watauga River, and in the next fifteen years frontiersmen established themselves in the valleys of the French Broad, the Nolichucky, and the Holston. Many of these early settlers traveled westward over the mountains from Morganton, North Carolina. The natural route would have been to follow the valley of the French Broad out of North Carolina into Tennessee, but Cherokee Indians blocked this way, and the reaches of the French Broad in Tennessee had to be approached from the north. In the years after the Revolution these settlements in eastern Tennessee were extremely isolated and faced continual danger because of their encroachment on the lands of the Cherokee south of the French Broad. The settlements of eastern Tennessee found it easier to communicate northward into Virginia, along the major Indian trail into the Shenandoah Valley, than eastward to North Carolina. Not until the late 1790s when Indian claims had been cleared did settlers even enter the western borders of North Carolina in large numbers, although there was considerable encroachment on Indian lands before that date. After Indian cessions in 1791 the valley of the French Broad was freed for as far as what was to become Knoxville.[18]

Even more distant from the East were the pioneers in the other center of early Tennessee settlement, along the Cumberland River. This area had first been settled in 1779, when James Robertson led a small party through the Cumberland Gap and along the valley of the Cumberland to found Nashville. The growth of the settlements was at first very slow. Not until 1788 was there even a road connecting the Cumberland settlements with those in eastern Tennessee.[19]

The major handicap to the settlement of both eastern and western Tennessee was the hostility of the Indians, particularly the Cherokee but also the Creeks. By an act of May 1783 North Carolina simply declared that all lands within her jurisdiction, with the exception of some between the French Broad and Tennessee rivers, had been forfeited by the Indians. Although North Carolina indicated that she would later meet with the Cherokee to discuss this appropriation, nothing was done. Instead the state's officials sanctioned a period of wild speculation in 1783 and 1784;

claims to millions of acres were entered under a new generous land law, and the Cherokee were long to suffer from the encroachments of those who claimed a right to their lands.[20]

The clashes with the Indians in Tennessee were increased because of inability of the settlers, the state of North Carolina, and the United States government to agree on a unified Indian policy. By the Articles of Confederation the United States government had the power to negotiate with all the Indians who were outside the bounds of the individual states. But as North Carolina did not finally cede Tennessee to the United States government until 1789, her officials felt no obligation before that time to abide by any arrangement made between the Cherokee and the national government. The Tennessee settlers complicated matters still further by often ignoring North Carolina as well as the United States. Isolated, exposed to Indian attack, neglected by North Carolina, the Tennesseans felt they had ample reason to act independently.

In the summer of 1784 settlers in eastern Tennessee moved toward the formation of the independent state of Franklin. They were initially inspired by the news that North Carolina had ceded her land claims to the Confederation government, although this cession was later rescinded. Franklin, under the leadership of John Sevier, managed to maintain a precarious independence until 1788, although North Carolina gradually reasserted control. Attempts to place Franklin under a very democratic constitution were blocked by Governor Sevier and his supporters, and the state made use of a slightly modified version of the North Carolina constitution.

During its few years of independence eastern Tennessee carried on its own Indian policy. The settlers considered that they were struggling for their existence unaided by either North Carolina or the United States. Their attitude was that they should take all they could from the Indians, regardless of the objectives of general American Indian policy. In June 1785 at the signing of the treaty of Dumplin Creek the Cherokee were persuaded to yield lands south of the French Broad and Holston rivers. Many of the Indians disagreed with the cession, and Franklin was soon engaged in Indian warfare.[21]

While the frontiersmen wanted Indian land on which to settle, the United States wanted peace. The Confederation government was desperately short of money and authority, and simply had no way of waging a general Indian war in the South. Accordingly, when Congressional commissioners were sent to negotiate with the Cherokee in the fall of 1785, they were ordered above all to avoid war.[22] The treaty of Hopewell on the Keowee River in November 1785 confirmed to the Cherokee much of the land they wanted to retain; the Franklin treaty of Dumplin Creek was repudiated, and the wishes of North Carolina ignored. Land speculator William Blount, who was present on behalf of North Carolina, argued that the treaty violated the state's rights. The southern states were more interested in land than in peace. They wanted to provide for the frontiersmen, aid the land speculators who frequently sat in the legislatures and executive mansions, and gain revenue from the sales. North Carolina even tried in April 1786 to persuade Congress to disavow the Hopewell treaty, but the attempt failed. The frontiersmen acted more directly. In July 1786 the fast-failing state of Franklin secured further land cessions from the Cherokee at the treaty of Chota Ford. The frontier settlers of North Carolina continually violated the treaty of Hopewell, and Congress was able to do nothing about it.[23]

The clash of jurisdictions in Tennessee at last came to an end in 1789 when North Carolina ceded its western land claims to the central government. In May 1790 the territory south of the River Ohio was created, and the settlers of the future state of Tennessee were bound more tightly to the federal government. It could hardly be said that the lot of the Indians had been much improved by these developments, for appointed as the governor of the new territory was that arch land speculator William Blount. It was his task to maintain boundaries against encroachment and conduct any new negotiations ordered by the federal government. The poacher now assumed his new task as gamekeeper.[24]

In 1791 at the treaty of Holston the federal government obtained more land from the Cherokee southeast of the Clinch River in an effort to encompass the illegal American settlers. Even this did not bring an end to encroachment on Indian land, and a subdivision of the Cherokee, the Chickamauga, began to direct bitter attacks against the exposed American settlements in western Tennessee. Not until the mid-1790s was there comparative peace on the Tennessee frontier. The federal government contributed to the difficulty by its delay in running the boundary agreed on at Holston in 1791; it was not clearly marked until 1797, and by that time many settlers, by accident or design, were on the Indian side of the line. The United States caused bitter resentment by using troops in an attempt to remove these settlers, and in 1798 it negotiated the treaty of Tellico to obtain more land for encroaching frontiersmen.[25]

In spite of the Indian warfare Tennessee continued to attract settlers. Its population doubled from 35,691 in 1790 to over 77,000 in 1795. Most of these immigrants came from Virginia and North Carolina, and by the latter date the population included over 10,000 slaves. Eastern Tennessee had grown far more rapidly than the western parts of the state, but this was soon to change when it became apparent that its rugged terrain and climate were more suitable to subsistence farming than the production of a cash crop, and that the lack of any convenient export route by water would restrict its economic growth.[26]

The Cumberland settlements in western Tennessee were just beginning their most dynamic growth at the time Tennessee became a state in 1796. By that time Nashville was connected by road eastward to Knoxville, and

Fort Natchez in 1790. (The New-York Historical Society)

more tenuously southward to Natchez. Yet on both of these routes much of the distance to be traveled was through a wilderness. Eastward, the cabins started to thin out half a dozen miles from Nashville, became very scattered, and finally some sixty miles away disappeared. Southward, on the famous Natchez Trace, the last Tennessee cabins were only ten miles or so from Nashville, with the wilderness stretching to sixty miles north of Natchez. Nashville itself had about sixty families, and the banks of the Cumberland River were well cultivated on both sides for a considerable distance. The cultivation of cotton, on which the prosperity of the area was soon to depend, was rapidly increasing in importance.[27]

Although Tennessee still contained vast unoccupied areas in 1796, the days of sharpest danger from the Indians were over. For much of the period since the Revolution the area had been in a state of crisis. Now there was a chance for comparatively peaceful, orderly development, and the opening up of new lands throughout the state.

In the years after the Revolution, while pioneers struggled to establish themselves in Kentucky and Tennessee, the remainder of the Southwest saw more land speculation, diplomatic maneuvers, and Indian war than settlement. Georgia was largely unsettled in 1783, and to her west, through the region that was to become the modern states of Alabama and Mississippi, were powerful Indian tribes. These tribes were supported by the Spanish in the territory west of Mississippi and along the Gulf.

Georgia had a population of only from 40,000 to 50,000 in 1783. Much of the state was occupied by the powerful Creeks, and settlements were confined to a long strip of land bordering South Carolina between the Ogeechee and the Savannah rivers and a connecting strip on the Atlantic between the Savannah and the St. Marys. After the Revolution Georgia pursued a rapacious and unwise Indian policy. Between 1783 and 1786 the state persuaded chiefs representing a minority of the Creek nation to cede large areas of land east of the Oconee River.[28] These cessions were repudiated by most of the Creeks, who were skillfully led by Chief Alexander McGillivray, born of a Scotch father and a Creek mother. Indian war raged on the Georgia frontiers, and by the fall of 1787 even the town of Savannah was being fortified. In the view of one resident the state by the end of 1788 was "the most *exposed*, and *impotent*, of the *whole Family*." [29]

The difficulties of Georgia were partly the result of her own blundering, but they were considerably increased by the confidence and strength that the Creeks gained from Spanish support. Georgia's aggression played into the hands of the Spanish, who as a result of their conquests in the Revolution claimed at least as far north as 32° 28' and refused to acknowledge England's cession of land to the United States as far south as the 31st parallel. Moreover, Spain had hopes not merely of adjusting the boundary in her favor, but also of winning control of much of the Mississippi Valley. The United States government was impoverished and ill-united after 1783. It was in no position to support the settlers of the Southwest in their desire for land and safety from the Indians.

After 1783 trade with the Indians of the Southwest was carried on mainly from Spanish territory, much of it through the firm of Panton, Leslie & Company, in which Alexander McGillivray was made a partner. To the trade links was added more direct political support. In the spring and summer of 1784 at Pensacola, the Spaniards concluded agreements with the Creeks, the Chickasaw, and the Choctaw. These tribes placed themselves under Spanish protection and received aid to resist pressure from Georgia.[30]

The influence Spain could exert on the Southwestern frontiersmen through her control of the Indians was in the long run less effective than her control of the Mississippi Valley trade routes. The westerners could not export their bulky farm produce eastward over the mountains. It was essential to them that they have the right to ship their produce down the Mississippi to the port of New Orleans. This was of equal importance to the Kentuckians, who could reach the Mississippi by the Kentucky and the Ohio rivers, and to the settlers in western Tennessee who wanted to send produce down the Cumberland-Ohio-Mississippi route.

After the Revolution the Confederation government was anxious to solve its outstanding problems with the Spanish, but with practically no army, no money, and no commercial control over its own states it was negotiating from a position of weakness. The problem became acute in 1784, for in that year Spain closed the Mississippi to navigation by the Americans.

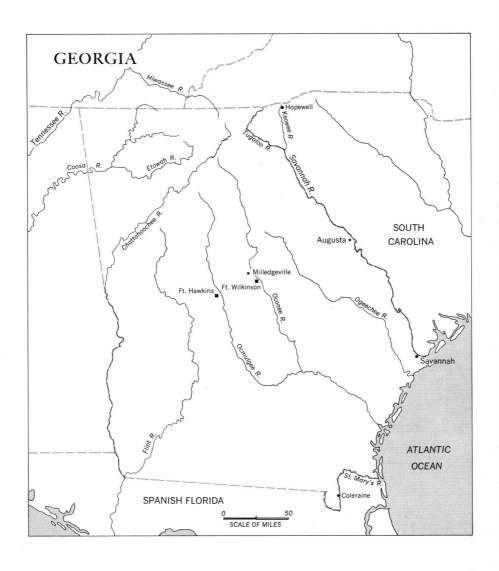

If this blockade were maintained, the settlers who were pushing west into the Mississippi Valley could not achieve economic prosperity.

In 1785 the Spanish minister to the United States, Diego de Gardoqui, met with the American secretary of foreign affairs John Jay to discuss the difficulties between the two countries. They were able to agree on trade between the United States and the Spanish peninsula, but as a concession to Gardoqui Jay asked the Confederation Congress for permission to sign an agreement by which the United States would give up the navigation of the Spanish portion of the Mississippi River for thirty years. This proposal was supported by a majority of states, but southern opposition made it impossible to secure the two-thirds vote needed for approval. Hopes of a treaty were abandoned.[31]

Although this proposal was not approved, the extent of its eastern support profoundly shocked the westerners. The Kentuckians and Tennesseans who had braved a wilderness and were fighting Indians to establish homes had received little help from the East, and now it seemed quite clear that many in the Confederation Congress thought so little of western interests that they were prepared to give up the navigation of the Mississippi. Western leaders had ample reason to despair of an American government that sent them no troops, advocated peace with the Indians, and was half-prepared to acquiesce in the closing of the only export route for western produce. Some now began to think of an agreement with Spain that would ensure their future safety and prosperity, and were quite willing to listen to Spanish overtures; in this way the "Spanish conspiracy" was born.

After the failure of his talks with John Jay, Gardoqui in 1786 began to seek out southwestern leaders who were despairing of American intentions. To John Brown, the representative of the Kentucky district of Virginia in the Confederation Congress, Gardoqui pointed out the advantages that would accrue to the West if separated from the United States and tied to Spain: in particular free entry to the port of New Orleans would be assured. Gardoqui also talked to Dr. James White, a delegate to the Congress from North Carolina, and White apparently led Gardoqui to believe that many westerners might be prepared to throw their allegiance to Spain if given the right concessions within the Spanish empire.[32]

The real leader of the negotiations with the Spanish in these years, however, was James Wilkinson, one of the shrewdest frontier rogues of the whole period. Wilkinson, who moved west to Kentucky after the Revolution, quickly assumed a leading position in trade and politics. Although his first overtures to Gardoqui met with a cool response, he descended the Mississippi on a well-laden flatboat in the early summer of 1787, spent the summer in New Orleans, made a good impression on Spanish Governor Esteban Miró, and was given the power to grant licenses to those in Kentucky who wanted to trade through New Orleans. In return for this Wilkinson gave his allegiance to the Spanish. He convinced the Spanish governor that there was solid sentiment for separation in Kentucky and that he would be able to organize it if he had the trade of the Mississippi to offer.

Wilkinson's contact with the Spanish government continued sporadically for years, and in the spring of 1788, using his power to grant licenses for trade, he sent twenty-five flatboats down the river to New Orleans. In a letter to Miró, Wilkinson held out the hope that Kentucky, which was moving toward statehood, would rather unite with Spain than keep its ties with the United States. But he also suggested that if this were to be accomplished Spain would have to stop supporting the Creeks against the United States.

Spain now decided to woo rather than coerce the westerners. For a time she not only pursued a peaceful policy toward the Indians of the Southwest, she also attempted to attract American settlers to settle in Spanish territory by allowing them freedom from imperial taxation and military service, and liberty to practice their religion. To complete the relaxation it was announced that the Americans could ship their goods down the Mississippi on the payment of a 15 percent import duty, and it was also agreed that to win Americans to the Spanish cause this duty could be reduced to 6 percent.

For a time in 1788 the Spanish also tried to interest the people of Tennessee in the possibility of uniting with Spain. Discussions were entered into with leaders in both eastern and western Tennessee, and the Cumberland settlements even named their district "Miro" after the Spanish governor. But in the long run it was clear that although some were anxious to gain any advantages they could by negotiations with the Spanish, the great majority of westerners were not prepared to sever their connections with the United States. Wilkinson and his supporters met firm resistance in Kentucky when they talked of actual separation. Yet Wilkinson maintained his contacts with the Spanish and continued to receive a pension from their government. This continued even after he became a lieutenant colonel in the United States army in 1791. The Spanish throughout the first half of the 1790s still had hopes that they could win the allegiance of the Kentucky settlers.[33]

The main reason that the Spanish were able to win friends in both the Kentucky and Tennessee regions was that the American government had failed in its responsibilities to the settlers of the Southwest. The export trade depended on the vagaries of the Spanish government, and the area west of Georgia was still a no-man's land over which the Spanish, the Indians, and the state of Georgia contended. The Confederation government had neither the power to win the commercial and territorial concessions the settlers of the Southwest desired nor the money to raise troops to protect them from Indian attack.

Hopes of an eventual solution to the westerners' problems brightened in 1789 with the formation of a new and more powerful American government, yet this government could do little to solve the basic difficulties between Georgia and the Indians. Although the treaties with the Creeks between 1783 and 1786 had been unfairly negotiated by Georgia with a minority of the nation, Georgia proceeded to survey and settle part of the ceded areas. There were now numerous settlers on the land between the Ogeechee and Oconee rivers which McGillivray and the main body of the Creeks considered had never been ceded.[34]

As the new United States government after 1789 hoped to avoid general war with the southern tribes, the federal authorities were obliged to negotiate in an attempt to achieve a compromise to end the sporadic warfare between the Creeks and Georgians. After earlier failures, a measure of agreement was reached at the treaty of New York in 1790. McGillivray came to New York hoping that he had more chance of a reasonable agreement from the United States than from the state of Georgia. The treaty gave back to the Creeks land south of the Altamaha River which Georgia had taken from them in the treaties after the Revolution, and defined the other Creek boundaries. For the land that remained in the possession of Georgia they were given an annuity of $1500. McGillivray himself was bribed handsomely. He was appointed an honorary brigadier general in the United States army, and given a salary of $1200 a year in secret articles attached to the treaty.[35]

Federal attempts to bring moderation to Georgia-Creek relations achieved little success. Georgia frontiersmen ignored the boundaries established at the treaty of New York and moved on to land guaranteed to the Creeks. The Indians continued to raid the frontiers of Georgia, and from 1793 a new Spanish governor, the Baron de Carondelet, renewed Spanish support for the southern tribes. Carondelet judged that the advance of the American frontier was threatening the future safety of Louisiana, and that it was necessary to take measures for its defense.[36]

The state of Georgia had ambitions far beyond its meager resources in these years after the Revolution. In reality Georgia was a thinly populated state, for the most part occupied by the Creeks, who were fiercely resisting the advance of the frontiersmen. Yet the state pursued an Indian policy better designed to infuriate than conciliate and also periodically asserted her claims to a large part of the southern half of the Mississippi Valley.

Since the end of the Revolution, the Georgia legislature had proved particularly responsive to the importunities of land speculators, and in satisfying them frequently ignored both the Spanish and the Indians. In 1784 the legislature supported William Blount and other speculators in their efforts to develop land in the Great Bend of the Tennessee River, and in 1785 it even created an ephemeral Bourbon County out of the land between the Yazoo River and the 31st parallel, including Natchez. That these efforts came to nothing did not dissuade the Georgia legislature from trying again, and in the early years of the new federal government Georgia made two attempts to create vast domains in modern Alabama and Mississippi for the Yazoo land companies; companies which involved not only speculators in Georgia, the Carolinas, and Virginia but also the Georgia legislature itself.

The first grants to the Yazoo companies were made in December 1789. They covered a huge area, extending from the land in the Great Bend of the Tennessee granted to the Tennessee Land Company, to lands along the Mississippi for the South Carolina Yazoo Company, and to lands in what is now northwestern Alabama and northern Mississippi for the Virginia Yazoo Company. The lands were sold by Georgia for less than one cent an acre, but the speculators were unable to take advantage of the grants. Spain was clearly unwilling to permit the carving of domains out of lands she claimed, and the federal government viewed with hostility attempts to weaken its power in the Mississippi Valley.[37]

Georgia once again was not disheartened by her lack of success, for in the winter of 1794–1795 the Yazoo speculations were revived in a different form. Four companies applied in the late fall of 1794 for tracts in the Alabama-Mississippi region that eventually amounted to some 35,000,000 acres. Initial opposition in the Georgia legislature softened when every man but one was bribed, and in January 1795 the grants were made. The speculators quickly resold a large amount of the land to many who had not been involved in the original speculation, but these purchasers ran into difficulty in the following year when a committee of a new Georgia legislature decided that the grants had been obtained by extensive bribery, and also that the lands granted had been guaranteed to the Choctaw and Chickasaw Indians in 1786 by the Confederation government. As a result of the investigation the Georgia legislature canceled its Yazoo acts. For the next twenty years the question of recompense for Yazoo purchasers caused bitterness in American politics; the final settlement was not made until 1814.[38]

While Georgia pursued her chimerical ambitions, the fate of the lower part of the Mississippi Valley was further complicated after 1792 by the outbreak of general European war and a revival of French interest in the region. Although this for a time meant additional embarrassment for the American government, the revolutionary wars ultimately made possible a solution of outstanding difficulties with Spain.

By early 1793 England and Spain were allied in a struggle against revolutionary France, and in that year the United States received the new French minister, Edmond Genêt. Genêt came with instructions to use the United States as a base for attacks on Spanish and British colonies and trade in the New World. The French minister misconstrued his tumultuous reception in Charleston to mean that he could act as he wanted in the United States, and he planned expeditions to attack Louisiana and New Orleans from Kentucky, and the Floridas from Georgia. He commissioned Elijah Clarke of Georgia to lead the Florida expedition, and George Rogers

Clark of Kentucky to attack New Orleans. In the winter of 1793–1794 Clark advertised for recruits in Kentucky, but the United States was determined to maintain her neutrality in the European struggle and forbade further action.[39]

Spain, however, was in difficulties. Her alliance with England was collapsing, and she was afraid that as she drew nearer to France, the United States and Great Britain might find common cause to threaten Spanish possessions in the New World. This threat seemed much nearer with the signing of Jay's Treaty between England and the United States in November 1794. Manuel de Godoy, who was in charge of Spain's foreign policy, first tried to draw the United States into an agreement with France and Spain. This effort failed, and after negotiations between Godoy and American envoy Thomas Pinckney a treaty was concluded between Spain and the United States at San Lorenzo on October 27, 1795.

It was agreed in this treaty that the Spanish-American boundary in the Southwest would run along the 31st parallel to the St. Marys River. Spain also acknowledged the right of the citizens of the United States to navigate the Mississippi and granted to them for a three-year period the right of depositing their goods at New Orleans free of duty before shipping them abroad; this provision could be renewed after three years. Spain also agreed to try to restrain the Indians. The treaty represented a major diplomatic success for the United States and ruined Spain's hopes of an effective conspiracy in the American Southwest. Spain, however, was slow to comply with the terms of the treaty. Not until the fall of 1797 was the evacuation of posts in American territory north of the 31st parallel ordered, and not until the early months of 1798 were the men at Natchez and Walnut Hills withdrawn.[40]

For more than a decade after the Revolution, American settlements in the Southwest endured a variety of dangers. The most serious of these was the threat of separation: the danger that Spain would use her powerful strategic position and the weakness of the American government to win the allegiance of the trans-Appalachian settlements. By 1796, with a new American government functioning effectively and after the signing of the treaty of San Lorenzo, this threat had ended. The settlers of the Mississippi Valley had secured export rights on the Mississippi, and the stronger United States government, backed by an increasing population west of the Appalachians, was in a position to resist any attempt to renew the blockade.

Danger from the Indians had not ended, but now that Spanish backing had been removed after San Lorenzo, and with the rapid increase of population in Kentucky, Georgia, and Tennessee, the Indians had far more to fear from the settlers than the settlers from the Indians. From 1795 the American government was less worried by the prospect of a successful Indian attack than it was by the possibility that the Indians would be exterminated by the advance of American pioneers. Concerned regarding the blow this would deliver to national prestige, the government increasingly turned to a policy of attempting to combine frontier expansion with civilizing of the Indians; civilizing meant transforming them into American farmers. It was hoped that in this manner land would be obtained with less conflict and that both pioneer and Indian would be satisfied.[41] This did not prove possible for the Indians, but for the states and territories of the Southwest the period of crisis was over; the emphasis was now to be on growth rather than survival.

◁ **2** ▷

Northern Expansion,
1783–1795

*A*t the heart of northern expansion in the years after the Revolution were
the farmers of southern New England. They found many reasons to leave
their homes in the last years of the eighteenth century. From the very
beginning the soil on which they settled had given New Englanders ample
reason to look for new opportunities. It forced upon them a harsh struggle
for existence. In the early days the farmers could at least look for the most
desirable spots, but population growth put great pressure on available land.
As in much of western Europe the younger sons of farmers needed new
farms, and in New England even many of their fathers hoped to move to
an easier and more profitable life.

The difficult terrain and population growth were not the only stimulants
to emigration. New England farmers suffered from high taxes and complained bitterly that their interests were neglected by the state governments.
In an age of revolution, when ideas of freedom and equality were in the air,
they found it hard to accept the political, religious, and social control which
was imposed upon them. Many began to move out immediately after the
Revolution, and in the following years the roads from New England were
crowded with farmers seeking new lands.[1]

Although many New Englanders moved to new lands beyond the Appalachians after 1783, a steady stream also migrated northward to the New England frontier of Vermont and Maine. New Hampshire had long existed as a separate colony, and although settlers still moved into her unoccupied areas, there was a lack of desirable land. Vermont and Maine offered the greatest opportunity for those moving north.

Northern New England was not easy to settle, although it had no large hostile Indian population. The terrain was mountainous, and the best locations were often in the valleys, but under the population pressure farming expanded outward into marginal hill country. The whole area was covered by a dense growth of timber, but those settlers who equated growth of trees with fertility were destined for disappointment. As the pioneers moved out of the river valleys into the uplands, they were soon to find that once the original covering left by the forests had been farmed out the soil underneath was not particularly fertile. Moreover, the winters were long and harsh, and the growing seasons, short. With hostile climate, dense forest, hilly terrain, and difficulties in reaching markets, the settlers found that their often rich-appearing land involved great hardships.

Settlers had been moving into Vermont since the French and Indian War. Connecticut had been the main source of these early pioneers; those from the eastern part of the state usually followed the Connecticut River into southeastern Vermont, while a smaller group moved from western Connecticut into southwestern Vermont. Other pioneers were usually from Massachusetts, Rhode Island, or New Hampshire. As the settlements in eastern and western Vermont were separated by the barrier of the Green Mountains, these regions developed independently of each other and with their own particular characteristics. The western part of the state had a reputation for unorthodoxy and radical views, and it was from this area that Ethan Allen brought his Green Mountain boys to fight in the Revolution; it was also to this western region that Daniel Shays and his followers fled after the failure of their uprising in Massachusetts in 1786. Vermont was also the haven for some 5000 Loyalists who in the American Revolution fled northward to avoid persecution.[2]

The years after the Revolution saw Vermont's most dramatic development, a development that was soon over. The population was estimated at some 30,000 in 1781, but by 1790 it was 85,425 (the state entered the union in 1791), and by 1810 it was 217,985. In the 1780s Vermont provided a frontier for the New England settlers who did not wish to risk their lives moving westward toward the lands of hostile Indians. As more newcomers arrived, settlers gradually established themselves over the whole of the state. The process was aided by a high birth rate, and in 1800 over 50 percent of Vermont's population was under the age of sixteen.

The period of expansion was a short one, for the state simply did not have the resources to support a constantly increasing population. There was insufficient good farm land, and the West offered a more attractive lure as the Indian menace was quelled and orderly government created. Moreover, beginning in 1807 Vermont was beset by other problems as America's difficulties with Great Britain cut off the state's regular trade with Montreal. From 1808 not only did pioneers show reluctance to enter the state, they also began to leave; in the next fifty years Vermont provided many settlers for new settlements in the West.[3]

While Vermont had its brief moment of glory, Maine also shared in the advance into northern New England. At the time of the Revolution this remote section of Massachusetts had a population of between 40,000 and 50,000, but after the war there was a rapid development aided by a liberal Massachusetts land policy. After 1784 the state gave lands to genuine settlers in townships away from the rivers, and set only moderate prices for riverside townships. There was some large-scale speculation east of the Penobscot River, but also a steady increase in the number of actual pioneers. By

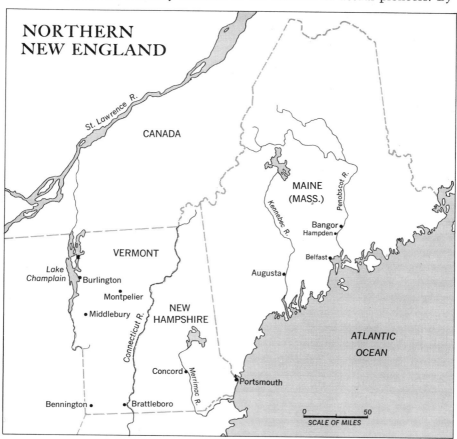

NORTHERN
NEW ENGLAND

St. Lawrence R.

CANADA

MAINE
(MASS.)

Penobscot R.

Kennebec R.

Bangor
Hampden

Belfast

VERMONT

Lake
Champlain
Burlington

Augusta

Montpelier

Middlebury

NEW
HAMPSHIRE

Connecticut R.

ATLANTIC
OCEAN

Concord

Merrimac R.

Portsmouth

Bennington

Brattleboro

0   50
SCALE OF MILES

1790 the population was 96,540, and the number of incorporated townships increased from 34 in 1775 to 126 in 1800. New settlers came in from Massachusetts and New Hampshire in such numbers that much of the desirable land in the state had been taken up by 1815, and Maine emigrants were beginning to swell the tide to the Ohio Valley.[4]

In these frontier areas of northern New England hard-working settlers made heroic efforts to farm all but the poorest land. They were temporarily successful, but in the next generation farms were abandoned and lands regained by the wilderness as it was discovered that farmers had been too optimistic in their hopes of new settlements and fertile soil.

The emigration to the north was somewhat overshadowed in the years after 1783 by the rush into the unoccupied lands of western New York. Until the end of the Revolution much of the state of New York remained unsettled. Although immigrants had been entering the region since the seventeenth century, settlement still extended only some one hundred miles west of Albany. In the colonial period pioneers had often preferred to enter Pennsylvania rather than New York, where much of the desirable land along the Hudson had been taken up by large landowners, and western New York was occupied by the powerful Iroquois confederacy. The great days of the Iroquois came to an end in the Revolution, when many of them joined the British. As American settlement advanced into western Pennsylvania and Ohio, the Six Nations found themselves particularly vulnerable to American attack.

As the menace of the Six Nations declined, the growing population of New York and New England looked covetously at the lands of western New York. Revolutionary troops had brought back tales of rich rolling country and beautiful rivers, but before population could flow into the area the conflicting claims of New York and Massachusetts to the region had to be resolved. Until they reached agreement firm land titles could not be obtained. In November 1786 representatives of the two states met in Hartford, Connecticut, and agreed that sovereignty would be given to the state of New York, while land ownership would be divided evenly between the two states. Massachusetts was given most of the land west of Lake Seneca and some 230,000 acres in the Susquehanna River region.[5]

This agreement immediately set off a series of speculations in the lands of western New York. In April 1788 a group originally led by Oliver Phelps and Nathaniel Gorham agreed to buy the whole Massachusetts tract west of Lake Seneca, amounting to some 6,000,000 acres, for £300,000. The two associates had the task of dealing with the Indians, and in July 1788 they obtained the rights to some 2,600,000 acres in a treaty at Buffalo Creek. Yet, like so many land speculators, Phelps and Gorham overreached themselves. In the spring of 1790 they had to give back to Massachusetts the area to which the Indian title had not yet been extinguished. The land that had been obtained from the Indians had already been subdivided, and a large amount sold at a land office at Canandaigua, New York, to actual settlers and speculators. A huge area of some 1,300,000 acres was sold to Robert Morris of Philadelphia, but the tract soon changed hands again, this time going to English speculators Sir William Pulteney, Patrick Colquhoun, and William Hornby. Morris also bought from Massachusetts the land given back by Phelps and Gorham and sold it to other speculators; much of the land came into the possession of a group of Dutch bankers known as the Holland Land Company.[6]

The main development in the early 1790s occurred east of the Genesee River, particularly in the Pulteney purchase. The Genesee River which flows north out of northern Pennsylvania to empty into Lake Ontario near modern Rochester was bordered by over 2,000,000 acres of rich land. For the most part the region, like the rest of western New York, was heavily forested, but it was also studded with large plains of high grass and rich soil, a fact not immediately appreciated by settlers who thought of fertility

The Hudson River. Engraving by C. Tiebout. *New York Magazine,* June 1791. (The New-York Historical Society)

Falls of the Mohawk, six miles from Albany. From Maulevrier, *Voyage dans l'Intérieur*, 1796. (The New-York Historical Society)

in terms of forest cover. In 1790 the whole population of the great Massachusetts tract amounted to only 1075, and these were all east of the Genesee.

The settlement of the region was given a great stimulus by the activities of the European speculators who were able to invest capital otherwise unavailable in the early days of the frontier. Instead of waiting for the natural expansion of pioneers into the region, the European speculators attempted to hasten the process by a "hothouse" technique. Particularly ambitious was Charles Williamson, the agent for the English Pulteney interests. Throughout the 1790s he made great efforts to attract settlers to the Genesee region, spending $1,000,000 to accomplish this end.

Williamson, and agents for other speculators, issued pamphlets and handbills and placed articles in eastern newspapers to paint the wonders of life on the Genesee. Like all promotional literature it exaggerated, but it was not a matter of all promotion and no accomplishment. The speculators offered favorable credit terms to potential emigrants; five years was a common term, and this was often extended to avoid extensive foreclosures. Williamson also actively promoted development within the region itself.

He had roads built, erected mills, and started towns at Williamsburg, Bath, and Sodus Bay. At Bath just three years after it was laid out there were already thirty or so houses, well-stocked stores, a good tavern, and extensive saw and flour mills in the vicinity. Settlers moved in ever-increasing numbers into the land east of the Genesee River, although to the west there was still a wilderness.[7]

In the area from the Mohawk Valley to Lake Seneca, New York had already made plans for settlement during the Revolution. From the Lake eastward the state laid out a large military tract of some 1,500,000 acres to provide for land grants to its Revolutionary soldiers. Settlement did not really begin there until after 1790, and by that time many of the soldiers had sold their rights to speculators and others, creating a considerable confusion in title. Within a few years there was a rapid increase in population.[8] South and east of the military tract, New York sold most of its lands to speculators, but they quickly encouraged actual immigration into the region. The roads west, from Albany along the Mohawk Valley and from Catskill toward the Susquehanna, were soon filled with emigrants. "All this country begins to be inhabited," wrote one traveler in the Mohawk Valley above Fort Schuyler in 1792, "everywhere one hears the axe, everyone is busy felling trees!" [9]

These years before 1795 even saw the first attempts to promote settlement in the less desirable northern areas of the state. Speculators tried to develop lands east of Lake Ontario and along the St. Lawrence River. The most ambitious of all the speculators in northern New York was Alexander

Macomb, who in July 1787 bought from the state of New York what was known as the "St. Lawrence Ten Towns," situated directly downriver from Ogdensburg on the St. Lawrence. Connected with Macomb in this speculation were a prominent group of early Americans, including Secretary of War Henry Knox, Gouverneur Morris, and Robert Morris. The speculation was ambitious, but the development slow, and in 1800 the Ten Towns contained under two persons a square mile. There was a similar slow growth in the other speculations in which Macomb was involved in northern New York. The 4,000,000 acres he bought in 1791 and quickly resold to other speculators were also not particularly attractive to settlers. They preferred the easier life of western New York to the harsh climate and difficult terrain of much of the northern part of the state.[10]

The expansion into the unsettled areas of the long-established northern states included a movement into northern and western Pennsylvania in the years after 1783. At this time these areas were still largely unsettled, although frontiersmen had advanced westward along Forbes' Road from Harrisburg to Pittsburgh. After 1783 pioneers moved slowly into all the northern counties of Pennsylvania, and more rapidly into the southwestern corner.

Pennsylvania had long had a more diverse population than that of New England, and this diversity was reflected in the growth after 1783. The Scotch-Irish at one time dominated the settlements along Forbes' Road to Pittsburgh. Even after 1783 their influence remained strong, although now New Englanders and New Yorkers flooded in as part of the general exodus that was taking place in the northeast, while some of the Pennsylvania Germans moved farther west. In the southwestern corner of the state there were also Southerners, who had come up along Braddock's Road from Maryland to establish farms south of the forks of the Ohio. The terrain, particularly in northern Pennsylvania presented major difficulties, but it attracted many settlers who did not wish to risk the dangers of hostile Indians and who wished to settle in an area that was already part of an organized state government.

As in New York, land speculators were exceedingly active, and they were given an excellent opportunity by the Pennsylvania land law of 1792. Although a limit of 400 acres was set on single purchases, speculators made a variety of applications and obtained large quantities of land at under twenty cents an acre. The main Pennsylvania speculators—John Nicholson, Robert Morris, and the Holland Land Company—were unsuccessful in these years. Nicholson, whose speculations involved 3,000,000 to 4,000,000 acres, eventually went bankrupt and died in prison; Robert Morris went down with him. The Holland Land Company became involved in massive title disputes and was unable to sell its lands at a profit. In general the results of speculation were far less satisfactory in Pennsylvania than in western New York. The settlement of the northwestern part of the state was retarded by

Lancaster, Pennsylvania, on the road west from Philadelphia. From Maulevrier, *Voyage dans l'Intérieur,* 1796. (The New-York Historical Society)

arguments over land titles, and in some cases farms were abandoned because of title difficulties.[11]

Western Pennsylvania grew steadily in the decade after the Revolution, although most pioneers after traveling from the East were prepared for the further adventure of floating down the Ohio to newer lands. After 1795 the influx of thousands of pioneers destined for the Ohio Valley created a ready market for the boats and products of Pittsburgh and the produce of the surrounding countryside, bringing increasing prosperity to western Pennsylvania.

In the lands north of the Ohio River there had been practically no settlement in the years before the Revolution. The only real exceptions were those settlements that had been established by the French before 1763; Detroit, Mackinac, Prairie du Chien, Kaskaskia, Cahokia, Vincennes, and other smaller communities. Yet the Old Northwest was far from unknown to the Americans. From before the middle of the century fur traders had lived and traveled south of Lake Erie, and from the eve of the Revolution settlers had gone down the Ohio to Kentucky. All described a rich and bountiful land. In 1783 pioneers were poised to cross to the north bank of the Ohio, but until the end of the decade there were few American frontiersmen in the Old Northwest. They were stopped by the policy of the Confederation government and by the hostility of the Indians, backed by the British.

The Confederation government became directly involved in the formation of policy for western settlement as a result of land cessions from the individual states. Even while the struggle with England was still in doubt the revolutionary colonies had quarreled bitterly over the status of the land of the Mississippi Valley. Seven of the original thirteen states—Virginia, North and South Carolina, Georgia in the South, and Massachusetts, Connecticut, New York in the North—claimed large areas of the Mississippi Valley either on the basis of their colonial grants from England or, in the case of New York, on the doubtful authority of cession by the Iroquois Indians. Many of the original charters granted overlapping claims, giving grants "from sea to sea," and all the territory over which the United States had sovereignty in the Mississippi Valley was claimed by one or another of the states.

During the Revolution the six states without lands had pressed for cession of the individual state claims in the Mississippi Valley to the central government. It was argued that these lands were being won by a common effort and that it would be unfair for certain states to have western lands as a source of revenue while others had to depend on their own resources. Although many of the arguments on the surface concerned the unity of the states, the whole issue was complicated by the role of the land speculators. Those speculators who hoped to profit by state-granted lands ardently opposed cession to the central government, whereas the speculators who had not gained recognition by the state governments pressed enthusiastically for the land cessions, hoping to gain a more favorable hearing from Congress.

This argument over the fate of the western lands delayed the ratification of the Articles of Confederation, for Maryland declared in 1778 that she would not ratify them until the western lands were ceded to the central government. She was influenced both her desire to share in the benefits of the sales and by the aims of influential middle state speculators in the Indiana and Illinois-Wabash land companies, who hoped to negotiate with the central government for western land. Virginia with her massive claims was the key state, but she did not wish to cede her lands if this merely meant helping land speculators from other states. When after considerable pressure, and New York's cession of her shadowy claims, Virginia ceded her lands north of the Ohio in 1781, she imposed the condition that no private claims to the ceded land would be recognized. Maryland ratified the Articles of Confederation, but for three years speculators tried to persuade Congress to ignore the conditions attached to the Virginia cession.[12]

After considerable argument it was at last agreed that Virginia could deny the right of the land companies to benefit from her cession. In December 1783 she repeated her cession of all her claims northwest of the Ohio to the Confederation government, keeping control over Kentucky and two tracts beyond the Ohio; lands between the Scioto and Little Miami rivers were retained as the "Virginia military reserve" to reward her revolutionary soldiers, and "Clark's grant" of some 150,000 acres in what is now southern Indiana was kept for the soldiers who had served under George Rogers Clark.[13] In March 1784 the Virginia cession was accepted by Congress from the Virginia delegates.

Once Virginia had acted, the cession of other claims northwest of the Ohio soon followed. In 1785 Congress accepted the Massachusetts cession of land west of the state of New York, and in September 1786 that of Connecticut. The latter state kept a Western Reserve of some 3,800,000 acres stretching westward 120 miles from the Pennsylvania boundary along the southern shore of Lake Erie. This became an area of strong New England influence in the new state of Ohio. Except for Virginia, the southern states were slower to cede their claims. South Carolina's cession of her nebulous claims to land south of the 35th parallel was of no importance, and North Carolina did not finally cede Tennessee until 1789. Georgia was even more reluctant to give up her western ambitions, and not until 1802 did she cede her claims to the great area south of Tennessee.[14]

The eagerness of the Confederation to secure lands beyond the Appalachians stemmed as much from a desire for money as for national unity. Those frontiersmen who thought they deserved land at a nominal cost as a reward for taming the wilderness were to be sorely disappointed. The government desperately needed any revenue it could obtain, and in any case many in the East feared that a generous land policy would depopulate their own states and dissipate American strength over thousands of miles. Revenue, not the wishes of the frontiersmen, dominated the thoughts of the Confederation.

The first attempts to create a policy for the lands being ceded by the states were made in 1784 and 1785. Congress did not have an entirely free hand, for in order to obtain the cession of state claims the Continental Congress had in October 1780 passed a resolution stating that the lands ceded to the United States would be disposed of for the common benefit of the states, "and be settled and formed into distinct republican states." [15] How this was to be accomplished was being discussed even while the details of the Virginia cession were being worked out, and in March 1784 a committee headed by Thomas Jefferson suggested a most influential plan. It recommended that the eastern half of the Mississippi Valley be divided into rectangular areas which would eventually become states—among them Assenisipia, Pelisipia, and Cherronesus. The original inhabitants of each area were to gather together to form a temporary government by adopting the constitution and laws of one of the existing states, and could elect a delegate to Congress who could speak but not vote. When there was a population of 20,000 free inhabitants the area could draft a permanent constitution, and when the population equaled that of the least populous of the thirteen original states it could be admitted to the Union. There was to be adult male suffrage, and slavery was to be prohibited. The report was adopted by Congress in 1784 with several changes. Most important was the failure to provide for the ending of slavery.[16]

As the Confederation government did not yet have firm title to the land of the eastern half of the Mississippi Valley and as many objected to the details of the new law, the 1784 ordinance had no immediate effect. The argument now revolved around the question of the method by which the public domain which was being created north of the Ohio should be sold. Some advocated the New England system of prior survey and the sale of townships to groups of settlers, and others espoused the southern practice of land warrants specifying the amount of land but not the location, with the settler himself delineating his own boundaries.[17]

A comprehensive system for the survey and sale of land—the Ordinance of 1785—was finally passed on May 20. The Ordinance set up a rectangular system of prior survey with range lines six miles apart. The ranges were to be divided into townships six miles square, and each township was to be divided into thirty-six sections of 640 acres. Section sixteen in each township was to be reserved for the support of public schools, and four other sections were to be set aside for future disposal by the national government.

The system of survey boded well for future security of title, but the arrangements for sale by auction were of little use to the individual frontiersman. The price for land was set at a minimum of $1 an acre, and the least that could be bought was 640 acres. Moreover, alternate townships were to be sold as a whole, and the auctions were to be held in the East, far away from most pioneers. The frontiersmen wanted small plots of cheap land on credit and auctions near their own homes.[18]

Instead of this, the national government in 1785 began to use troops against its own frontiersmen northwest of the Ohio. Since the Revolution pioneers had begun to move out of western Pennsylvania and Virginia across the west bank of the Ohio River into what is now the extreme eastern portion of the state of Ohio, south of Steubenville. Some of them even sailed farther down the Ohio, to settle on the Muskingum, the Scioto, and the Miami. These were "squatters," with no legal right to the land on which they settled; they were in great danger from the Indians, and they quickly discovered that if the Indians did not burn their cabins the government would. In 1785 Colonel Josiah Harmar was ordered to use force to expel the squatters, and he carried out his instructions by pulling down or burning the cabins of many of these frontiersmen northwest of the Ohio. Even with this extreme action the government was not completely successful, for as soon as the troops left many of the settlers returned to rebuild their cabins.[19]

Though the tiny American army was useful in removing frontiersmen and their families, it had insufficient strength to remove the Indians from the land which the government now hoped to sell under the provisions of its Ordinance of 1785. The Indians of the Northwest had not suffered severe defeat in the Revolution. The Delawares and Wyandot, of what is now eastern and central Ohio, could not retain all their lands if the settlement of the new national domain were to take place. Even more dangerous to the United States were the Shawnee of western Ohio, who had been at war with the Americans since 1774 and showed every sign of continuing their fierce resistance in the years after 1783. Also ready to fight on this frontier were the Mingo (the Ohio Seneca), who had their villages at Sandusky, and the great northern tribes of Ottawa and Chippewa, some of whom hunted south of Lake Erie and even had villages in what is now northwestern Ohio. Moreover, the educated Joseph Brant of the Six Nations was prepared to use his skill and British backing in an effort to organize resistance, and the tribes farther west could also be called upon for aid. Along the Wabash were the Miami, the Wea, the Piankashaw, and other tribes, and to the north of that river were numerous Potawatomi. These tribes were as yet little touched by the advancing American frontier and were far less impressed by American power than the tribes farther to the east.

American difficulties in negotiating with or defeating the Indians of the Old Northwest were much increased by the policy of the British in the years between 1783 and 1794. The major problem was that although the British had agreed in the peace treaty to withdraw from their line of military posts south of the newly established Canadian-American border they did not in fact do so. Of great importance for the control of the Indians were

Joseph Brant, Mohawk chief. Engraving by J. R. Smith after a painting by G. Romney. (The New York Public Library)

the posts at Mackinac, Detroit, and Niagara. Farther east the British also retained posts at Oswegatchie and Oswego on Lake Ontario and at Dutchman's Point and Point-au-Fer on Lake Champlain. The immediate decision to stay in the posts was taken by the British authorities in Canada; the main responsibility falling on General Frederick Haldimand, governor in chief of Quebec. Haldimand was influenced in his decision both by a desire to avoid an Indian uprising which might follow the sudden withdrawal of British power from the West and by his willingness to implement the wish of the Canadian fur traders to retain the posts through which they controlled the trade adjoining the Lakes. He was supported in his decision by the British government, which justified the retention of the posts on the grounds that debts were still owed by Americans to British subjects. As a result of this retention, the Indians were still in direct contact with British emissaries, received British supplies, and had ample reason to believe that British power merited their respect.[20]

The British not only retained possession of the Northwest posts, but until 1794 they also actively influenced the Indians against the United States. Beginning in 1783 the British encouraged the Indians to resist American demands for land and backed an Indian confederacy under the leadership of Joseph Brant. In the years after the Revolution the United States faced Indians in the Northwest who had not been defeated in the Revolution and who were receiving considerable encouragement from the British.[21] In view of these difficulties the impoverished Confederation government might well have pursued a policy of extreme caution in the Old Northwest. Instead, assuming that the American victory in the Revolution would overawe the Indians, the Confederation conducted an aggressive Indian policy regardless of the weak American army. Ignoring colonial precedents, the government leaders took the attitude that the British cession of land westward to the Mississippi included not only territorial sovereignty over the region but also the actual right to the soil on which the Indians lived.

Between 1784 and 1786 the United States dictated treaties to those Indians who had claims to land in what is now eastern and southern Ohio. In October 1784 at the treaty of Fort Stanwix, the Six Nations yielded all their claims to land west of Pennsylvania. At Fort McIntosh on the Ohio in January 1785, the Delawares, Wyandot, Chippewa, and Ottawa agreed to be confined to an area that is now north central and northwestern Ohio. At the mouth of the Great Miami at the temporary Fort Finney in January 1786, the Shawnee agreed to live on lands west of the Great Miami.

At these treaty councils there were no negotiations in the real sense of the word. The tribes were told that the British had ceded the land on which they lived but the United States would allow them to retain some of their lands. The Indians were overawed by the occasion and by troops at the council ground, did not understand the talk of "sovereignty" and "right of soil," and later refused to carry out the provisions of the treaties they had signed.

By 1786 the Confederation government had obtained the area northwest of the Ohio from the states, had passed ordinances by which it could be governed and parts sold, had obtained considerable cessions from the Indians, and had taken steps to move illegal squatters. In appearance this was a coherent policy. In reality few actual settlers could afford to buy land on the government's terms; the Indians were disgusted at the treaties and were still raiding south as far as Kentucky; squatters came back as fast as government troops chased them out.[22]

An apparent way out of the government's immediate problems developed in 1786 and 1787. Since the end of the Revolution Brigadier General Rufus Putnam had shown an interest in acquiring a tract of land in the West for the settlement of New England Revolutionary veterans. It was hoped that this could be acquired by the use of depreciated federal debt certificates, which the government would accept at face value. Putnam interested his friend Brigadier General Benjamin Tupper in his western project, and Tupper traveled west to look at the Ohio country. In January 1786 Tupper and Putnam called for interested Revolutionary veterans to meet in Boston in March. There the Ohio Company was formed, with a proposed capital of $1,000,000 in depreciated continental certificates which were to be exchanged for stock in the company. At first it was envisioned that those who purchased stock would migrate to the Ohio country, but in the long run less than one-third of the shareholders actually emigrated.[23]

Even with the use of depreciated continental certificates, a year was required to raise a quarter of the necessary capital. With this on hand it was decided to begin negotiations with the Confederation Congress on the grounds that once the Company was in actual possession of a valuable tract it would be far easier to attract additional investors. In the early summer of 1787 the Reverend Manasseh Cutler traveled to New York to open negotiations. The purchase of a large tract, on terms contrary to the provisions of the Ordinance of 1785, was made possible by the machinations of the secretary to the Board of the Treasury, William Duer, and by the readiness with which Manasseh Cutler accepted his suggestions.

The crux of the arrangement was that the Ohio Company, as well as applying for 1,500,000 acres for itself, would also apply for an option on another 5,000,000 acres for a newly formed Scioto Company, in which Duer and other politicians would participate. The Scioto Company was eventually established with thirty shares, of which thirteen were controlled by Cutler and Winthrop Sargent of the Ohio Company, thirteen by Duer and his associates, and four were to be sold in Europe. It was also agreed that the Ohio Company would pay $500,000 when the land was granted, $500,000 when it had been surveyed, and the balance in six installments—all of it in depreciated certificates. Duer promised to make up any deficit in the initial payment in exchange for the Scioto arrangement. As he had influential support, Cutler was able to deal strongly with Congress in the summer of 1787, and in October the Ohio Company was sold 1,500,000 acres along the Ohio River. It turned out to be more when surveyed, and the company actually obtained its lands for some eight cents an acre. The Scioto Company received an option on a vast area west of the Ohio Company purchase.[24]

The efforts of Duer and Cutler in the summer of 1787 also helped to bring about the passage of a new measure for the government of the public domain. The Jefferson Ordinance of 1784 had undergone criticism both from those who thought it did not provide for a sufficiently strong control over the frontiersmen and from those who feared the creation of too many western states. Since 1785 Congress had discussed possible revisions of Jefferson's ordinance, and by the time Cutler arrived in New York to obtain land for the Ohio Company Congress had almost agreed on a revised plan. As the Ohio Company wanted to be able to ensure its investors that an orderly form of government had been adopted for the territory northwest of the Ohio, Congress now had good reason to enact a new measure without further delay. The Northwest Ordinance was passed on July 13, 1787.

The Ordinance stated that the territory northwest of the Ohio was first to be governed as one unit, but would eventually be divided into not less than three or more than five territories. These territories would pass through two stages before being allowed to form a constitution and enter the Union. In these two stages all effective power would rest in the hands of the central government through its appointees, although the inhabitants of the area were guaranteed fundamental liberties through a bill of rights written into the Ordinance, and slavery was prohibited.[25]

Although there has been a tendency in recent years to emphasize the undemocratic features of the Northwest Ordinance, it did provide in practical fashion for the policy of amalgamation first expressed during the Revolution itself; new areas would not be treated indefinitely as colonial dependencies—dependencies which would in the course of time want to break away—but as territories eventually to be fully equal to those in the East.

The New Englanders of the Ohio Company wasted no time in establishing themselves on the lands they had obtained from Congress. In the winter of 1787–1788, one party set out from Massachusetts and another from Connecticut. After traveling overland, fifty or so settlers gathered at Sumrill's Ferry on the Youghiogheny River some thirty miles southwest of Pittsburgh. There they spent the early months of 1788 building their own boats and finally in April set off down the Youghiogheny River to the Ohio. With a good New England sense of history they named their main boat *Mayflower*. On April 7, 1788, they landed near the mouth of the Muskingum River, where the United States had already constructed Fort Harmar and

Fort Harmar, Ohio, in 1790. From *The American Pioneer*, 1842. (The New-York Historical Society)

founded Marietta, named after Marie Antoinette in remembrance of French aid in the Revolution. Most of these settlers were Revolutionary veterans, and they were obliged to make use of their military experience in the following years.[26]

Since the treaties of 1784–1786, Indian hostility had increased. The Indians disavowed the treaties they had signed and raided when they could. The few regular troops on the Ohio were totally inadequate for offensive warfare, and before 1790 the only expeditions northwest of the Ohio were sent by the Kentuckians. Some of the easterners resented these Kentucky raids, arguing that they merely increased Indian hostility, but a committee of the Confederation Congress commented in 1786 that "the offensive operations commenced by the inhabitants of Kentucky are authorized by self preservation and their experience of the imbecility of the fœderal government." [27] Confronted by hostile Indians and beset by financial worries, the Confederation government decided that it would have to abandon the policy of claiming all Indian lands in the northwest by cession from Great Britain. It would be much cheaper to pay for lands than finance a military expedition. In January 1789 in two treaties at Fort Harmar, the government obtained a confirmation of the earlier cessions from part of the Indians in the Old Northwest, for a payment of goods to the value of $9000.[28]

These treaties were of no use to the settlers huddling together for protection at Marietta. The Shawnee had refused to negotiate after 1786.

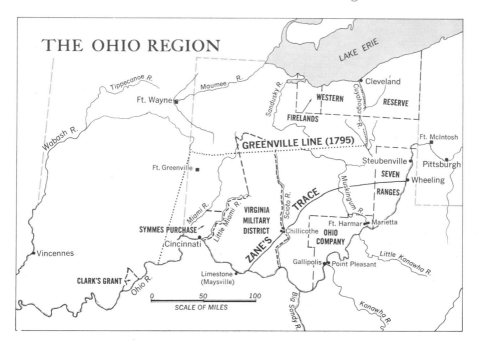

Many other Indians disavowed what had been done at Fort Harmar, and from 1789 the sporadic warfare of the post-Revolutionary years assumed an even fiercer aspect. In Kentucky and north of the Ohio pioneers carried their guns wherever they went and strengthened their cabins. At Marietta rangers employed by the Ohio Company scoured the surrounding country for hostile Indians.[29] Any frontier hopes that the new and more powerful government formed in 1789 would soon provide protection and punish the Indians collapsed in 1790 and 1791.

In 1790 the new federal government authorized an expedition against the Indians northwest of the Ohio. It was organized by General Josiah Harmar in consultation with Arthur St. Clair, the recently appointed governor of the Northwest Territory. Their plan was for a two-pronged attack against the Indian villages in what is now northeastern Indiana. The west wing of the attack, consisting of a small group of regulars and 300 militia from Virginia and Pennsylvania under the command of Major John Francis Hamtramck, marched from Vincennes at the end of September. He found that the Indians had deserted their Wabash villages, and his column achieved little. Meanwhile General Josiah Harmar led a force of some 300 regulars and 1200 militia northward from Fort Washington (now Cincinnati) to attack the Indian villages in the region of what is now Fort Wayne, at the portage between the Maumee and the Wabash. Harmar moved very slowly. He burned the Indian villages at the Maumee-Wabash portage in the middle of October but then by detaching parts of his army managed to lose two engagements with the loss of some 180 men. The Indians, with good reason, considered they had been victorious, and the expedition had done nothing to demonstrate American strength to the hostile tribes. The Indians were now confident, and the American task was made more difficult by the British Indian Department, based in Detroit, which was both supplying the Indians and helping them gather to resist the American expeditions.[30]

In 1791 Secretary of War Henry Knox decided it was essential to try again; the frontiers of the Northwest and Kentucky were now completely unsafe. In the early summer militia forces made diversionary attacks against the Indian villages on the Wabash to keep the Indians away from the American frontiers, and in October Arthur St. Clair led an expedition northward from Fort Washington to establish a post at the Maumee-Wabash portage. It took St. Clair a month to move one hundred miles north of Fort Washington, and on November 4 his force was overwhelmed by a sudden Indian attack. Over six hundred of his men were killed; the rest fled back to Fort Washington, taking days instead of weeks to cover the ground. It was the worst defeat ever inflicted upon the United States by the Indians. They were now triumphant, and no place on the frontier was safe.[31]

The Ohio Company settlers lived in a state of siege in their early years in the West. Marietta was across the Muskingum from Fort Harmar and was laid out, with Yankee thoroughness, as a village of wide streets and ample squares. But the inhabitants spent most of their time in one of two stockades. The strongest was the Campus Martius, with blockhouses at each corner, built to resist any Indian attack. In the first years there were food shortages, attacks of smallpox, and fear of Indian assault, but all was not gloom. One resident spoke of the garrison life having "broken up former fixed habits of industry, and led to a fondness for sports and social meetings where drinking was practiced, and hours spent in jovial conviviality." To

Camp Martius, Marietta. From S. P. Hildreth, *Pioneer History.* (Ohio Historical Society Library)

most travelers, however, the New Englanders of southeastern Ohio were a refined, circumspect element in frontier society.[32]

In spite of the extreme danger from the Indians, settlement began to expand beyond Marietta in these early years. Outposts were begun at Belpre, farther south along the Ohio, and at Waterford, up the Muskingum; but in the winter of 1790–1791 expansion northward was stopped when Indians attacked the new settlement at Big Bottom, killing twelve and capturing five. Waterford was now in imminent danger, and the inhabitants retreated into a fort. As late as 1793 there were probably less than 500 pioneers living in the Ohio Company settlements.[33]

For all their hardships those who settled under the auspices of the Ohio Company were far better off than those who put their trust in its bastard offspring the Scioto Company. Unlike the Ohio Company, the Scioto Company was intended purely for speculation not settlement, but it embarrassingly obtained settlers when the agent sent to France to sell stock to French speculators instead sold nonexistent land to optimistic Frenchmen. These unfortunates arrived in the United States in the spring of 1790 to the consternation of American partners in the enterprise who had an option but had bought no land; the Company failed in 1792.[34]

Over a thousand Frenchmen arrived in the United States to occupy the nonexistent Scioto lands. They soon became aware of their misfortune, but it was agreed that they could settle within the Ohio Company purchase at a settlement to be called Gallipolis. Some four hundred took advantage of this offer and went to Gallipolis in the late fall of 1790. Instead of the city, abundant fields, and balmy climate they had been promised in France, they found a few huts precariously perched on the edge of a great forest.

The settlers were mostly artisans from Paris and Lyons, knew little about frontier farming, and suffered considerably from hunger. As if this and the danger from the Indians were not enough, their settlement was also located at the edge of a swamp. The fevers were soon killing more than the Indians. Some fled, but there were still 250 or so there at the end of 1792. This number had been reduced to under 150 by 1796, by which time all visitors agreed that there were few more dismal places to be seen in the West. One visiting Frenchman called it an "abode of wretchedness," and Pennsylvanian Andrew Ellicott who had little good to say of any of the settlements of the Ohio thought "of all the places I have yet beheld, this was the most miserable." Congress granted surviving families some lands on the Little Scioto, but few tried more pioneering.[35]

The Congressional sale of land to the Ohio Company encouraged other speculators to bid for land north of the Ohio. The biggest of these was Judge John Cleves Symmes of New Jersey. Symmes, who became one of the judges of the Northwest Territory, originally obtained from Congress 1,000,000 acres between the Great and Little Miami rivers in what is now the southwestern corner of the state of Ohio. He had difficulty meeting his

View on the road from New-Windsor to Morris-Town, New Jersey. Many left this placid farm country for the dangers beyond the Ohio. (The New-York Historical Society)

payments, and eventually kept about 300,000 acres; even so some settlers suffered from his habit of selling lands outside his official boundaries and his carelessness in recording claims.[36]

The first settlement within the Symmes purchase was made by a small party of twenty-six men who in November 1788 founded Columbia near the mouth of the Little Miami. It was an unfortunate location, as it was frequently under water, but these pioneers showed remarkable confidence in establishing themselves in such a place at such a time. At the end of December another small party founded the settlement of Losantiville, opposite the mouth of the Licking River on the other side of the Ohio; its name was changed to Cincinnati in 1790. In February 1789 Symmes himself led a party to found North Bend on the Ohio River west of Cincinnati, and very near to the modern Indiana line. The early emigration into the Miami purchase was a New Jersey enterprise, but there were also settlers from Kentucky and from western Pennsylvania.

Symmes was displeased by the lack of government support at the time of his initial advance north of the Ohio. In the spring of 1789 he complained that although the Marietta settlements were far less exposed than his own over two hundred troops were stationed there while he had been given only one ensign and seventeen troops for protection. He admitted that some in Kentucky called his Miami purchase the "Slaughterhouse," but complained that the Kentuckians were trying to prejudice strangers against his settlements. His irritation at the lack of military support lessened in the summer of 1789 when Fort Washington was built in the vicinity of Losantiville. The fort provided the protection the Miami settlements so badly needed, and helped to bring about an increase in population in the following years. Symmes' purchase was excellent farming country; good timber interspersed with many prairies. In spite of all the Indian difficulties, its population was some 2400 by 1793, and Cincinnati was developing as an important town on the lower Ohio with a population of several hundreds; its growth was considerably helped by the use of Fort Washington as a base for government expeditions against the Indians.[37]

Apart from Marietta, the Miami purchase, and Gallipolis, there were few pioneers north of the Ohio before 1795. Even the squatters who had crossed to the north bank after the Revolution were at times frightened away by Indians confident after their victories over Harmar and St. Clair. The only other region that began to be occupied during these years was the area in eastern Ohio whose survey had been authorized under the Ordinance of 1785. The first basic geographer's line ran forty-two miles west from the junction of the Ohio River with the Pennsylvania boundary. At first seven ranges were to be surveyed south of this line, bounded on the east by the Ohio River. The survey of the seven ranges began in the spring of 1785. The surveyors were harrassed by the Indians, and it was not until the summer of 1787 that land from the first four ranges was on sale in New York. The auctions resulted in the sale of less than 73,000 acres. Although the survey was completed in 1789, the dangers and the price of the land dissuaded settlers, and for several years there were only a handful of them on the Ohio below Fort Steuben.[38]

The land northwest of the Ohio could not expect a rush of settlers until the constant danger from the Indians was removed, and the Indians would not cease resisting the American advance across the Ohio until they had been defeated in battle. After their overwhelming victory over St. Clair they were too confident to concede anything in negotiations, and American attempts at sending peace missions, from 1791 to 1793, were designed more to delay and lessen Indian attacks than actually to achieve a peaceful settlement. They also served to convince the people in the East that everything possible was being done to avoid war.[39]

Any slight hope of peace evaporated completely in the face of increased British intervention in the Old Northwest. In March 1792 the British minister in the United States, George Hammond, was told by his government that he could offer mediation in the American-Indian conflict. The basis of an agreement should be no American settlement west of the Muskingum River and the guarantee of Indian territory beyond that river in the Old Northwest as a neutral barrier state. Hammond did not formally make this offer, as he feared the American reaction, but the British authorities in Canada went further than their government in England. When in 1792 two American envoys went to Niagara in the hope of sailing on the lakes to Detroit to persuade the Indians to make peace, the British refused them permission to proceed even though both Detroit and Niagara had officially been ceded in 1783. Other efforts to achieve a lasting peace in 1792 were also unsuccessful; two of the peace messengers, Captain Alexander Trueman and Colonel John Hardin, were killed by the Indians before they could deliver their message.[40]

The Indians did agree to meet the Americans to discuss a new treaty in 1793, but they stated categorically that the boundary was to be the Ohio River; all those settlers who had crossed to the north bank would have to leave. In the negotiations at the mouth of the Detroit River in the summer of 1793 the discussions never passed the preliminary stage. The Indians were aided throughout by members of the British Indian Department at Detroit and would not budge from the Ohio as a boundary. They told the American commissioners:

> We desire you to consider, brothers, that our only demand is the peaceable possession of a small part of our once great country. Look back, and review the lands from whence we have been driven to this spot. We can retreat no farther, because the country behind hardly affords food for its present inhabitants; and we have therefore resolved to leave our bones in this small space to which we are now confined.[41]

The last faint chance of peaceful agreement had gone. The American government was prepared for the failure of the negotiations and even while

Detroit in 1780. By David Meredith. (Detroit Public Library)

General Anthony Wayne. By Edward Savage. (The New-York Historical Society)

Detroit in 1794. Watercolor by E. H. (Burton Historical Collection, Detroit Public Library)

these efforts were being made General Anthony Wayne had been organizing an expedition against the northwestern Indians. Mindful of the St. Clair catastrophe, he had gone about the task in a careful and methodical manner, taking pains with the training of his men and the organization of supplies. When news of the failure of the 1793 negotiations reached him, it was too late in the year for military operations, but he moved north from the Ohio and established Fort Greenville. There he spent the winter of 1793–1794, waiting for the next campaigning season.[42]

While Wayne waited, the Indians, with the help of British Indian agents Alexander McKee and Matthew Elliott, prepared to wage their last great fight for the land of the Old Northwest. The agents freely distributed supplies and helped to gather the Indians from as far away as Mackinac and Saginaw Bay. Even Lord Dorchester, the governor in chief of Canada, delivered an inflammatory speech to the Indians in February 1794, and shortly afterward the British rebuilt their old Fort Miami near the rapids of the Maumee, in what is now northwestern Ohio, and garrisoned it with a small party of British troops. But, for all these preparations, the Indians suffered a setback in the early summer of 1794. A costly mistake at the end of June was the Indian attack on Fort Recovery, which had been constructed by Wayne on the site of St. Clair's defeat. The Indians traditionally disliked attacking entrenched positions and were perhaps driven into this attack by overconfidence. They were beaten back and thus suffered their first setback in years.

Wayne finally marched his main force from Fort Greenville late in July. The Indians chose to defend themselves in a grove of fallen trees near the rapids of the Maumee, and were bolstered by a detachment of militia

The Treaty of Greenville, August 1795. Believed to have been painted by an officer of Wayne's staff. (Chicago Historical Society)

from Detroit. Their traditional fasting before the battle worked distastrously for them, as Wayne delayed his attack for three days. When his troops finally moved forward on August 20, 1794, many of the Indians were away collecting provisions. By the time they ran back, the armies were fiercely engaged. The Wyandot put up a particularly brave struggle, but the Indians finally fled in confusion downstream, hoping to find shelter in Fort Miami. They discovered, however, that while the British had been prepared to encourage and give provisions, they were not prepared to risk outright war with the United States. The gates of Fort Miami were closed to the Indians, and they had to continue their flight toward the mouth of the Maumee.[43]

Wayne's victory at the battle of Fallen Timbers was rounded off by two treaties. In November 1794 John Jay, who had been sent to England to discuss the crisis precipitated by British actions at sea against American neutral commerce and by British interference in the Old Northwest, signed a treaty which included the surrender of the Northwest posts. In the next two years Great Britain withdrew from American soil; Detroit and Mackinac were abandoned to the Americans in the summer of 1796.[44] Meanwhile the Indian tribes defeated at Fallen Timbers had in August 1795 signed the Treaty of Greenville by which they ceded what is now southern and eastern Ohio, and a strip of southeastern Indiana, to the United States. Moreover, the United States prepared for further expansion in the Old Northwest by obtaining some sixteen reservations for posts on the Indian side of the boundary line and the right of communication between them.[45]

The battle of Fallen Timbers was a turning point in the history of the Old Northwest. Those few pioneers who had clung tenaciously to the north bank of the Ohio were in the next twenty years to be joined by hundreds of thousands of hopeful emigrants. Settlement could thrust up the river valleys away from the Ohio, and the river itself became for the first time a safe highway. The years of crisis and desperate defense were over.

◁ 3 ▷

Southern Settlement, 1796–1815

*I*n the years after Wayne's victory at Fallen Timbers in 1794, the most dramatic frontier growth was in the Old Northwest. Ohio changed from almost complete wilderness in 1790 to a state populated by over 581,000 in 1820. This dramatic illustration of the frontier process tends to obscure the exceedingly rapid increase in the recently settled areas of the South in the same period. By 1810 Kentucky had a population of 406,511 and Tennessee, 261,727; in 1820 their combined population was nearly 1,000,000[1]

This great growth of population did not mean that the whole area westward from Virginia and North Carolina had passed out of the frontier stage. Much depended upon the ease of access to a particular region, the fertility of the soil, the availability of water, and the strength of Indian resistance. Within Kentucky some areas were highly developed, while pioneers were living in others much as the first settlers in the region had lived in the 1770s and 1780s. Moreover, there was no clear progression from civilization to wilderness as one advanced westward. What is now West Virginia stayed far more primitive than central Kentucky throughout this period. A traveler commented in 1802 that "All that part of Virginia situated upon the left bank of the Ohio is exceedingly mountainous, covered with forests, and almost uninhabited." Game still roamed freely, and settlers from Ohio crossed to hunt bears every winter. As pioneers did move into western Virginia they hugged the banks of the Ohio and its tributaries, engaging in subsistence farming more than the production of cash crops for a market.[2]

The main towns of western Virginia were Wheeling and Charleston. Wheeling in its early years had been renowned for its gambling and drinking, but by 1814 the town was respectable enough to make a decent impression on a visiting minister, who was pleased to see "females of respectable appearance walking four or five miles to meeting."[3] Wheeling prospered from the emigrants who came there to take passage down the Ohio and from the goods that were shipped through there rather than through Pittsburgh; although farther from the eastern source of supply, Wheeling had the advantage of being downriver from Pittsburgh and consequently suffered less from low water in the dry seasons. By 1814 it had over a hundred cabins and houses and a number of large stores, and although it had little industry, it was the center of commerce for the surrounding country. Charleston developed later than Wheeling, but by 1810 it was about as large and was also a commercial center.[4]

In the years after 1800 travelers down the Ohio generally agreed that the Virginia side was less prepossessing and less developed than the northern bank, and those from the North or from England were usually quick to point out that this could be attributed to the evils of slavery. A traveler who took this point of view in 1803 was also, although he did not realize it, giving his reactions to two different stages in the development of the frontier:

> *Here*, in Ohio, they are intelligent, industrious, and thriving; *there*, on the back skirts of Virginia, ignorant, lazy, and poor. *Here* the buildings are neat, though small, and furnished in many instances with brick chimneys and glass windows; *there* the habitations are miserable cabins. *Here* the grounds are laid out in a regular manner, and inclosed by strong posts and rails; *there* the fields are surrounded by a rough zigzag log fence. *Here* are thrifty young apple orchards; *there* the only fruit that is raised is the peach.[5]

Although nonsoutherners continued to ascribe the differences between the Virginia and the Ohio banks of the Ohio to the existence of slavery in the South, slavery was in fact not extensive in western Virginia.[6]

The reflections on the evils of slavery which were inspired by the contrast between Ohio and the western regions of Virginia tended to be modified as travelers reached Kentucky. Here progress was rapid, in spite of a slave population of 126,732 by 1820. Most observers, favorably impressed by Kentucky development, were less caustic in their remarks on the slave system than they had been farther upriver. Scotsman John Melish said in 1811 that the slaves in Kentucky appeared "better fed, better lodged, and better clothed than many of the peasantry in Britain," although he was perhaps telling more of the condition of the British working class in the early nineteenth century than of the actual condition of the slaves. Early Kentucky resident Daniel Drake writing in the 1840s considered that the treatment of slaves in early Kentucky was far worse than at the time he was writing.[7]

Anyone landing at Limestone (later Maysville), Kentucky, after 1800 found conditions far different from those of twenty years before. Limestone itself remained fairly small, but the route from Limestone to Lexington had been transformed; one traveler in 1807 commented that "the country on every side appears to be better improved than I have observed it in any part of America."[8] Washington, four miles from Limestone, had some two hundred houses as early as 1802, and by the time of the War of 1812 these were mostly of brick. Near Lexington in this first decade of the nineteenth century the roads became wide and in good condition; everything was cultivated; and the whole vista appeared more like the settled areas of the East than a frontier.[9]

Lexington was praised by most visitors. The streets were broad, and many of the houses were of brick. By 1815 it was a trade center of great importance, and had hemp industries, schools, churches, and a population of between 6000 and 7000. The country around Lexington was among the most developed west of the Appalachians. On the thirteen-mile road from Lexington west to Versailles in 1811 "the country was really beautiful, and the improvements, which have nearly all been made within twenty years, present a most pleasing picture of the progress of society. There are finely cultivated fields, rich gardens, and elegant mansions, principally of brick, all the way."[10]

The other Kentucky towns were smaller and less important than Lexington. Frankfort, the state capital, was renowned in these years for its state prison, where prisoners were continually occupied in useful tasks. But one visitor complained in 1810 that there were "elegant accommodations provided for those who make the laws, and those who break them, but there is no house of God."[11] Louisville developed only slowly before 1815. The early complaint of the prevalence of fever and ague continued, but gradually the population increased. Settlers numbered over 2500 by 1815, and the town's prosperity was to develop rapidly with the coming of the steamboat.[12]

Although the towns helped the countryside attain economic prosperity, the basic task of winning the frontier was carried out on the farms. The towns were little more than the long-term investments of frontier promoters until sufficient rural population had arrived to create a demand for imported goods and provide farm produce for export. In these years after 1800 rural Kentucky engaged in far more than subsistence farming and exported tobacco, hemp, and a variety of other products to New Orleans. The region around Lexington and between the Kentucky and Licking rivers was most developed, but the whole area of north central Kentucky, along the Ohio as far as Louisville, was becoming intensively farmed. In the southern part of the state, development was much slower. The infertile and broken "barrens" from the Green River to the Tennessee line still had a small and scattered population in 1812; the pioneers concentrated in the areas where water was available. Western Kentucky was far less prosperous than the central parts of the state, and one cleric's view of the region was that "the great mass of the people are very rude, ignorant, and vicious." [13] For all its increase in population, Kentucky still presented the full range of frontier development in 1815.

Tennessee did not grow as rapidly as Kentucky in the years after it became a state in 1796; the development of eastern Tennessee was hampered by mountainous terrain and inadequate communications, and even western Tennessee was less accessible to settlers than the states directly adjacent to the Ohio. On his way through the hills of eastern Kentucky into Tennessee in 1803, Methodist Bishop Francis Asbury wrote:

> A man who is well mounted will scorn to complain of the roads, when he sees men, women, and children, almost naked, paddling bare-foot and bare-legged along, or labouring up the rocky hills, whilst those who are best off have only a horse for two or three children to ride at once.[14]

The real American pioneers were not the Daniel Boones and Davey Crocketts killing Indians and running fleet-footed through the wilderness, but women and children trudging barefooted on rough western roads.

To add to the difficulties of a rugged terrain and inadequate communications, Tennessee still faced the resistance of numerous Indians in the years after 1796. Much of the state was in the possession of the Cherokee, and the federal government had the difficult task of obtaining more and more land while preventing Indian war. Although the policy was eventually disastrous for the Indians, the government achieved its objectives in the years before 1815. This was done by a combination of methods. The government kept up a steady pressure on the Cherokee, offering them annuities for their lands and, if necessary, resorting to the bribery of influential chiefs to secure cessions. Once a cession was obtained the government attempted to maintain the established boundaries against the American settlers in order to avoid Indian hostility at illegal encroachments. When the frontiersmen increased in number and preventing encroachment became too difficult, the government persuaded the Indians to make additional cessions.

In order to reconcile the Indians to the reality of their ever-decreasing lands, the government also attempted to persuade them to adopt the ways of American civilization. This was no elaborate policy; it mainly involved providing a few agricultural implements and teaching the women how to spin and weave. The object was to persuade the Indians to accept the concept of private property and to live on small farms rather than roam over a large hunting area. This policy had more success among the Cherokee than among other southern tribes, but the acquisition of land was always more important than the bringing of civilization.

Treaties with the Cherokee in the years from 1798 to 1806 were negotiated mainly with the object of obtaining the Indian-owned land that separated the settlements of eastern and western Tennessee. After the treaty of Tellico in 1798 the Cherokee for a time resisted further cessions. But in two treaties at Tellico in October 1805, after gifts to individual chiefs, the Indians ceded the land separating eastern and western Tennessee and also the remainder of their lands between the Cumberland and Duck rivers. The following year in Washington these cessions were increased by land between the Duck River and the Tennessee. Even the Chickasaw of western Tennessee came under pressure, and in July 1805 at Chickasaw Bluffs they ceded land north of the Tennessee River.[15]

The two cores of settlement in Tennessee continued to be in eastern Tennessee along the river valleys of the Holston, the Clinch, the French Broad, and their tributaries, and in western Tennessee along the Cumberland. Population thinned as it expanded outward from these centers. Although both soil and communications were poorer in eastern Tennessee, the full effect of these handicaps was not felt until after 1815 when the cotton economy of the western parts of the state became more highly developed. Knoxville was the most important town in eastern Tennessee. It was a flourishing settlement with a population of over 1000 and considerable trade by 1815.[16]

Along the Cumberland in western Tennessee and in the area east of the Tennessee and north of the Duck rivers, cotton became the dominant crop, and there was a considerable expansion of the slave system in these years. Nashville had a population of over 1100 by 1810, and was a trade center of great importance, exporting via the Cumberland, Ohio, and Mississippi rivers. Only in the extreme west was Tennessee still a wilderness in 1815.[17]

After Pinckney's treaty of 1795 the two most notable areas of frontier development in the lower South were within the state of Georgia and in the areas along the Mississippi River. The turning point for Georgia was the cession of her western land claims to the federal government in 1802. As a condition of this cession the state received a pledge from the government that Indian claims to land within Georgia would be quieted as soon as possible. In 1800 Georgia's population was 162,686 (including 59,699 slaves) and the main westward drive was toward the land in the forks of the Oconee and Ocmulgee rivers.[18] The federal government met with stubborn resistance in its efforts to negotiate with the Creeks for large land cessions. At Fort Wilkinson in June 1802 the Creeks would cede only about half of the land in the forks of the Oconee and Ocmulgee, and land south of the Altamaha River and above Rock Landing. Not until November 1805, after considerable pressure by negotiators, did the United States obtain the rest of the land in the Oconee-Ocmulgee forks. As with the Cherokee the federal government attempted to combine the acquisition of land with the bringing of civilization. This effort was less successful among the Creeks than among the Cherokee.[19]

Georgia pursued a generous policy in the granting of land to her frontiersmen; in 1803 a law provided for land to be distributed by lottery for the payment of only a recording fee. Population continued to increase—it was over 250,000 by 1810—but the presence of the Indians, who still owned over half the state in 1815, and the counterattraction of Kentucky and Tennessee for southern emigrants prevented any dramatic thrust westward. Cotton cultivation spread slowly across the state, and although the state capital was located at Milledgeville, well away from the coast by 1815, population began to thin out some fifty miles or so to the west on the road to Fort Hawkins.[20] Georgia, already a state at the beginning of the Revolution, was unable to occupy even half of her official limits by 1815.

Much of what is now the states of Alabama and Mississippi was ceded by Georgia to the federal government in 1802. This whole region labored under severe disadvantages. As western Georgia was still unsettled, the only connections eastward by land were through Indian country. There were additional problems to the south and west. The land along the Gulf of Mexico, New Orleans, and the whole area west of the Mississippi was in foreign hands. Without American control of the rivers running into the Gulf the development of this area was severely hampered. This situation was dramatically altered by the Louisiana Purchase of 1803.

The Louisiana Purchase was precipitated by the secret Treaty of San Ildefonso of October 1, 1800. In this treaty Spain agreed to retrocede the Louisiana territory to France. Now a major power, not moribund Spain, would control American commerce on the Mississippi River. All the old problems of the 1783–1795 period could well be repeated; this time with a far more dangerous opponent. By 1802 definite news of the Louisiana cession had reached the United States, and in October the Spanish, who were still in control of the area, precipitated a crisis by suspending the American right of deposit at New Orleans. No longer could the westerners land their goods at New Orleans, store them, and export them by sea without the payment of duties. The American frontiersman blamed not Spain but France for this decision, assuming that it had been ordered by the new owners, and demanded prompt action to preserve American rights.

To avoid the possibility of war, Jefferson in 1803 sent James Monroe to France to join Robert Livingston in an effort to purchase New Orleans and the Floridas. Independent of any American action, Napoleon had decided even before Monroe arrived in France that he would sell the whole of Louisiana. Napoleon's colonial ambitions had been dealt a severe blow by the failure of his army to take control of Santo Domingo, and he now had less use for Louisiana. Moreover, England and France were near a renewal of their war; Napoleon knew he would find it very difficult to hold Louisiana against British naval strength, and if he was to campaign in Europe, he needed money. Accordingly, he determined to sell the whole of this great area stretching to the Canadian border and the Rockies to the Americans; Monroe and Livingston exceeded their instructions in agreeing to buy the whole of the territory for $15,000,000. These treaties, which were signed on May 1 but dated April 30, ended the constant threat to American settlements in the lower half of the Mississippi Valley. They opened up a great area for settlement across the Mississippi River, and doomed Spanish control of the Floridas.[21]

A strange irony was that the purchase of Louisiana, which effectively ended any real threat of separatism in the Mississippi Valley, was followed by the most famous of the southwestern conspiracies, that of Aaron Burr. It is justly famous in that it involved a vice-president, but as a western conspiracy it was hopeless from the beginning. In 1805 and 1806 Burr discussed with the British, the Spanish, and the westerners a plot whose details changed to suit the hearer: it would separate the western states from the Union, or bring about an invasion of Mexico; or result in seizure of the President; or involve the capture of Washington and an expedition to create an independent Louisiana. Burr's ambitions collapsed pathetically in December 1806 when only one hundred men were ready to sail down the Mississippi to carry out his schemes. Burr was acquitted of treason, although if such plotting had been carried out twenty years before by a man of his national prominence it could have been dangerous. As it was, the plot was merely a strange interlude in the history of the West which damaged local political reputations but had no chance of success.[22]

The Louisiana Purchase, although placing the Spanish possessions east of the Mississippi River in jeopardy, did not suddenly solve the commercial problems of what are now Alabama and Mississippi. The rivers running into the Gulf were still controlled by Spain, and the most desirable areas for settlement from the point of view of communications were directly east of the Mississippi. It was this part of the region that developed most in the years before 1815.

In 1783 settlement within what is now the state of Mississippi was concentrated around the post of Natchez. Some settlers had been there as early as the second decade of the eighteenth century, but the permanent development of the region had begun after the British won possession of it in 1763. The American Revolution helped the population growth, for Loyalists fled from the eastern seaboard to find refuge on the Mississippi. By 1788 the population of the Natchez district was over 2600 and was helped immediately after that date by the Spanish policy of encouraging immigration by special privileges, including freedom from imperial taxation and a guaranteed market for tobacco. Although the Spanish government ended this policy

Aaron Burr. By John Vanderlyn. (The New-York Historical Society)

of artificially raising the price of tobacco in 1790, the population had reached 4300 two years later. These settlers increasingly turned to the cultivation of cotton.[23]

In 1795 Spain agreed to relinquish all the land north of the 31st parallel, but it was 1798 before she allowed the agreed boundary to be surveyed and Congress was able to create the territory of Mississippi. This territory at first was limited to former Spanish lands south of the Yazoo, but after Georgia ceded her western claims in 1802 the boundary was extended north to the Tennessee; its eastern limit was the Chattahoochee.

At the time of the Spanish cession the population was concentrated in the Natchez region, and as late as 1800 the total population of what is now Mississippi amounted to only 7600. Although there was slavery and the production of cotton as a cash crop was becoming increasingly important, the region in many ways had hardly passed out of the most primitive frontier condition. "Plantations" for the most part consisted of a log cabin, a few slaves, and a cotton patch. In 1797 travelers out of Natchez had to manage their journey so as to arrive before night at a plantation where pasture for their horses would be available, for it was not always to be had. The visitors slept on the floor, wrapped in their blankets, and usually dined on a "mess of *mush* and milk" and some fried bacon. Although the territory had been settled for so long, commented one traveler, it had "all that inattention to neatness, cleanliness, and the comforts attending thereon, that there is in a country just cleared." Even the residents protested in 1799 against "the present ruinous State of the roads and bridges throughout the whole of this Territory." [24]

In the years after 1798 settlement was restricted by the distance from eastern centers of population and by confusion over land titles. There were no surveyed government lands, and not until 1803, after Georgia had ceded her western claims, were land offices established in the territory and long-established residents given firm titles. Between 1803 and 1810 settlers began to enter the territory in increasing numbers, often coming downriver from Kentucky and Tennessee. By 1810 the territory had a total population of over 40,000 (including 17,088 slaves); the greatest number of settlers were still along the Mississippi, particularly in the river counties south of Natchez.[25]

Natchez waxed rich on Mississippi River commerce; its wharves were crowded with boats from the Ohio, and its merchants shipped out the cotton of the region to New Orleans. The riverfront had long been notorious for its vice, and was a favorite haunt of the Mississippi boatmen. But by 1815 the town had a population of over 2000; substantial houses had been built; and there were Methodist and Presbyterian churches.[26] Even though much of the territory was still occupied by the Indians, it was on the verge of statehood by the time of the War of 1812.

The eastern portions of the Mississippi Territory, now much of the state of Alabama, attracted little immigration before 1815, but the foundations were laid for a rapid development after that date. Prior to 1800 the only American settlements were north of Mobile on the Tensaw, Mobile, and Alabama rivers, and farther north around Fort Stephens on the Tombigbee. There had been a few French before 1763, but the first important increase in population came during the Revolution, when Loyalists from the Carolinas and Georgia moved in.

The Spanish withdrew from Fort Stephens in the spring of 1799, and in 1800 Washington County was created within Mississippi Territory to cover the whole area between the Pearl and the Chattahoochee rivers; the Alabama region had a population of only some 1250, including nearly 500 slaves. Americans who had entered since the Revolution had often come to evade justice.[27] In 1804 it was said:

> The present inhabitants (with few exceptions) are illiterate, wild and savage, of depraved morals, unworthy of public confidence or private esteem; litigious, disunited, and knowing of each other, universally distrustful of each. The magistrates without dignity, respect, probity, influence or authority.—The administration of justice, imbecile and corrupt.[28]

Before the United States occupied Mobile in the War of 1812 there were few areas in the West in a worse position for communications than the infant Alabama region. The Spanish charged a tariff on all goods entering or leaving through Mobile, and hundreds of miles of wilderness separated the settlements from Georgia in the east or the Mississippi in the west. The post road established in 1805 to connect Fort Stoddert on the Tombigbee with New Orleans was for many years only a primitive track.[29]

An entirely separate settlement began to develop in what is now Alabama after 1806, when the Cherokee ceded the land south from the Tennessee boundary to the Tennessee River. This area quickly attracted settlers from Georgia, and in 1808 Madison County was created to cover the region. It proved popular to cotton planters, and by the beginning of 1809 had over 2200 inhabitants.

The whole of the Alabama region had no dramatic development in these years. In 1810 the population was still only just over 9000, and the area was hard-hit by the War of 1812. The outlying settlements were particularly exposed to the attacks of the Creeks, agriculture was disrupted, and many lives were lost. The war did, however, make possible quicker progress in the following years by bringing about the occupation of Mobile and control of its outlet to the Gulf. But in 1815 the region was not highly developed. Corn still competed with cotton as a crop; numerous cattle were kept; and pelts obtained from the Indians were still exported through Mobile.[30]

The most prosperous, and also the most unusual, frontier development in the lower Mississippi Valley in the early nineteenth century was that of

Louisiana. From the beginning of the eighteenth century the land directly west of the Mississippi had been under French control, and at New Orleans and along the lower reaches of the Mississippi there was considerable settlement. In 1763 New Orleans and the land west of the Mississippi had been ceded to the Spanish, who held it for the next forty years.[31]

The retrocession of Louisiana from Spain to France in 1800 did not immediately affect population patterns in the region. The French merely received it from the Spanish shortly before transferring it to the Americans in December 1803. At this time the population of the Louisiana territory was over 40,000, including many slaves. Most residents were of Spanish or French descent, but there were some Americans. The main settlement stretched southward along the Mississippi from Baton Rouge, which was still Spanish. There was an uninterrupted chain of plantations, sheltered behind a continuous levee, all the way to New Orleans.[32]

New Orleans was by far the greatest city of the Mississippi Valley with a population of over 10,000; more than half were slaves or free Negroes, and the rest, a mixture of French, Spanish, American, English, Scotch, Irish, and a variety of other nationalities. Although large and long-established, New Orleans was still in these years a curious mixture of European city and frontier town. During the day the river at the levee was crowded with the boats of Kentuckians and Tennesseans, rough and ready backwoodsmen ready to drink and carouse in this great metropolis; but on a summer night the gravel walk along the levee, shaded by orange trees, was used as a promenade by fashionable New Orleans residents.

The houses in the main streets near the river were of brick, with open galleries and gardens crowded with shrubs and flowers, but back from the river they soon gave way to wooden, ill-kept cabins. When the Americans took over the town, the streets were unpaved, and in wet weather pedestrians avoided the mud by balancing on the narrow wooden drains used to carry off water and filth; the rain at least cleared the stench. The houses could not have cellars, for any hole in this sodden soil filled with water mixed with delta mud; all the drinking water was taken from the river.

As late as 1808 a band of poor, debauched, practically naked Indians lived near the city. All of them, women and children included, were constantly drunk, and there were daily scenes of "riot, obscene dances and intoxication." Yet, at the same time the town supported two French theaters, with a "brilliant audience" on Sunday evenings.[33]

Even vice in New Orleans was not only the rough and ready debauchery provided for the boatmen here and all along the river. It was the common thing for New Orleans gentlemen to keep a free colored concubine. "These in most cases are selected from the mixed breeds," commented one outspoken American military man, "except among the Spanish settlers, who prefer a fat black wench to any other female!"[34] The new American Governor William Claiborne thought the citizens were "uninformed, indolent, luxurious—in a word, illy fitted to be useful citizens of a Republic." The gay indolence was one side of New Orleans, but another was the periodic yellow fever which killed a great many of the American newcomers.[35]

The contrasts that were present in New Orleans were echoed to a considerable extent in the rest of Louisiana. Although the river front from Baton Rouge to New Orleans presented a succession of plantations and a high degree of cultivation, the land away from the river was often no more developed in these years than most other areas of the Mississippi Valley. Much of Louisiana was still a frontier wilderness, but in the years after 1803 settlement of the unoccupied areas proceeded rapidly.

The counties of Opelousas and Attakapas, west of the Atchafalaya River, proved particularly attractive to new American settlers; they joined a number

View of New Orleans from the plantation of Marigny, November 1803. Oil by J. L. Boqueto De Woiserie. (Chicago Historical Society)

of French who were already well-established in the region. The extensive rich prairies interspersed with scattered groves of wood and cut by many small streams provided ideal country for grazing cattle. Most of the settlements were on the River Tache and the other waterways. Attakapas County, which extended north from the Gulf to Opelousas, profited from its cattle and cotton, and increasingly from its sugar cane; by 1812 many of the planters were living as well as established plantation owners along the lower Mississippi.

Lands in the Opelousas were not as low lying as those in the Attakapas, and were also not generally as fertile, but the country was beautiful and much healthier than the areas farther to the south. There were immense meadows, plantations scattered along the waterways outside the fringe of woods, and great herds of cattle roaming over the prairies. Cotton was an important crop, and the cultivation of sugar cane was developing. The cattle were driven to New Orleans for sale.[36]

The Opelousas region stretched northward to the Red River country, which was also becoming increasingly interesting to pioneers in the decade after the United States acquired Louisiana. By 1812 settlements were scattered sporadically along the Red River Valley from its mouth on the Mississippi all the way to Natchitoches, over two hundred miles away, and even beyond. The French long established there had been joined by numerous American pioneers. They raised corn and cotton and kept cattle, hogs, and horses; in the neighborhood of Natchitoches "innumerable herds of cattle and horses" were to be seen in every direction. Apart from Natchitoches the main settlements were at Avoyelles, about sixty miles from the Mississippi, and at the rapids, another sixty miles or so up the river.

Northern Louisiana was less developed in these years, but cotton was being grown in Catahoula and Ouachita counties, and in Concordia there was extensive grazing of cattle and the raising of corn. There were also scattered settlements on the routes to the Red River.[37]

By 1810 the Territory of Orleans (modern Louisiana) had a population of 76,556, of which 34,660 were slaves, and in that year its bounds and population were increased by the addition of part of West Florida. The most developed area of West Florida was north of the town of Baton Rouge, and there the old inhabitants, including Revolutionary Loyalists, had been swamped by the recent American immigration from Mississippi Territory, and even farther up the river. America had long shown a diplomatic interest in the region. In 1810, when the inhabitants rose in revolt, declaring their independence from Spain and their desire to join the United States, President James Madison quickly issued a proclamation in October annexing West Florida west of the Perdido River to the United States.[38] In 1812 Louisiana came into the Union as the first state of the trans-Mississippi West. This was no typical frontier state. Its long occupation by the French and Spanish had given it a distinctive character, but Americans from Mississippi Territory,

Kentucky, and Tennessee came in large numbers to push back the bounds of the frontier.

Most of the land obtained in the Louisiana Purchase of 1803 was un-occupied except by Indians, but farther up the river, in what is now the state of Missouri, the purchase included some long-established French settle-ments as well as some far more recent American advances. After 1803 the region did not have the dramatic growth of the Ohio Valley, but it gained

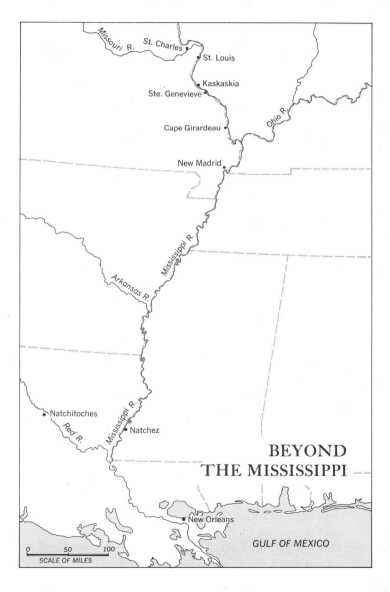

BEYOND THE MISSISSIPPI

population slowly. Many frontiersmen of the Ohio Valley who disliked the increasing population, the disappearing game, and the advancing civilization, came out to the Missouri country to renew their struggle with a virgin frontier country.

The area of settlement in this Missouri country stretched from the Arkansas River, in what is now the state of Arkansas, to north of the mouth of the Missouri; but there was comparatively little settlement on the Mississippi below the mouth of the Ohio. A few hundred hunters and pioneer farmers lived along the Arkansas River, separated by a wilderness from the pioneers to the north at New Madrid. This settlement of New Madrid had been established by American speculator George Morgan, with Spanish encouragement, in 1789, and the pioneers of the region had originally lived on the peltry trade. By 1815 they were concentrating more on agriculture, growing cotton and tobacco as well as the ever-present corn and flax.

The town of New Madrid itself never lived up to the hopes of its promoter and early settlers. The river kept eating away its banks, and the cabins had to be moved farther and farther back. The inhabitants kept corn and cattle for their own consumption and sent cotton to New Orleans, but it was not of good quality. The men had to trade with the Indians for peltry and hire themselves out as boatmen, while their wives raised a little corn to keep themselves alive until the return of their husbands who "eat, drink and dance as long as their money lasts, and then take another trip to obtain a fresh supply." The settlement was dealt a major blow in the winter of 1811–1812 when an earthquake that rocked the whole Mississippi Valley hit this area with particular force; many residents fled.[39]

The Cape Girardeau district (in present southeastern Missouri) was not settled until the mid-1790s, but Americans came in steadily after that date, settling for the most part on the land ten or twelve miles back from the river and on the waters of the St. Francis. They raised corn, flax, cotton, and tobacco and sent pork and beef downriver to New Orleans. The Ste. Genevieve region to the north had a population of over 1000 by 1815, and exported lead and salt throughout the eastern half of the Mississippi Valley. Formerly a quiet French rural community, Ste. Genevieve was the despair of frontier preachers during these years. Nearly everyone gambled, and dances begun at dusk often continued until ten or eleven o'clock the next day. Even when dancing the rough and ready frontiersmen did not leave their weapons behind. A concealed knife could "fall out of the bosom, or from behind the girdle, while its owner was dancing with a lady, without her betraying the least sign of surprise or displeasure."[40]

A wagon road connected Ste. Genevieve with lead mines fifty miles or so to the west. These were scattered over a considerable area, and the lead was smelted on the spot in the woods. It was a tumultuous region in which "the continual broils and quarrels among the workmen, as well as the proprietors, keep up a constant scene of warfare." As at Ste. Genevieve knives were carried, usually well concealed, and often pistols as well. Although many of the miners were French, the region attracted adventurers from most parts of the United States.[41]

Settlements were scattered along the river north of Ste. Genevieve, but the next main concentration of population was in the St. Louis area. Many Americans came into this part of Missouri, and by 1815 they were in the majority. Apart from St. Louis the centers of population were Carondelet and St. Ferdinand, and as in the rest of the Missouri territory the French tended to stay in the towns and villages while the Americans expanded the farming area, growing corn and trading pork, beef, and a few peltries. St. Louis itself had long been an important fur trading center, but it experienced some loss of prosperity in the early nineteenth century owing to the diminishing game on the lower Missouri. It flourished again, however, as more population moved into the region, and as fur traders went farther up the Missouri.

After 1810 the Missouri pioneers began to push farther west. St. Charles had been the old limit of settlement on the Missouri, and in the 1790s the Frenchmen who lived there hunted and traded with the Indians and hired themselves out as boatmen. They were very poor, and a visiting fellow countryman commented in 1796 that "it would be difficult to find a collection of individuals more ignorant, stupid, ugly, and miserable." [42] After 1810 new pioneers pushed beyond St. Charles to the Gasconade River. They also went north beyond the mouth of the Missouri up the Mississippi, and there was even a thrusting of pioneers way into the interior of the territory with the development of the settlement in the Boonslick area after 1807.[43]

Although Missouri had a population of over 20,000 by 1815, it had not passed out of the first frontier stage. Its long-established French villages existed alongside the American farming settlements rather than as leaders or even partners of these communities. Traders in the towns concentrated on exporting lead, salt, and peltries, and the Missouri farmers still often exported their own produce down the Mississippi and did not depend on middlemen. The Missouri frontiersmen were on the cutting edge of the frontier throughout this period.

By 1815 the southern frontier extended from the western regions of Virginia and North Carolina to Missouri, and from central Georgia to central Louisiana. Within this area there was great divergence in the extent of development. It was not possible to travel westward passing in orderly stages from civilization to wilderness. In 1815 frontiersmen were living in the first stage of development and contending with virgin soils or forests in central Georgia, western Virginia, and western Tennessee, in Louisiana, in Mississippi and Missouri territories, and in what is now Alabama. At the same time landowners in the Lexington area of Kentucky or on the banks of the lower Mississippi were often living as richly as planters on the eastern seaboard. The concept of a continuous frontier running in a great arc around the western edge of American settlement simply did not apply on the southern frontier in these years. There was a series of disconnected frontier cutting edges scattered over the whole area from Virginia, North Carolina, and Georgia to Louisiana and Missouri. Even this is an oversimplification, as within a state such as Kentucky one pioneer in 1815 might still be building his log cabin on land never before farmed while twenty miles away a prosperous eastern plantation owner might be buying up a farm that had been improved for twenty years. In all areas, the desirable land—fertile, convenient terrain, well-watered—was developed first, and pockets of less desirable land were left to be pioneered when the pressure for land became greater.

Population distribution on the frontiers of the South in these years was determined by a variety of factors. Some were legacies from the colonial period. The concentration of population in the upper South had made possible the advance through the Cumberland Gap; the late settlement of Georgia in the colonial period meant there was simply insufficient population in the immediate post-Revolutionary years to bring a rapid advance westward. Legacies of eastern population concentration could only be overcome by favorable river systems. The Ohio took innumerable pioneers down to Kentucky, or on again to Louisiana or Mississippi Territory, or up the Cumberland to Tennessee. Indian tribes also played their part in the distribution of population and the rates of expansion. Although Georgia was not heavily populated, its settlement would have proceeded much more rapidly if the Creeks had not occupied so much of the state. In the same way the development of central Tennessee was delayed by the presence of the Cherokee. Kentucky, on the other hand, was not occupied by powerful Indian tribes, and although the settlers suffered much from Indian raids, they did not have to remove Indians from the land on which they wished to live. The nature of the soil and terrain also determined the details of the frontier advance. Undesirable areas such as the barrens of southern Kentucky and northern Tennessee were only developed when more desirable lands were taken up. Settlers flowed rapidly into the bluegrass of Kentucky when they were only meandering onto the less desirable soils of western Virginia. Least definable of all, some areas caught the imagination of the emigrants, and they would be satisfied with nothing else. For many it would have been easier to find new lands in Virginia and North Carolina in 1785 than to trudge along rocky tracks, across streams, up mountains, and through the Cumberland Gap to plunge down into the great forest spread before them, but "Kentucky" was a magic word, and nothing else would do. The same feeling was to send pioneers across the whole continent in the 1840s.

◁ 4 ▷

Northern Settlement,
1795–1815

*A*fter 1795 the movement of settlers into northern New England was overshadowed by the emigration westward. By 1810 pioneers were even leaving northern New England. Some crossed Lake Champlain (on the ice in winter) to northern New York; others pushed on to western New York and beyond the Ohio. As this happened, the cutting edge of the frontier moved out of Ohio into Indiana and Illinois.

In western New York most settlers continued to move to the lands east of the Genesee River. Around Utica by 1811 "the houses were so thick, that it was for a considerable way like a continued village. Many of the buildings were elegant, with fine orchards attached to them, and the plots of ground adjoining were fertile and elegantly cultivated."[1] The New York military tract east of Lake Seneca had an estimated 30,000 settlers as early as 1804; many of these were from New England, but there were also pioneers from eastern New York, Pennsylvania, and New Jersey. West of Lake Seneca toward the Genesee there was the same bustle of settlement and growth, particularly along the route of the Mohawk Turnpike, which stretched westward from Albany to Utica and Canandaigua, and then on to Avon on the

View of Utica, New York, from the hotel, September 1807. Watercolor by Baroness Hyde de Neuville. (Stokes Collection, The New York Public Library)

Genesee River. The whole region had a flavor of New England, with its white houses, churches, and neat farms. Only in the hilly section of the southern Genesee country were the New Englanders in a minority. Here it was easier for the Pennsylvanians to advance northward, and the New Englanders concentrated on the more gentle slopes farther north.[2]

The land west of the Genesee River was little developed prior to 1800. Owned by the Holland Land Company, it was not until 1797 that this area was ceded by the Seneca at the treaty of Big Tree. In its tracts farther east—south of Lake Ontario and north of the Mohawk River—the Holland Land Company had attempted a "hothouse" development in the manner of the Pulteney interests, but finding that these efforts had not brought a return commensurate with the cost, it was more cautious west of the Genesee. After 1797, however, the surveying of the region was able to proceed under the direction of agent Joseph Ellicott. From 1802 an office in Batavia sold land to settlers on liberal credit terms, and settlers began to move in as roads were extended west to Buffalo.[3]

The majority of new settlers were New Englanders, but there were also Germans from Pennsylvania and Scotch and Irish immigrants. By 1811 the houses on the turnpike between Batavia and Buffalo were so numerous that it was said "that the traveller is never out of sight of one, and inns are to be found at the end of every two or three miles." Buffalo had a population of some five hundred, and although the buildings were mostly of wood there were some "good brick houses, and some few of stone." The town greatly benefited from the influx of settlers destined for places farther to the west.

Settlement northwest of Buffalo, along the Niagara River, was not heavy before the War of 1812; it was less developed than on the British side of the river, and immigration that began on the eve of the war was blocked during the conflict by the fierce fighting, during which Buffalo and Black Rock were burned to the ground.[4]

Although western Pennsylvania did not have the dramatic growth of western New York or Ohio—the majority of those who had journeyed that far preferred to travel on down the Ohio River—its expansion continued during these years. In 1790 there had been some 75,000 settlers in western Pennsylvania, the majority in the southwestern counties, and by 1810 this population had reached 210,000. Slowest to expand was the northwestern part of the state, but within this section the river and portage route south from the village of Erie (Presque Isle) by way of French Creek and the upper Allegheny River developed because of the trade southward to the headwaters of the Ohio. Much of the trade was in salt, and it suffered a severe

Advertisement from *The Albany Gazette*, December 17, 1810. (The New-York Historical Society)

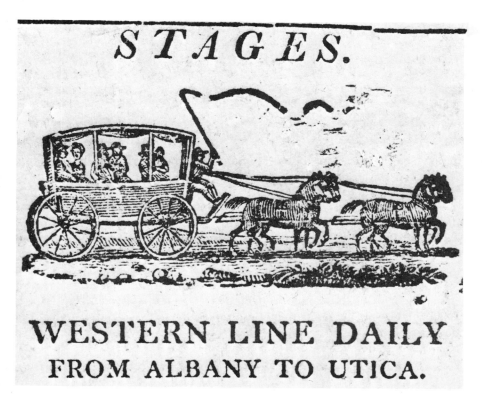

View on the Susquehanna. From Maulevrier, *Voyage dans l'Intérieur*, 1796. (The New-York Historical Society)

blow with the rapid growth of the salt works along the Kanawha after 1810. West of Erie population increased only slowly before 1815.[5]

The boom area of western Pennsylvania was around Pittsburgh. Until 1795 Pittsburgh's development had been slow, but after that date the great influx of settlers on their way west brought prosperity. The town, providing for the settlers passing through and serving as entrepôt for goods from the East on their way to settlements down the Ohio, was fast becoming a western industrial center. Pittsburgh was a bustling, thriving settlement but presented an unusual appearance for a western town. Since its early years the readily available coal had been used by the residents as a cheap fuel. Visitors talked of the pall of smoke, and by 1815 Pittsburgh had a problem which became more common a hundred years later. The smoke that hung over the town descended "in fine dust which blackens every object; even snow can scarcely be called white in Pitsburgh." Its population in 1815 was about 7000; there were numerous factories; and Pittsburgh showed every sign of the great development to come. It had come a long way from the straggling cabins, fur traders, and drunken Indians of 1783.[6]

In 1794 settlers still clung precariously to the north bank of the Ohio River, but Wayne's victory in that year and the Treaty of Greenville in the next made possible a rush of population that soon grew to a torrent. Before 1800 pioneers still moved mainly to the Marietta region and the Miami country. The only important new development was in the large Virginia military district between the Little Miami and the Scioto rivers, which had been reserved by the state of Virginia for the claims of her Revolutionary veterans. Nathaniel Massie had founded Manchester, the district's first town, in 1791, but settlement of the area had hardly begun before Wayne's victory. Land warrants for most of the Virginia military district had been issued before 1800. These had usually been sold to speculators, and one-third of the district was owned by seventy-five individuals. In spite of this, the region gained an influx of settlers from Virginia and Kentucky, and they adopted the land system of the South, ignoring the neat townships of New England and the federal government in favor of piecemeal location of land claims. Chillicothe, founded in 1796, became the main town, and the whole district quickly took on a southern character. It also soon produced several able leaders to join Nathaniel Massie. Thomas Worthington, one of the most prominent of the politicians of early Ohio, moved into the Scioto Valley in 1797, and with him came his brother-in-law Edward Tiffin. These Vir-

Pittsburgh. Signed by Joseph Warin, probably by General Victor Collot. The second oldest known view of the city. (Stokes Collection, The New York Public Library)

ginians were soon to find themselves clashing politically with the New Englanders in Ohio.[7]

The Connecticut Western Reserve, situated in the northeast corner of the state along Lake Erie, also began its development after the Treaty of Greenville. Connecticut kept 500,000 acres at the western end of the Reserve, the "Firelands," for its citizens who had suffered property damage during the American Revolution. The remainder was sold to the Connecticut Land Company, and Moses Cleaveland was sent by the Company to negotiate for the Indian claims and to survey the land. At Buffalo in the early summer of 1796, Joseph Brant and other chiefs agreed, after accepting a small payment, to permit some settlement; and Cleaveland and his tiny party founded Conneaut on Conneaut Creek. That summer they began the task of surveying, and also founded Cleaveland on the Cuyahoga River. The Connecticut Land Company resold much of its land to other speculators, but most of the settlers were to be from New England—the majority from Connecticut. The region grew slowly in the early years, and in 1800 the population was little more than 1000.[8]

The year 1800 was a turning point in the history of Ohio, for statehood became possible when the "Territory Northwest of the River Ohio" (Northwest Territory) was divided by the creation of Indiana Territory. More important from the point of view of potential settlers was the change in the United States land laws. Although the Ordinance of 1785 insured an orderly system of survey and the establishment of title, for the most part it prevented individual frontiersmen from obtaining their land directly from the federal government. Few pioneers could pay $640 for their farm, and individual settlers avoided the lands of the federal government or moved on as squatters.

Revision of the 1785 ordinance was not a simple task. Those in the East who feared the loss of population wanted to make it more difficult, not easier, to move west. The first land surveyed—the Seven Ranges—was only sparsely populated before Wayne's victory. But the needs of the individual settlers were again ignored when, by the land act of May 18, 1796, the additional national domain acquired at the Treaty of Greenville was ordered to be surveyed and put on sale. The only concession to the frontiersmen was that provision was made for land sales in the West; land west of the Great Miami was to be sold at a land office in Cincinnati and lands east of the Scioto, in Pittsburgh. The remaining land in the Seven Ranges was to be sold at Pittsburgh and Philadelphia. In its other features this act was disastrous to the individual settler. The price was raised to two dollars an acre with useless credit facilities, one-twentieth to be paid immediately, a half in thirty days, and the rest in one year. If the farmers did not have the cash to pay immediately, they were hardly likely to have it after only one year on their virgin land.[9]

Under the terms of the land act of 1796 less than 50,000 acres were sold, and in the following years there was a noticeable increase in the number of squatters northwest of the Ohio, particularly in the valley of the Scioto and beyond the Great Miami. These settlers began to petition the government for a change in policy, and they received aid from the congressional delegate of the Northwest Territory William Henry Harrison. Under his sponsorship a new act was passed on May 10, 1800. It change the mode of selling lands and the method of payment. Although the land east of the Muskingum River was still to be sold in amounts of not less than one section, that west of the river could be sold in half sections of 320 acres. Also, in a definite attempt to put the land offices near to the places of settlement, lands were to be sold at Marietta, Chillicothe, Steubenville, and Cincinnati. The most vital change, however, was in the system of payment: the price was kept at two dollars an acre, but generous credit terms were granted. The pioneer could pay one-fourth in forty days after the sale and the other three-fourths at the end of the second, third, and fourth years. There was in addition another year's grace before he was supposed to forfeit his land. For $160 down and closing fees the settler could obtain his land.[10]

The land act of 1800 began a new era in the history of government land sales; nearly 750,000 acres were sold under this act by the end of 1802. Moreover, the new Republican administration that came to power under Jefferson in 1801 was prepared to go still further in encouraging western settlement. In 1804 the minimum area that could be purchased was reduced to a quarter-section of 160 acres, and although the price remained at two dollars an acre, the various fees, except for survey, were abolished. As stimulants to settlement the new laws were a great success, but difficulties arose from the inability of settlers to complete their payments within five years. As a result the government was obliged either to reclaim the lands or grant extensions. Although forfeiture was occasionally enforced, the bitterness and hardship it caused made the government reluctant to follow this course. Instead, from 1806, Congress regularly passed relief acts to extend the time during which payment could be made. Because of these difficulties the credit system was eventually abolished in 1820, after twenty years of aiding western growth.[11]

The combination of peace with the Indians, new land laws, and the admission of Ohio as a state in 1803 brought a rush of population to the Old Northwest. Improved roads accelerated the movement. A great many of the settlers from the East came first to Pittsburgh; the Northerners, along Forbes' Road, and the Southerners, on Braddock's Road. In the fall of 1804 Braddock's Road was "crowded with wagons and pack-horses carrying families and their household stuff westward."[12] The main route through Ohio was Zane's Trace which began at Wheeling, ran westward through Zanesville and Chillicothe, and reached the Ohio River opposite Limestone. It had existed as a packhorse route in the early 1790s, but in 1796 Ebenezer Zane opened the route for wagons. From Wheeling there was a connection by road eastward to Pittsburgh and Philadelphia. These western roads were extremely primitive. "We have concluded the reason so few are willing to return from the Western country," wrote one young woman in western Pennsylvania in 1810, "is not that the country is so good, but because the journey is so bad." [13]

Attempts to create more efficient land routes to the East were mainly in the planning stage before 1815. When Congress in 1802 passed an enabling act authorizing the Territory of Ohio to apply for statehood, it was agreed that 5 percent of the proceeds from the sale of public lands in the state would be used to finance roads to and through the state from the navigable waters emptying into the Atlantic. Also, it was decided that 2 percent of this would be used to finance a national road linking Ohio with the East. There was considerable delay while politicians argued over the desirability of the plan and attempted to decide the exact route the road would take from Cumberland, Maryland, to Wheeling, Virginia. It was not until 1811 that arrangements were made for completing the first ten miles, and it was 1818 before the road reached Wheeling.[14]

Before the completion of the national road, settlers were obliged to follow the main state routes or find their way across the country as best they could. Once they reached the Ohio many who wanted to settle in the western parts of the state still depended on the Ohio River; settlers also went by water up the various tributaries of the Ohio and in the north used Lake Erie to reach the Western Reserve. The flow of settlers seemed never ending. In 1805 it was "truly astonishing" to one traveler; and five years later in 1810 a girl on her way across western Pennsylvania commented: "From what I have seen and heard, I think the State of Ohio will be well fill'd before winter,—Waggons without number, every day go on—One went on containing *forty* people—We almost every day, see them with 18 or 20." [15]

Between 1800 and 1810 the population of Ohio increased from over 45,000 to over 230,000. For those who had known the Ohio River in the 1780s or the early 1790s, the change was particularly noticeable. Instead of unbroken forests, countless animals, and hostile Indians, the banks were studded with farms and villages. Below Marietta, on a Sunday, the banks on the Ohio side "were alive with people going to or returning from places of worship, or seated in groups in their best apparel." [16] Less than twenty years after the Marietta pioneers had huddled in their forts and the Miami purchase had been called the "Slaughterhouse," the whole northern bank of the river from Marietta to the Indiana line abounded in settlers. "Thirty years ago," wrote one traveler in 1811, "the whole country on the banks of this river was almost an entire wilderness. Twenty years ago, a friend of mine descended, and could hardly get provisions by the way. When I descended, I found its banks studded with towns and farm-houses, so close, that I slept on shore every night." [17]

The southeastern corner of the state was not as popular as many other areas farther along the Ohio, for except for the riverbottom lands the soil was generally inferior to that in other areas of the state. Steubenville was the main town in the region. It had been laid out in 1797, and within ten years was called "a handsome, flourishing town." By 1812 it had between 150 and 200 houses, many of them of brick, and over 800 inhabitants. It carried on a good deal of trade with the surrounding farmers and had about a dozen stores, which were very well stocked. Many of the early settlers in this region had simply crossed over from western Pennsylvania, although they had seldom been in that region for very long.[18]

Farther down the river the New Englanders continued to dominate the Marietta district. Marietta itself flourished in the early years of the nineteenth century as a large shipbuilding industry developed there, sending ocean-going vessels down the Mississippi to the Gulf. When that industry declined with restrictions on American commerce after 1807 and a number of ship disasters at the falls of the Ohio, the town settled into moderately prosperous trading but no dramatic growth. The population reached 1500 by 1810, and to avoid the flooding to which the original town was liable, houses were built on the opposite bank of the Muskingum, where Fort Harmar had stood in more dangerous times. "Marietta may be considered as New England in miniature," it was said in 1807 by a New Yorker, "her inhabitants are sober, honest, religious and industrious, while dissipation and irrational amusements are not known in her friendly circles."[19] Four years later an Englishman described the inhabitants as "sober, industrious, intelligent, and discreet." In fact, as though always convinced by outer demeanor, travelers almost invariably referred to the New Englanders as "sober and industrious." It became a truism of frontier description, and at times the laudation was carried to extremes, as when the same English traveler said that "the mass of the New England people get a virtuous education; they are generally handsome in their persons, active, hardy, and industrious; and it is the very flour [sic] of them who emigrate."[20]

As immigrants to Ohio came from a variety of states and tended to congregate in different sections, it was possible to draw distinctions between the characteristics of the population in different areas of the state. Certainly, in the years before 1815 Ohio appeared to be no frontier "melting pot." Shrewder visitors to the Ohio Valley observed that whereas Kentucky, with its dominant population from the upper South, could be said to have a distinct character of its own, Ohio had no distinct character but rather a variety of characters. That the observers usually gave most praise to the New Englanders of the Marietta region may perhaps be attributed to the fact that in their stress on education, religion, and sober outward demeanor the New Englanders appealed to those two groups of visitors whose impressions have usually been perpetuated—travelers writing for publication and ministers. Typical were the New England ministers who praised the Ohioans who had originated in the northeast and then commented that the immigrants of

German extraction, together with emigrants from Maryland, Virginia, and Kentucky, were too often loath to support schools and the gospels, "and too fondly cherish that high toned and licentious spirit, which will suffer neither contradiction nor opposition, and which is equally inconsistent with civil and religious order." [21]

The areas that proved most popular with the Virginians and Kentuckians were the Virginia military district and the Miami purchase. Chillicothe, the main town of the former, was a very influential early Ohio town. It was surrounded by prairies which produced excellent wheat, and was on Zane's Trace from Wheeling to Limestone. At first the settlers suffered a good deal from fevers, but by 1812 there were over 1400 inhabitants, mainly from Virginia and Maryland with some from Pennsylvania. The town had a fine situation on the west bank of the Scioto, and its well-painted houses and good order belied those who contrasted the Virginians unfavorably to the New Englanders.[22]

Southerners also moved quite heavily into the Miami country of southwestern Ohio, although the region had originally been settled by emigrants from New Jersey. It was an excellent farming country, and the inhabitants sent wheat, flour, beef, and pork in large quantities to the New Orleans market. Instead of the one county that had originally been enough for this region, by 1815 eleven stretched northward toward Fort Recovery. Cincinnati thrived on the extensive trade of this hinterland, on trade to the south along the Licking River Valley, and on the Ohio River traffic. By the end of this period it began to develop its own manufactures, and in 1815 had a population estimated at anywhere between 4000 and 6000. Nearly a quarter of the houses in the town were of brick, most two stories high. One of its residents thought that its mixed population found common ground in their "industry, temperance, morality, and love of gain." [23]

The years after 1795 saw the pushing of settlers away from the Ohio and up the valleys of its tributaries into the interior. Yet in 1815 the great majority of the population were still in the southern half of the state. The main area of settlement in the north, the Western Reserve, had not made dramatic progress. The settlers still lived for the most part in log cabins. Most developed was the southeastern part of the Reserve, where dairy produce was sent to Pittsburgh, but along Lake Erie settlement was sparse. Cleveland (Cleaveland) was unimportant; the mouth of the Cuyahoga was blocked by a sand bar, and the stagnant waters proved fertile breeding grounds for mosquitoes. In October 1811 a visitor to a tavern in Cleveland found the people looking "pale, sickly, and dejected," after a summer of fevers.[24] Farther west along Lake Erie, the northwestern corner of the state was the least developed. The Maumee river region was an important battleground in the War of 1812.

The great majority of the Ohio inhabitants were farmers, but over the state were scattered innumerable small towns and villages. These acted as

Cincinnati in 1800. Lithograph by Strobridge after a painting by A. J. Swing.
(The Cincinnati Historical Society)

trading centers for the surrounding countryside and grew as the countryside developed an agricultural surplus and began to demand imported manufactured goods. Much of the southern part of the state had by 1815 passed out of the most primitive frontier stage. In the country the more prosperous farmers were moving out of their log cabins into frame houses, were exporting a surplus, and were buying imported manufactured goods as well as making their own necessities. In the towns and villages the richer inhabitants lived in brick houses, and there were usually several churches, a school, and in the county seats brick courthouses. Although log cabins and small-scale farmers still dominated in the southern counties, the main cutting edge of the Ohio frontier was moving into the northern and northwestern parts of the state.

In the rest of the Old Northwest in these years the most important growth was in Indiana, where the population began to increase rapidly by 1815. Illinois also began to obtain more settlers, but Michigan and Wisconsin had changed little from the time that they were owned by the French.

When Great Britain ceded the Old Northwest to the United States at the end of the Revolution, the center of population in the Indiana region was Vincennes and its immediate area. Here lived several hundred Frenchmen, still disappointed at the disappearance of French rule, impoverished by the war, but possessed of the Gallic capability for enjoyment. The Kentucky historian John Filson who visited Vincennes in the winter of 1785 thought that "no people on earth live more cheerfully than the people of this place[.] balls and reveling take their nightly round, Vice and profanity become Common and habitual." Most American visitors were less tolerant of the French and attacked them for their vice and indolence.[25]

After the Revolution some Americans began to move into the region; by 1787 there were perhaps 900 French and 400 Americans in the Vincennes area, and there had been some friction, leading to violence, between the two groups. The Vincennes inhabitants had suffered in the war; their fur trade was disrupted by Indian troubles; and they lost property in 1786 when Kentuckians who were seeking Indians showed no respect for what was now American territory. Early in the 1790s, after the area became a part of the Northwest Territory, Vincennes was described as generally wearing an "aspect of distress." The town occupied an area of about half a mile square on the east bank of the Wabash and was surrounded by a large plain. It had narrow streets, log cabins, described by one visitor as "low, Old, and ugly," and only a few houses of more than one story, many "in decay'd & even ruinous condition." Many families emigrated to Detroit or to the Spanish side of the Mississippi, and after Wayne's victory over the Indians, when some of the settlers went to live on outlying farms, a large number of cabins in Vincennes were deserted.[26]

Although Knox County was established at Vincennes in 1790, the Indiana region in general was neglected by the territorial government and

for the most part was still a wilderness in these years. Buffalo were still seen
on the Indiana bank of the Ohio, and there was practically no settlement on
the river below the falls. In 1796 Clarksville, the center of the grant of
150,000 acres given to Clark and his troops on the north bank of the Ohio
opposite Louisville, consisted of "Six Cabbins and One Logg Hous with a
Stone chimney." [27] The journey from Clarksville to Vincennes was one of
the worst in America, "owing to the quantity of Trees overturned by storms,
to the thick brushwood through which one is obliged to pass; to the numbers
of Flies by which one is devoured." [28] Settlers going to Vincennes usually
landed at Pigeon Creek and drove their cattle over a path to the post rather
than attempt the difficult journey up the Wabash from the Ohio.[29]

When in 1800 Indiana Territory was created, it included land westward
to the Mississippi and northward to the Canadian border, but what is now
the state of Indiana had a population of only 2500, of whom over 1500 were
in Vincennes and its vicinity. Most of the other settlers were along the Ohio
in the southern part of the state on Clark's grant, where some 900 pioneers
lived.[30]

After 1800 there was a slow but noticeable growth in the population of
Indiana. Many of the new settlers came from Kentucky. The expansion of
population in that state and the great confusion over land titles helped to
send Kentuckians, who had often only recently come from the backcountry
of the South, northward over the Ohio. Some of the emigrants from Kentucky were also men opposed to the institution of slavery and were ready to
resist when other immigrants hoped to introduce it into Indiana.[31]

The main streams of immigration continued to flow into the Vincennes
region along the Wabash and into Clark's grant along the Ohio. Pioneers
also came in increasing numbers into the southeastern corner of the state
ceded by the Indians at the Treaty of Greenville. There were very few
urban settlements. The prosperity of Vincennes began to revive, but Clarksville remained practically deserted. Its place was taken by Jeffersonville,
directly opposite to Louisville on the Ohio.[32]

Some squatters had begun to settle along the north bank of the Ohio in
southeastern Indiana after Wayne's victory, and within a few years frontiersmen began to move into the Whitewater Valley in greater numbers. Most
of them were Southerners, and among them were numerous Quakers who
disagreed with the practice of slavery and moved to the Whitewater from
the back country of North Carolina. As in Ohio there were some exceptions
to the general American settlement. In 1802 a group of French Swiss made
a determined attempt to bring wine-growing to the north bank of the Ohio
when they established Vevay, but this outpost remained small.

With the expansion of settlement around Vincennes, along the Ohio,
and in the Whitewater Valley, southern Indiana gradually developed primitive communications between the regions. The most important road was
that between the falls of the Ohio and Vincennes; this was usually called the

"Buffalo Trace," and pioneers began to establish homes along it. Population also expanded along the water route of the Ohio; particularly in the stretch between the Gore and Clark's grant, although it thinned out farther down the Ohio. Throughout Indiana the early settlers were mostly Southerners. Some brought their slaves in violation of the Northwest Ordinance and in the vicinity of Vincennes made a determined attempt to keep them, causing a major political argument in the young territory. Yet, although some successful attempts were made to evade the prohibitions against the introduction of slaves, the number involved was small—less than 250 in 1810, when the Indiana population as a whole had increased to 24,520.[33]

By 1810 this Indiana frontier was once again facing the problem of renewed Indian hostility. This resistance was provoked by the efforts of Governor William Henry Harrison to expand American boundaries in the Old Northwest. The pressure began in 1802 and increased considerably after February 1803 when President Jefferson ordered Harrison to obtain all the land he could westward to the Mississippi. Jefferson feared that as France had obtained Louisiana, French influence would soon cause a stiffening of Indian resistance. Yet, though the Louisiana crisis soon came to an end, Harrison continued his pressure on northwestern lands, and was given ample encouragement by the central government. In a series of treaties between 1803 and 1809, Harrison obtained considerable cessions in the modern states of Indiana and Illinois, and his acquisitions even extended into Missouri and Wisconsin. Many of the northwestern Indians refused to be a party to these cessions, and those who actually signed the treaties often considered they had been browbeaten into agreement. With the renewed pressure on their lands, there was a steady growth in Indian resistance in the Old Northwest. In 1805 an Indian confederacy arose under the leadership of the Shawnee Tecumseh and his brother the Prophet.

While the Prophet tried to persuade the Indians to throw off white influence, Tecumseh argued that land belonged in common to all the Indian tribes and that a cession by any one tribe was invalid. Tension increased as Harrison persisted in persuading individual tribes to yield land. Finally in the fall of 1811 when Tecumseh was away attempting to recruit the southern tribes, Harrison marched a force northward out of Vincennes toward Prophetstown on the Tippecanoe River in northwestern Indiana. He camped within a few miles of the town, and at dawn on November 7, the Prophet launched his warriors against the American camp, promising his Indians immunity from the American bullets. Indians fell, along with the Prophet's reputation, and after a fiercely fought engagement the Indians left the field. This was an evenly fought battle, but Tecumseh's confederacy had been dispersed, and his attempt at a large organized resistance was succeeded by sporadic warfare on the frontiers.[34]

The renewed Indian threat and the outbreak of war in 1812 were not enough to stop the flow of settlers into Indiana. By the end of the war population estimates ranged anywhere from 35,000 to 60,000, with the latter figure probably nearer the truth. These Indiana pioneers had not for the most part achieved the moderate prosperity that was being enjoyed by the settlers of Ohio. Most of them were still in log cabins, engaged in subsistence farming, and living more as the Ohioans had lived in the 1790s. One observer wrote in 1807 of "the necessitous circumstances" of most of the people of Indiana Territory, and in 1814 a visiting minister wrote that "very many of these are poor people, and destitute of the Scriptures." They found life on the outer edge of the frontier a hard one.[35]

The progress of the Illinois country was slower, and existence was even more difficult than in Indiana in the years before 1815. The Illinois settlements, which were situated along the east bank of the Mississippi River from Kaskaskia to Cahokia, had in the French and even in the British period enjoyed a reasonable prosperity from the proceeds of the fur trade combined with a little farming. But like Vincennes these Illinois settlements suffered a variety of misfortunes after being taken over by the Americans. The basic calamity was the decline in the fur trade, but they were also hurt by a lack of efficient law, Indian attack, and even depredations by the Americans.

After its capture by the Americans in 1778, the Illinois country was left to its own devices until the creation of the Northwest Territory. When Governor Arthur St. Clair went there early in 1790, he found the inhabitants disgusted at the manner in which they had been treated by the American government. Their land titles were in great doubt; they were worried about losing their slaves in view of the passage of the Northwest Ordinance; and the great increase of Indian hostility had not only destroyed their hopes of a profitable trade but had also brought constant attacks. They had cultivated their fields under guard, yet settlers were killed and horses stolen. To add to their problems the Mississippi had for several years overflowed its banks. As a result of all these difficulties, there had been a gradual exodus of French inhabitants across the river into Spanish territory.[36]

At Kaskaskia in 1795 it was said that "nothing is to be seen but houses in ruins and abandoned." [37] As many of the more prosperous had left, those remaining were often as much Indian as French, and in appearance they could hardly be told apart. Everywhere were signs of poverty. Prairie du Rocher and Cahokia were no better than Kaskaskia. Many had abandoned the settlements, leaving behind the poorer residents married to the Indians. French visitors of this Revolutionary generation tended to be even more critical than the Americans. One Frenchman thought the residents were "traffickers, adventurers, hunters, rowers, and warriors; ignorant, superstitious and obstinate," and that living like Indians they had become "indolent, careless, and addicted to drunkenness, they cultivate little or no ground, speak a French jargon, and have forgotten the division of time and months."[38] An American visitor to Prairie du Rocher later agreed that in appearance the French seemed like "their savage neighbours," but he thought that their native politeness came through in talking to them.[39] Travelers rarely stayed long enough to discover that these distant pioneers had often taken on some of the values as well as the outward primitiveness of the Indians, and that their life did not have the casual brutishness which was assumed by those making a cursory visit.

From the Revolution there had been a trickle of American immigration into the Illinois country. This trickle began to widen a little after 1790, and by 1810, after the creation of Illinois Territory in the previous year, the total population had reached 12,282. Most of the new immigrants came from the South, particularly from Kentucky. There was still a heavy concentration of settlers along the Mississippi River, but new settlers were also establishing themselves on the Wabash and on the Ohio. By the time of the War of 1812, Illinois settlement was spread some thirty miles up the Wabash and forty down the Ohio. The growth of the region was restricted more severely than Indiana, however, by the Indian hostilities on the frontier from 1811 to 1814. There were frequent raids and murders, and pioneers were loath to lead their families into this region until the coming of peace. By 1815 Illinois had a population of around 15,000. The territory benefited from the navigable rivers on its borders, but internal communications were little developed.[40]

In the rest of the Old Northwest such settlements as were there were relics of French fur trading establishments and strategic posts and attracted only a few adventurous Americans. The largest was at Detroit. In the middle of the eighteenth century there had been some 500 settlers in Detroit and another 2000 scattered along the Detroit River between Lake Erie and Lake St. Clair. Although this population fluctuated in the next thirty years, the total did not change very much, and in 1812 Detroit had only some 1700 settlers with another 2000 scattered along the river. The population also remained basically French, although a ruling class of Americans came in after the British evacuation of the post in 1796 and the creation of the territory of Michigan in 1805. But the incoming population was small, and it had little impact on the rest of the country. In 1801 the postmaster general turned down the idea of a new post route from Pittsburgh to Detroit. "The distance is very considerable," he stated, "the Inhabitants at Detroit are not very numerous, the route is thro' a Wilderness and only marked by Indian foot paths and without accommodation for a post rider." The main line of American expansion ignored Michigan Territory until well after 1815.[41]

In the rest of the Old Northwest the small settlements were even more isolated, mere clearings in a vast wilderness. To the north at Mackinac the British and French-Canadians had long controlled the fur trade. It was only on the eve of the War of 1812 that American influence began to take over. To the west there was a small settlement at Green Bay, which had been reached as far back as the 1630s by the French. At the other end of the Fox-Wisconsin portage there was the somewhat more substantial settlement of Prairie du Chien, which like the settlements in the Illinois country had declined after being taken over by the Americans. But the country around these posts was in the hands of the Indians.

On the northern frontiers in these years from 1783 to 1815 the pattern of expansion was somewhat less erratic than in the South. Northwest of the Ohio before 1815 a traveler could as he journeyed westward pass from later to earlier stages of frontier development in something approaching an orderly progression. Yet, far to the east there were large enclaves, particularly in northern New York and northwestern Pennsylvania, little removed from the wilderness.

Moreover, as on the southern frontier, there could be striking differences in development within a few miles. Variations in terrain, water supply, and fertility attracted or diverted settlement in the early years. This later meant that well-established farmers and pioneers clearing virgin land could exist in the same local area. These later pioneers, however, had numerous advantages not shared by those on the outer edge of the frontier. They had no fear of the Indians, could obtain provisions locally, and perhaps secure the money to buy things by working for local farmers. Small luxuries that made life far easier were also available, and stock was less likely to be in danger from wolves or other wild animals.

The frontiersmen of the first wave of settlement, those of Ohio in the early 1790s or of Indiana and Illinois in the early nineteenth century, had to contend with mounting Indian resistance and dangers, were obliged to depend on their own resources, and faced a much longer struggle to reach prosperity than those who took up lands in an area already reasonably settled. Yet many of them cherished the opportunity of freeing themselves from the restraints of an old-established society. They dreamed of obtaining the choicest stretches of land and a plentiful supply of game to supplement their crops. Although their life seemed poor and barren to the travelers from the East, the frontiersmen often became enough attached to it to move on to another frontier rather than take advantage of an advancing society. They left the main profits and the ordered society to those who were less adventurous and who preferred to buy at least partially cleared and settled land. By 1815 these more prosperous farmers were well-established in much of western New York, western Pennsylvania, and southern Ohio.

◁ **5** ▷

The Organization of Government

*T*he organization of government for the vast areas settled after 1783 was often carried on in an atmosphere of bitter controversy. Some of the disputes echoed the previous history of American westward expansion. Throughout the colonial period newly settled areas commonly complained that officials were too far east and that the administrative structure was being extended too slowly to provide efficient government. The complaints of lack of efficiency had frequently been coupled with the accusation that longer settled areas showed great reluctance to share their power. New settlers were not necessarily striving for a more democratic government; they were often asking for a more efficient government, a government in which the decisions, democratic or not, were made in consultation with leading local citizens.

The problem of providing administration for new settlements was complicated by the American Revolution. Along with the long-existing problems of the slowness with which new areas were allowed to take a full part in government and the complaints at the lack of efficiency, there now developed a general demand for a more democratic suffrage in all parts of the country. When new constitutions were drafted early in the Revolution some of the states revised their voting qualifications to make them more liberal, and the Pennsylvania constitution of 1776 became particularly influential in other states. Although the victory of those who wanted a more democratic suffrage was not to come in all the states until the middle of the nineteenth century, the years after the Revolution brought a general struggle for the liberalization of the franchise. And this desire for more democratic voting laws naturally became one of the problems that surrounded state-making in the western states—states which cannot be viewed in isolation from the rest of the country. Most of the states of the Atlantic seaboard had bitter fights, often successful, to liberalize their constitutions in the years before 1815. Although in some states conservative forces were able to block the moves for reform, there were in others basic changes. Georgia in 1789 gave the vote to all free white males who had paid a tax during the previous year, as did Maryland in 1802. South Carolina by 1810 had adopted a more democratic suffrage.[1] The areas settled after 1783 were involved in this struggle for a more democratic suffrage; indeed they were settled by many of the Revolutionary generation who had been active in reform in their own states, and the problem was compounded by the usual demand of new areas for a more efficient government.

The only area east of the Appalachians which established a separate government in these years was the state of Vermont, and even here basic decisions had been taken prior to 1783. Although Vermont was not admitted into the Union until 1791, the region had in fact existed as a separate government since the early days of the Revolution. The Vermont constitution of 1777, although somewhat changed in 1786, was not substantially modified until the 1830s. It was based on the Pennsylvania constitution of 1776. The most liberal feature of the 1777 Vermont document, and in this it went beyond that of Pennsylvania, was the granting of universal manhood suffrage. The constitution also set up a single house legislature, although representation was based on towns rather than population. The executive consisted of a governor and council, and the governor did not have a veto power. After 1786, however, the executive could delay the laws passed by the legislature. Although the influence of Connecticut, particularly in the legal system, was strongly felt in Vermont, the area well represented those desires that had helped to produce the Revolution. In Vermont it was not so much that the environment created a frontier democracy, rather that the distant frontier attracted many in southern New England who disagreed with established authority.[2]

Apart from Vermont, Kentucky was the only frontier area which in this period had to create a government separate from an existing state rather than under the direct authority of the federal government. As Virginia did not include Kentucky in her western land cession of 1784, it was governed as a Virginia county. Its citizens in the years from 1783 to 1792 were almost constantly discussing the possibility of separate statehood, yet they found difficulty in agreeing on the precise form this separation should take. The debate began to take a practical form in 1784; by that time Kentuckians had ample reason to question the benefit of the eastern connection. Virginia had been unable to protect Kentucky from the repeated attacks of the Indians, who still posed a continual threat to the infant settlements. Moreover, settlers fighting for their lives in the Bluegrass Region had ample reason to complain of other aspects of Virginia control. The governmental system was particularly aggravating to distant pioneers; to argue legal matters in Richmond, Virginia, involved time and trouble that few were prepared to take. Land speculators had additional reasons for supporting separation, for in May 1784 the Virginia legislature had put a tax of 5 shillings per 100 acres on all land grants over 1400 acres. This may well have influenced some in their desire to end the Virginia connection, but, as in so many other areas across the Appalachians in this period, the need for more adequate government accounted for most support for separation.[3]

In summoning the first convention in 1784 the Kentuckians ignored the Virginia law that only those with freeholds had the vote, a provision unworkable in Kentucky where there was such confusion over land titles that very few could prove a clear title to the land on which they lived. Accordingly, it was arranged that delegates to the first convention at Danville would be selected by the militia, with a representation of one delegate for each militia company. In spite of some opposition, this broadening of the franchise went still further in the elections for subsequent conventions, when delegates were elected on the basis of general white manhood suffrage.[4] The first convention met at the end of December 1784, expressed its desires for separation, voiced its concern at governmental inefficiency, and protested the tax on land. It called for another convention to meet in the spring.

In the following three years several other conventions met to discuss separation, and in January 1786 Virginia accepted the principle, but there was still no final decision. The delay was caused both by the Indian warfare which removed leading Kentuckians from the discussions at crucial times, and by the impossibility of quick communication with Virginia. By the time Kentucky's petition for admission to the Union was presented to Congress in 1787–1788 that body was in the process of being superseded by the new constitution and would take no action.

It was not until July 1790, after the formation of a new federal government, that the ninth Kentucky convention made plans for actual separation and statehood. It provided for a constitutional convention, and asked Congress to admit Kentucky into the Union. Congress did this in February 1791, and in April 1792 a Kentucky constitutional convention met at Danville.[5]

This convention was typical of most in that the prosperous class was

well-represented. There existed a definite division between the conservatives, who wanted to preserve an aristocratic society, and the radicals who
wanted reform. The conservatives included those who had received large
land grants from Virginia and who wanted to perpetuate the planter aris-
tocracy; among the radicals were many who either owned no land or who
had difficulty proving their claims. After much discussion the constitution
gave a moderate victory to those who favored reform—notably in the provision that the lower house of the legislature be elected by free male suffrage and be reapportioned every four years on the basis of population and
in the provision for the popular election of militia officers and members of
local government. More caution was shown in the decision that the senate
and the governor were to be elected by an electoral college and that the
judges were to be appointed by them. The constitution was based quite
closely on Pennsylvania's of 1790. It was as democratic as any in the United
States, certainly more democratic than that of the parent Virginia.[6]

The advance into the wilderness had not created a brand new frontier
democracy, but as the frontier tended to attract those dissatisfied with
established institutions, Kentucky provided a modest victory for those who
favored reform. As has ever been the case, it was far easier to draft a new
constitution with reform features, even against conservative opposition,
than to alter an existing constitution.

Outside of Vermont and Kentucky the frontier areas that formed their
governments in these years had to evolve within the general framework
of government first laid down in the Northwest Ordinance of 1787 and its
subsequent modifications for areas outside the Old Northwest. The Northwest Ordinance was a conservative document, vesting all power during
the first stage of government in the hands of the federally appointed governor and judges. Even in the second stage, permitted after there were 5000
free adult males, the governor was given the power of absolute veto and
could prorogue or dissolve the assembly at will. There were also other careful checks on the legislature. By insisting that only free adult males who
owned fifty acres could vote for the lower house, the Confederation Congress set more stringent voting restrictions than existed in most of the eastern
states. The legislative council was far removed from popular will; the lower
house was to choose ten men, each owning at least 500 acres, from whom
Congress would choose five. These first two stages gave little power to the
frontiersmen. Indeed in the authority it gave to the governor it smacked
too much of royal government for western settlers who had so recently
fought against it.

The main hope of the frontiersmen for direct influence on Congress
rested in their territorial delegate. In the second stage of government the
council and the house combined elected a delegate to Congress. He had
the right to speak but not to vote. In the territory itself it was hoped that

the rights of the inhabitants would be protected by "articles of compact" which were written into the Ordinance. These articles guaranteed freedom of religion, *habeas corpus*, trial by jury, the right of bail in most cases, moderate fines, and no cruel and unusual punishments. The power vested in the officials of the territory would at least be tempered by this written statement of individual rights.[7]

The powerful post of governor of the Northwest Territory was given in 1788 to Arthur St. Clair, a Scotsman who had settled in western Pennsylvania. "Our country is to thin of inhabitants," he had said in August 1786, "we have not hands sufficient for the cultivation of our lands much less for manufactures of the most necessary kind. emigration therefore in our present situation is hurtful, and the settlemt. of the western country still more so as civilization and government does not advance with the settlers." [8] Secretary of the territory Winthrop Sargent and one of the judges, Samuel Holden Parsons, had been prominent in the foundation of the Ohio Company, and a second judge, James Mitchell Varnum, was yet another New Englander. The third judge, John Cleves Symmes, was a New Jersey man and the dominant land speculator of southwestern Ohio. The leadership of the Northwest Territory was hardly such as to encourage libertarian ideas.[9]

At Marietta in the summer of 1788, St. Clair began an arbitrary rule that lasted for over ten years. Almost immediately there was controversy, at first among the territorial officials. The judges and St. Clair argued about the legal code, and St. Clair and Sargent had clashing personalities; the journal of the proceedings of the executive in the Northwest Territory was described by Secretary of State Edmund Randolph in 1794 as "very little more, than a history of bickerings and discontents." [10] The quarrels, the frequent absences of administrators, and the lack of any local participation in the government caused bitterness among the settlers, and the territorial government continued to be inefficient and arbitrary. Some improvements were made: the laws of the territory were refined in "Maxwell's code" of 1795. But the frontiersmen could well argue that in no empire in the world would they have had less say in how they were governed.[11]

Opposition to St. Clair could hardly be stifled after Wayne's victory over the Indians ended a long-endured state of emergency, and in 1798 the governor permitted the move to the second stage of territorial government. In providing for the election he had to modify the fifty-acre freehold qualification for voting. Many did not yet have a clear title to their lands, and many were freeholders by virtue of small town lots; accordingly those having houses and lots worth fifty acres of land were allowed to vote.[12]

The creation of a territorial legislature stimulated rather than smothered discontent. It became obvious that the governor wanted to delay statehood for Ohio, and as party bitterness increased in the United States, St. Clair, a Federalist, was opposed by the majority of settlers in his territory who were Jeffersonian Democratic-Republicans. Opposition was particularly strong in the Virginia military district, where St. Clair had two formidable opponents in Virginians Thomas Worthington and Edward Tiffin. A further complication was added by St. Clair's efforts to ensure that in any division of the territory at least one region would support the Federalists. In this he was unsuccessful, for when Indiana Territory was created in July 1800 the dividing line between the old and new territories better suited the opposition.[13] St. Clair, however, still hoped for a further division to suit his point of view and continued his opposition to statehood. He argued that it would produce "nothing but misfortune." His view of the territory was a pessimistic one. To him it was a region of mostly poor men living "in a very wretched manner," too busy "to employ their thoughts on abstruse questions of Government and policy." [14]

Unfortunately for St. Clair, his opponents were not too busy to exert pressure on the new administration of Thomas Jefferson. Whether or not they had time for "abstruse questions" they knew enough practical politics to tell Jefferson that the territorial government under the Ordinance was "a true transcript of our old English Colonial Governments, our Governor is cloathed with all the power of a British Nabob." [15] With the Democratic-Republicans in power in Washington, St. Clair's reign was nearing its end. The United States Congress decisively rejected the move to alter the boundaries of Indiana and finally agreed to go ahead with the plan for a new state northwest of the Ohio River, although available figures gave Ohio a population of only just over 42,000. This was less than required for statehood, but the move was justified on the grounds that the rate of increase was such that the population would have reached 60,000 by the time Ohio entered the Union. In April 1802 an enabling act authorized the calling of a convention to write a constitution for the new state. The act stated that delegates could be elected by all free adult males who were taxpayers.

The Republicans were successful in their efforts to obtain a convention which would favor their views; 26 Republicans, 7 Federalists, and 2 doubtful were elected. The southern elements in Ohio had the most important role in the convention, and when it met in Chillicothe in November 1802 there was only one vote cast against becoming a state. In spite of this, St. Clair urged the delegates not to proceed but rather to take another census before moving to statehood. When Jefferson heard of St. Clair's efforts to obstruct the convention he dismissed him from office. The victory of the Republicans, and the anti-St. Clair party was complete.[16]

The constitution produced by this Ohio convention was much influenced by those of Tennessee, Kentucky, and Pennsylvania but was more liberal. Both houses of the legislature were to be elected by free white adult males who paid taxes, and even an effort to give the vote to free Negroes only just failed. Members of the lower and upper houses were to serve for only one and two years respectively; there was no property qualification for membership. The convention reacted to their experiences under St. Clair by depriving the governor of most of his power, just as the states of the eastern seaboard had reacted when given the opportunity to throw off the royal governors at the beginning of the Revolution. The Ohio governor was to be popularly elected, was to serve for only two years, and had no veto power. The judiciary was also made amenable to popular control; judges were to be elected for fixed seven-year periods by the combined vote of the legislature. County and township officials were to be elected by popular vote. All in all, this constitution was a democratic one, and it was completed by a bill of rights which outlawed slavery and religious tests. The Ohio constitution was undoubtedly influenced by the national triumph of Jeffersonianism after 1800, but the atmosphere which made it possible was created by the arbitrary rule of the 1790s.[17]

While the Ohio opposition was still attempting to end the dominance of St. Clair, there were already signs farther west that the type of government authorized by the Northwest Ordinance was destined to cause controversy between any governor and the residents of his territory. The inhabitants at Vincennes and in the Illinois country had derived little benefit from the distant government of the Northwest Territory. Administration was lax, and there was great difficulty in obtaining prompt action in the courts. Discontent became acute after the second stage of the territorial government was reached in 1798; particularly irksome was the increased cost of administration. The settlers along the Wabash and the Mississippi felt that they were paying heavy taxes but were receiving little in return and petitioned for a separate government. Some settlers even wanted to return to the first stage of territorial government in order to reduce taxes. As the western request for separation coincided with the desire of the Ohio area to become more compact for the purposes of statehood, Indiana Territory was created in July 1800; its governmental system was to be in all respects similar to that established for the Northwest Territory by the Ordinance of 1787.[18]

The governorship of the Indiana Territory was given to William Henry Harrison, who had become prominent in Ohio as one of the opponents of Arthur St. Clair and as the territorial delegate to Congress. It soon became apparent that whatever his reputation in Ohio, many in Indiana looked upon him as another St. Clair. An additional complication in Indiana was the argument over the introduction of slavery. Although slavery had been outlawed by the Northwest Ordinance, some of the most influential southern settlers along the Wabash and the Mississippi favored its legalization. Harrison gave them his support. A convention at Vincennes in December 1802 agreed to petition Congress for a ten-year suspension of the prohibition against slavery. The convention members requested that slaves brought in during this period should remain as slaves after it was over. It was argued that this was necessary to attract settlers to Indiana. Congress refused to suspend the antislavery provision, but in the following years the governor and judges permitted slavery under various guises.

In regard to slavery the convention had acted in support of a conservative southern position; the remainder of its actions showed a more liberal attitude. Notably, it asked that the suffrage be given to all free adult males, that land in southern Indiana be sold in small quantities at a cheaper price, and that squatters be granted the right of pre-emption. Harrison had ample reason to understand the pressures and attacks that would be leveled against a governor who for too long resisted the desires of the people to take part in government, and the Indiana pioneers benefited from the struggles of the Ohioans. In 1804 the governor approved a vote to decide whether or not the territory should advance to the second stage of territorial government. As no change had been made in the fifty-acre freehold provision, this vote was open only to freeholders. They decided in favor of an advance to the second stage, and Harrison called for the election of a legislature.[19]

This advance did not bring peace to the territory. In the following years Harrison and his Vincennes party were challenged by a vigorous opposition who disliked both the introduction of slavery, and Harrison's rule. "Under colour of strengthingng [sic] the government," one Indiana opponent of Harrison wrote, "the governor degrades the citizen much below what an American, especially an old Veteran, like me of *seventy six* can tolerate even in a Territorial goverment under the Auspicies of the United states." [20] The whole contest was marked by virulent political and personal attack, but unlike St. Clair in Ohio Harrison realized the advantages of occasionally yielding to popular pressure. He also mustered more supporters and had the backing of the administration in Washington. In spite of the accusation of government "by terror and corruption," Harrison kept his post as governor, while the years from 1803 to 1812 brought steady victories for those who wanted more popular participation in the territorial government.

In February 1808 the first extension of the suffrage occurred when Congress agreed that the vote could be exercised by every free white adult male who had lived in the territory one year and who owned fifty acres or a town lot worth $100.[21] It soon became obvious when the Indiana territorial legislature met in October 1808 that the reform forces were gaining great strength. The lower house passed a resolution in favor of the delegate to Congress being elected on the same basis as members of the lower house. They also asked that the delegate should try to obtain the repeal of the governor's veto and of his power to prorogue and dissolve the assembly at will. Even the legislative council showed a new spirit. It passed a resolution in favor of the election of both the delegate to Congress and the upper house by the same voters who were eligible to vote for the lower house. The legislative pressure was aided by continued petitions from the inhabitants, and in February Congress granted the same basis of election for lower and upper house, and territorial delegate. The power of apportioning representatives in the territory was given to the lower house rather than the governor, and Congress gave recognition to those on the Mississippi who had long called for their own government by separating Illinois Territory from Indiana.[22]

The Indiana inhabitants now concentrated on securing free white adult male suffrage and obtained it from Congress in March 1811 for those who had been in the territory one year and paid taxes. At the same time election procedures were reformed; sheriffs could be fined for failing to perform their duties, and polling was to be by townships rather than counties. It was also specified, in a direct blow against Harrison, that persons holding offices of profit from the governor of Indiana Territory (with the exception of justices of the peace and militia officers) would be ineligible to serve in the territorial legislature.[23]

In spite of the victories the pressures continued. Petitions requested the removal of the governor's veto power, and the legislature asked for the admission of Indiana to the Union. This legislative petition, in December 1811, stated that the Northwest Ordinance had established a colonial and "Monarchal" system, "little reconcilable to the principles which have governed the institutions of the different States of the Union." The legislators argued that they had enjoyed civil and political rights in their original states and now thought it hard "to be in a degree disfranchised as a people when they have done no crime, but by their migration thither confered a benefit to the United States." [24] Some in Indiana who opposed the request for statehood on the grounds it would cost too much and that in any case the territory did not have even half the population needed, were delighted when Congress rejected the request. Political passions in the territory were now partially submerged in the general excitement of the War of 1812. During the War the legislature was able to use the excuse of Indian attack to remove the state capital from Vincennes, long the center of the old Harrison clique, to Corydon in the southern part of the territory. With the end of the war Indiana's increase in population was such that the request for admission to the Union was renewed; this time with success.[25]

Indiana in its territorial phase soon discovered, as had Ohio, that the provisions of the Northwest Ordinance established an arbitrary government that was unacceptable to settlers who had held more power in the regions from which they had emigrated. By 1812 the inhabitants of Indiana had achieved considerable success in modifying the government that had been imposed on them in 1800. With the United States in the hands of the

Jeffersonians, the citizens of the territory were able to achieve success in winning back what they considered their inalienable rights and had also managed to achieve some of the reforms that had been advocated throughout the United States since the Revolution.

During the years from 1783 to 1809 the inhabitants of the Illinois country were unhappy about both their lack of prosperity and their inefficiency of government. In the 1780s they were left to their own devices, and their incorporation into the Northwest Territory brought little improvement. The whole administrative and judicial machinery was ill-designed for the inhabitants of distant Illinois. Roads were practically nonexistent, and the main links of the settlers were to other settlements on the Mississippi. Their inclusion in Indiana Territory when this was created in 1800 did not solve their problems. Kaskaskia, Cahokia, and the other settlements in Illinois were separated from Vincennes by prairies that were parched in summer and flooded in winter. The use of the Vincennes courts involved a long and difficult journey, and the Illinois frontiersmen felt isolated and neglected.

After 1800 the Illinois country became the scene of steady and almost continual protest against the Indiana territorial government. Like the settlers on the Wabash and the Ohio, the Illinois frontiersmen objected to the despotic rule of the governor and judges but were particularly critical of the inefficiency of their government. Some of them hoped, after the Louisiana Purchase, that they would be attached to upper Louisiana to form a separate government, but their petition to Congress was rejected. It was not until February 1809 that the Illinois settlers finally succeeded in persuading Congress to create a separate Illinois Territory west of the Wabash.[26]

Once again it was specified, as at the creation of Indiana Territory in 1800, that the government would be similar to that provided in the Northwest Ordinance of 1787. However, it was also stated that an assembly could be formed whenever satisfactory evidence was given to the governor that it was wanted by a majority of freeholders, even if there were not 5000 free adult males. In this provision the Illinois Territory reaped the benefit of the struggles of the Northwest and Indiana territories. The area was also fortunate in its appointment of Ninian Edwards as governor. Edwards had a Jeffersonian belief in popular government, and he was better able to cope with the problems arising from his arbitrary power than were St. Clair and Harrison.[27]

As early as 1812 Governor Edwards provided for a vote to discover if a majority favored the advance to the second stage of territorial government. This was approved, but few were able to meet the freehold requirement for voting, only some 200 or 300 out of a population of over 12,000. This common problem in the territories arose in acute form in Illinois because public lands were not yet on sale. When the inhabitants petitioned Congress to ask both for an extension of the suffrage and the right to elect the delegate to Congress, Governor Edwards wrote to representative Richard M. Johnson of Kentucky asking him to use his influence to secure this change.[28]

In May 1812 Congress gave the vote to free white males who had lived in the territory for a year and paid taxes; they were also allowed to choose the members of the upper house, the delegate to Congress, and the members of the lower house. Although Illinois was still to experience some harsh quarrels in the years immediately after the War of 1812, its passage through the first years of territorial government was eased by the willingness of Edwards to listen to the demands of his citizens and by the lessons learned in Ohio and Indiana.[29]

The least developed of all the areas which achieved territorial status in the Old Northwest in these years was the vast Michigan Territory. In 1783 the population in Detroit and along the Detroit River was basically French, although economic power in the community was held by the British who had assumed control after Detroit was taken over by England in 1763. Detroit, and what is now the Michigan area, were officially ceded to the United States at the end of the Revolution, but Britain's decision to retain control of the posts south of the Great Lakes meant that the inhabitants were still under British military rule. This situation produced considerable agitation among the Detroit merchant class, and from 1788 the area was given a British civil government, although it should have been under American rule.

Detroit's anomalous situation came to an end in 1796 when, following the signing of Jay's Treaty in 1794, the British evacuated the town. Detroit was placed under the government of the Northwest Territory; the newly created Wayne County included not only Detroit but also practically all of what is now Michigan and parts of what are now Ohio, Indiana, Wisconsin, and Illinois. The great problem under this new government was Detroit's distance from the center of administration. Marietta, Chillicothe, and Cincinnati were far away across unsettled country, and matters became worse in 1803. With the admission of Ohio to the Union, the Detroit area was placed within Indiana Territory. Vincennes was simply too distant for effective government, and moreover the Detroit area had again reverted to the first stage of territorial government, after being in the second stage under Ohio. As soon as the Detroit residents learned they had been tied to Vincennes they began to petition for a separate government, and in January 1805 Congress passed an act creating Michigan Territory.

Between 1805 and 1812 the dissatisfaction of the residents and the quarrels among the territorial officials created a situation similar to that in the Northwest Territory in the 1790s. There was considerable opposition to Governor William Hull and to the judges. The citizens objected forcefully to the manner in which their officials governed, while Hull and the most important judge, Augustus B. Woodward, were often in opposition. The latter eventually became leader of the movement for greater local participation in government. In the fall of 1809 the residents petitioned Congress to advance them to the second stage of territorial government and also asked that the governor should lose his power of absolute veto. Congress did not act on these requests, and the argument continued to the War of 1812. In that conflict Detroit suffered more from Hull's incompetence than from any authoritarian rule. After his surrender to the British in August 1812, Detroit remained under British control until the fall of 1813 when it was reoccupied by troops under the command of William Henry Harrison. Yet, even after the war, it was to be many years before the Michigan region was to have enough immigrants to reach statehood.

In these years Detroit was too isolated from the main settlements on the American frontier to be attached effectively to another area. It was inevitably on the outer fringes of any administrative unit of which it formed a part. Yet it was also too small to conduct its own affairs without intelligent guidance, and this was not given by Governor William Hull. In such a sparsely populated area as Michigan Territory, the inhabitants with power were few in number; all knew Hull and the judges; personal rivalries and cliques became all important. It was a narrow, clannish, political society.[30]

In the area south of the Ohio, with the exception of Kentucky, frontier governments were established along the lines laid down by the Northwest Ordinance. But in Tennessee (as in Louisiana) the situation was complicated by peculiar local conditions. Unlike the area north of the Ohio, where the creation of a government coincided approximately with the beginnings of settlement, Tennessee already had a population of some 35,000 by the time the "Territory South of the River Ohio" was created by Congress in May 1790. During the period of their control by North Carolina the frontiersmen of east Tennesse had already attempted to govern themselves in the Franklin experiment. But, in spite of population and previous history, Tennessee was given a first stage government with a governor, secretary, and three judges.[31]

The governorship of this new southwest territory was given to land speculator William Blount, who in the early years attempted to ignore population growth and keep affairs in control of the governor and judges. This produced some pressure for a representative assembly, but the opposition was not as great as in the Northwest Territory. Blount's skill as a politician and his powerful friends in the region helped weaken the opposition, and the acute danger from the Indians helped to reconcile the citizens to the need for centralized power. "No body will say that the Ordinance [for] the temporary constitution of this country is a good one," wrote Blount in May 1793, "but it is to be observed that it is temporary not permanent. If certain liberties are given up temporarily, temporary benefits are given in lieu, that is the expense of government, of which the people bear no part, not even the tax of an excise, for it is borne by the federal government." [32] Blount, however, found he could not indefinitely resist the demands of the Tennessee population for a legislature. In October 1793 he issued a proclamation announcing that an election would be held to elect a general assembly. The assembly met in February 1794, nominated ten from which the five council members would be chosen, and sent Dr. James White as the territorial delegate to Congress. The interests of the large-scale speculators and landowners were well represented on the council; they were already well represented in the governor's office. [33]

The population of Tennessee was increasing rapidly, and no sooner had the new territorial legislature met than there were demands for an advance to statehood. This movement was considerably aided by Blount's decision to back it, a move which would give Tennessee more influence nationally. In the early summer of 1795 the legislature ordered a census to determine whether there was the necessary population for statehood, and whether the people wanted it. Both of these conditions were soon met—the population amounted to 77,262—and in November 1795 Blount issued a proclamation calling for the election of a convention to meet at Knoxville in January 1796. [34]

The constitutional convention was presided over by William Blount. The usual argument flared between those who wanted the most advanced ideas incorporated into the constitution and those who favored a conservative policy, yet in the long run the constitution contained a number of the reforms demanded since the Revolution. The main models were the Pennsylvania constitution of 1790 and the North Carolina constitution, but Tennessee went further than North Carolina in allowing popular participation. Both houses of the legislature and the governor were to be elected by popular vote, and there was no property qualification required for voting. Moreover, representatives were to be apportioned by population rather than by area; a bill of rights was included; and militia officers were to be elected rather than appointed. The proponents of reform did not win a complete victory. The constitution required property qualifications for governor and legislators; justices of the peace were to be elected for life by the legislature; and the justices had the power to make most county appointments. Also a religious test was included in the constitution; officeholders had to believe in God. This was certainly not the extreme reform document that some in Tennessee had wanted since the time of the abortive state of Franklin, but it incorporated reforms desired by many all over the United States. [35]

At first the Senate was reluctant to accept Tennessee's application for admission to the Union, as she had gone ahead without consulting Congress. Also the Federalists had no desire to see another state in the West, but in June 1796 the admission was approved. Tennessee had a smoother political passage after 1790 than Ohio or Indiana. There had been no long period of tutelage; Congress had been obliged by the size of the Tennessee population to allow a rapid move to statehood. Moreover, Blount, unlike St. Clair or Harrison, had established his influence in the territory he governed before he was appointed governor.[36]

In the region to the south of Tennessee, the area of modern Mississippi and Alabama, political conditions in many ways more resembled those in Ohio, Indiana, Illinois, or Michigan than those of Kentucky and Tennessee. Here, as northwest of the Ohio, the new territorial organization was not imposed on populations already well-established and numerous but on sparsely settled areas that could not expect statehood in the near future. The organization of American government for the lower part of the Mississippi Valley only really became possible after 1795 when Spain at the Treaty of San Lorenzo finally agreed that the 31st parallel would be the boundary separating American and Spanish territory. Even then there was delay as Spain did not immediately comply with the terms of the treaty. In April 1798 Congress at last passed a bill creating Mississippi Territory. It was given the same government as that created for the Northwest Territory, except that slavery was permitted. Slaves, however, could be imported only from the United States.[37]

For governor of this new territory the President nominated Winthrop Sargent of Massachusetts and Ohio. Sargent had been prominent in the foundation of the Ohio Company and had served as secretary of the Northwest Territory until appointed governor of Mississippi Territory. He had not been a popular figure in the Northwest, and his frigid manner was hardly designed to please the citizens of the Natchez district. He journeyed to Mississippi in the summer of 1798 and immediately clashed with the inhabitants.

The objections of the Mississippians ranged over a variety of subjects. Most infuriating to the Republican United States was the contention of local inhabitants that the lax rule of the Spanish had allowed them more say in their government than was permitted by the United States; some showed their liking for Spanish rule by moving south and settling on Spanish territory. Having grown used to one system of government, the settlers also objected to the new code of laws put into effect by Sargent and his judges; they also claimed that they were paying more in taxes. Many wanted more voice in the appointment of civil and militia officers, and others complained that they had not been allowed time to bring their slaves out of Spanish territory before the prohibition against the importation of slaves from foreign countries had gone into effect.[38]

Yet when in October 1799 these slaveowners petitioned Congress for an advance to the second stage of territorial government, their arguments in many ways echoed those who were demanding reform in the East and on the other frontiers of the United States. They reminded Congress that many of the citizens in the territory had fought in the struggle against England (although they did not mention the many Loyalists who had settled there). The triumph of the United States, argued the Mississippians, had established the fundamental maxim in American politics that it was the birthright of every citizen to have a voice in the framing of laws and the passing of taxes. Congress, they argued, had composed "a form of Government in which not even a Shadow of this precious privilege is retained in its first Grade." They wanted to move to the second stage of territorial government and asked the federal legislators "shall the Congress of the United States refuse to their children the same measure of liberty and rights, which by force we have contributed to wrest from Britain?" [39]

In May 1800 Congress gave the territory of Mississippi a legislature, and in 1801 President Jefferson informed Sargent that because of the lack of harmony he was replacing him. His successor, William C. C. Claiborne, a Virginian who had made his career in Tennessee and represented that state in the fifth and sixth Congresses, was better fitted to appease the Mississippians than their short-lasting New England governor. [40]

The administration of Governor Claiborne brought greater calm to Mississippi Territory. The territorial legislature, which was Democratic-Republican in sympathy, had by early 1802 repealed most of the laws passed under the Sargent administration and substituted a new code. This eased the violence of opposition, but there was still dissatisfaction with the judges and a feeling that there would have to be greater popular participation in government.

A major source of complaint, as in all territorial areas, was the restriction on the suffrage. The voting rights in Mississippi Territory were confined, as in the Northwest Ordinance, to fifty-acre freeholders. In August 1802 the inhabitants asked that the vote be given to all adult males who had lived in the territory for six months and were United States citizens. The Mississippians further requested that the members of the council should be elected in the same manner as the members of the general assembly. These objections were not necessarily only out of a desire to give the vote to small, poor farmers. The fifty-acre rule also disqualified many citizens who possessed considerable property in goods, slaves, or cattle, but owned only small town lots. These were helped in 1808 when Congress agreed that the vote could be exercised by free white adult males who owned a town lot worth $100, but general free white male suffrage was not granted before 1815. As it was, voting laws were administered erratically. In some counties all the men were allowed to vote in spite of the laws; in others qualified voters did not exceed fifteen. The Mississippi legislature continued to ask for a change in the law until the end of this period. "The Laws are made for the common good," the legislators said in 1814, "they operate alike upon all. The life the liberty and the property of every man is affected by them, Every man therefore ought to have an agency in their formation."[41]

The situation in Mississippi Territory was complicated by the desires of the small settlements on the Mobile and Tombigbee, in modern Alabama. Far separated from the Natchez district, they had ample reason to want separate territorial status but hardly the population to support it. This dissuaded them neither from asking for a separate territory nor from spelling out the type of government they desired. A memorial to Congress in 1809 from settlers east of the Pearl River requested a new territory with a popularly elected governor and a legislature to be elected annually by all free adult males who had paid a tax and resided six months in the region. They wanted no practicing attorney or clergyman to serve as representative or senator. But they at least conceded to the conservative thought that legislators should be resident for one year with a freehold or real estate. The Alabama region was not to obtain its separate government in this period, but its citizens showed every sign of wanting to obtain the most modern possible constitution, embodying some of the main reforms demanded in the rest of the United States since the Revolution.[42]

From 1811 the territorial legislature of Mississippi was making serious efforts to attain statehood. The objections of the legislators to the excessive powers of the territorial governor echoed those of Ohio and Indiana:

> Our Legislative authority is but a cypher without his concurrence, [they wrote in 1814], He is commander in chief of our Militia, possesses without controul, the authority to appoint, all officers, civil and military: who hold their appointment during his will and pleasure. He is also possessed of an absolute veto on all Laws passed by the other two branches of the Legislature, and may prorogue or dissolve the General Assembly whenever in his opinion it shall be expedient, and there is none who can demand of him the reasons of his conduct. In theory the Government can scarcely be distinguished from that which prevails in the British North American Colonies. [43]

Congress would not agree to Mississippi entering the Union as a state in this period but permitted statehood soon after the end of the War of 1812. The sharp clashes at the very beginning of American rule in Mississippi can be attributed to a population which having grown used to Spanish rule was unwilling to accept silently the arbitrary decisions of untactful American administrators. Those who had built up local power resented the all-pervasive authority of the newcomers.

In the settlements beyond the Mississippi the problems of government were complicated by the presence of a large non-American population. After France ceded Louisiana territory to the United States in 1803, Congress in October authorized the President to rule it until Congress should decide upon its new government. The new system was established in March 1804 with the division of Louisiana.

The area south of the 33d parallel, which included the well-populated region along the lower Mississippi, was made the Territory of Orleans and given a somewhat different government from other territories. Instead of merely governor and judges, legislative powers were vested in the governor and thirteen residents of the territory who formed a legislative council. This council was to be appointed annually by the President from those who held real estate in the territory and had lived on it for at least one year. The governor, however, as in the other territories, was given extensive powers. He could, with the advice and consent of the legislative council, alter, modify, or repeal the laws which were then in force; and he could convene and prorogue the legislative council at will. This was a modified version of the first territorial stage, although the territory already had a population of over 40,000.[44]

For the delicate post of governor of the Orleans territory, Jefferson chose William C. C. Claiborne, who had managed to bring a modicum of peace to troubled Mississippi. Claiborne soon discovered that the inhabitants were displeased that they had been denied all real participation in government. Many also objected to the prohibition against the importation of slaves from outside the United States. Some of the Americans who moved to the lower Mississippi after the Louisiana Purchase took the part of the French in their objections; particularly vocal was Edward Livingston from New York. In the early summer of 1804 Livingston took the lead in organizing an appeal for the immediate admission of Louisiana as a state. Governor Claiborne did not think the territory was ready for statehood, but believed the representative system should be introduced as soon as possible. Three French agents visited Washington in February 1805 and presented the petition asking for the admission of the Territory of Orleans as a state. The request was not granted, but it advanced the cause of representative government.[45]

In March 1805 Congress authorized the establishment of a government like that of Mississippi Territory. This meant that the Territory of Orleans would obtain the standard second stage government as under the Ordinance of 1787, with the exception that slavery would be permitted. The establishment of a legislature, as in other territories, allowed the opposition to the governor to become more vocal. Claiborne's position was particularly difficult because most of the members were French and had no reason to condone arbitrary American rule. The legislators sent as delegate to Congress an opponent of the governor, Daniel Clark, and pressed for statehood in the following years. They tended to attack the nature of the governor's power in the territories rather than Claiborne himself. At times even praising the governor's cooperation, they nevertheless argued that the Ordinance of

1787 was originally intended for the government of a small agricultural society and was ill-suited to a populous, wealthy, and commercial area.[46]

In December 1810 an enabling act was introduced into Congress, and although it met opposition from the Federalists, was passed over their objections, becoming law in February 1811. In the winter of 1811–1812 a convention met and drafted a constitution which was most cautious in the extent of power it was prepared to place in popular hands; this is not surprising in view of the traditions left by French and Spanish rule. The most liberal feature of the constitution was the granting of suffrage to all free white males who had a one-year residence and paid state taxes. Membership in the legislature, however, required other qualifications: representatives had to possess property valued at $500 or more and have a two-year residence; senators had to own property valued at $1000, be two-year residents, and twenty-seven-years-old. The governor of the state was made a powerful official. He was to be indirectly elected, with the general assembly choosing him from the two who received the most votes in a popular election, and he had to own property valued at $5000. His power of veto could be overridden by a two-thirds vote of both houses, but with the advice and consent of the senate he could appoint judges, sheriffs, and a number of other state officials, including the attorney general. Judges were to serve during good behavior. It was stated, however, that the governor could not succeed himself after his four-year term, and there was also a bill of rights written into the constitution.

The Louisiana constitution was a cautious document. It was obvious that the prominent inhabitants who pressed hard for more self-government before 1812 had no desire to throw unlimited power into the hands of the general population. The constitution was approved by Congress in April 1812, and in that month the state of Louisiana was admitted to the Union. Within a week it was agreed that the land east of the Mississippi and south of the Mississippi Territory as far as the Pearl River was to be added to the state.[47] In spite of its Spanish and French population Louisiana passed through the territorial phase with less difficulty than many other territorial areas. Part of this can probably be attributed to the administration of Governor Claiborne, who did not have the rigidity of a St. Clair or Sargent.

The northern area of the Louisiana Purchase presented a more typical picture of sparse population and vast unoccupied areas in these years before the War of 1812. In March 1804 this great region north from the 33d parallel (the southern line of the modern state of Arkansas) became the District of Louisiana and was placed under the jurisdiction of the governor and judges of Indiana Territory. Its position was somewhat strange as it was not incorporated into Indiana. The governor and judges made separate laws for the District of Louisiana in October 1804, but even before these had been promulgated inhabitants of the district had signed a petition protesting their rule by distant officials. Congress reacted quickly to these protests—the case was a strong one—and in March 1805 established a separate Territory of Louisiana with a governor, three judges, and a secretary. There were several governors in its early years; the most notorious being the first, General James Wilkinson, who added to his enemies during his brief term in office and became deeply embroiled in the Burr conspiracy. [48]

Missouri, like the other territorial areas, soon demonstrated a desire to enter into the second stage of territorial government, and did so in June 1812 as the Missouri Territory. The vote was given to all free white adult male taxpayers with a year's residence; they could elect a delegate to Congress as well as an assembly. The legislative council was to consist of nine members; the lower house was to nominate eighteen, each owning 200 acres of land, and the President would appoint nine with the approval of the Senate.[49]

Missouri's second stage had several improvements over that of the Northwest Ordinance. The suffrage was extended, and the election of the delegate to Congress was taken out of the hands of the legislature. The struggles which had rocked the territories for twenty years had produced some modifications to avoid the most obvious objections. Missouri was ready to begin her struggle for statehood in the years after the War of 1812.

There seems good reason to suppose that the West in these years at the end of the eighteenth and the beginning of the nineteenth century reflected quite closely in the political field the interests and aspirations of the population of the rest of the country. That this was the case should be cause for no surprise. The West gained its population from the eastern seaboard, and in the few years that elapsed between the coming of the first main body of settlers and the demands for political advancement there was really no time for them to be transformed. The West did, however, attract a large proportion of those for whom the existing society was in some way unsatisfactory, and this helped to produce western modifications of old eastern constitutions. These constitutions were in general based on eastern models, but they also incorporated democratic reforms that had been demanded in the United States since the Revolution. There was no complete overthrowing of eastern models, because in all the western states there was a conservative group, often composed of many of the most prosperous, who resisted radical change.

The major complicating factor in the political development of the territories in this period was the conservative nature of the Northwest Ordinance. The constant complaints of tyranny voiced in the West in these years reveal not so much that the West was innately more democratic than the East but rather that the immigrants from the East discovered in the first two stages of territorial government they had far less say about the way in which they were governed than they had in their original states. It was often a case of waging a struggle to win back the rights that already existed in the original states. This peculiarity of western development meant

that often there were temporary alliances between local conserva
radicals; both protested against the arbitrary alien rule imposed b
Ordinance, even though they had different ideas of what self-governm
should entail. Local landowners might want a conservative government, bu
they could well object to the manner in which they were excluded from
power in the first stage of the Ordinance.

Under the provisions of the Ordinance much depended upon the rate
at which an area was developing and on the good sense of the governor.
The first two stages were particularly hard to bear when it seemed that an
area was unlikely to reach statehood in the near future; there was then
likely to be continual bickering at what seemed to be an interminable
authoritarian rule. The territories tended to have factions and cliques rather
than well-organized political parties. Much depended on local rivalries
and personalities, and a governor such as Harrison in Indiana who managed
to ally with a powerful local clique was able to defend himself against considerable opposition. A governor who neither built a powerful local party
nor was ready to advance any aspect of local desires for self-government
often found his position practically untenable. St. Clair in Ohio and Sargent
in Mississippi both managed to antagonize too many elements in local
society to be safe and were then doomed by a new administration in Washington.

There was in these years no surge of democracy peculiarly western
in nature, but there was throughout the territories a steady demand for
more popular participation in government. Although there were influential
conservatives, powerful cliques, and land speculators in the West, there
was also a great mass of people who had shown enough independence to
make a life in a new country. This mass of population was not content to
hand the entire control of political affairs to any particular interest group
and managed to make its desires felt both in changes in territorial government and in the state constitutions. After fighting a Revolution against
British rule, Americans were ill-inclined to accept a form of government
that gave them fewer rights than they had possessed as colonials.

◁ **6** ▷

The Life of the Settlers

On a frontier that stretched from Maine to Georgia and from the valleys of the Appalachians to the banks of the Mississippi, there was obviously considerable diversity in the details of the process of settlement. Once the settlers had passed out of the most primitive stages, they developed different crops, different ways of marketing, and different social systems. Yet for all the variations in climate, soil, terrain, and in the origins of the settlers, the lives of the frontiersmen in the early years of pioneering bore a marked similarity.

The many travelers who journeyed down the Ohio River in the years after the Revolution generally agreed that in discussing expansion across the Appalachians one had to talk of "waves of settlement." To some extent these travelers copied the idea from each other, but it is also clear that the history of many individual families of this period supports the idea of a fluid frontier, with some families moving four or five times, each time to a frontier that was about at the same stage of development. Most contemporary observers discussed several stages, or waves, of settlement by which an area would pass from wilderness to a settled farming community.[1]

The first wave in most areas was usually the hunters, who had no permanent residence in the area through which they roamed. To hunt a particular district they often built a crude cabin, or lean-to, of brush and

104

the bark of trees, supported on poles. At night there was a fire blazing on the open side, and the hunters slept on the ground rolled in blankets. They moved on when the game diminished, and except for spreading a knowledge of the country and acting as guides and hunters for actual settlers, they left little mark on the country through which they passed.

After the hunters came those who actually began to cultivate the land as well as hunt. By their contemporaries they were often referred to disparagingly as "squatters" or "backwoodsmen." One unfriendly observer wrote of them as "men of morose and savage disposition, and the very outcasts of society, who bury themselves in the woods, as if desirous to shun the face of their fellow creatures." They devoted much of their time to hunting, but they also began to clear the forest and plant corn. Instead of a lean-to, there was a crude log cabin, and instead of a lone hunter, there was often a large family. The clearing in the forest was often only three or four acres, and these pioneers grew only the corn that they ate themselves. When more settlers began to come into the area and the game decreased, some moved on again to the edge of the frontier. They were, wrote one traveler, "a race which delight much to live on the frontiers." [2] In 1802 one of them on his way down the Ohio to settle on the Missouri was dressed in "a waistcoat with sleeves, a pair of pantaloons, and a large red and yellow worsted sash." He also had a carbine, a tomahawk, two beaver snares, "and a large knife suspended at his side." [3]

These backwoodsmen usually did not own the land on which they lived. They were "squatters," and when they decided to go to a new frontier they sold their "improvements" to another wave of pioneers. The new settlers cleared more land and perhaps built a better cabin. But they too, often sold out after a few years and moved on, to be followed by more permanent settlers. These put up frame houses instead of log cabins, planted new crops and orchards, and prepared to stay permanently. Often, of course, there were variations in this pattern. Some settlers who made the first small clearing stayed on for fifty years, until the whole country had been transformed. More often the second-comers made a permanent home, but it was typical for pioneers who had taken the first steps in cultivating the wilderness to leave as population increased. One Quaker group that emigrated from North Carolina to Ohio at the beginning of the nineteenth century bought out a group of five or six squatters who had been on the ground for four or five years. They paid them for their improvements and for their help in building new cabins. "If any one has an idea of the appearance of the remnants of a town that has been nearly destroyed by fire, and the houseless inhabitants turned in upon those who are left," wrote one of the newcomers, "they can form some idea of the squatters' cabins that fall." [4]

When a settler moved into a wilderness area with his family, his first task was to provide a shelter for the coming winter. A man living in isolation on the very edge of the frontier was likely to spend the winter with his fam-

Drawings by Joshua Shaw, *ca.* 1800. (Museum of Science and Industry, Chicago)

"A birch canoe pol'd among rocks and stones against a rapid stream." From Campbell, *Travels*, 1793. (The New York Public Library)

ily in a temporary shelter; but in most areas, with the help of his neighbors, he erected a crude log cabin, unfinished inside, before the winter set in. It was built of tree trunks, notched at the ends, which were fitted together to make a one-room cabin some twenty to thirty feet long, and fifteen to twenty feet wide. A variety of woods were used; in Kentucky and Ohio buckeye was prized because there was less risk of breaking axes on the soft light wood. The roof was made of clapboards, and at one end of the cabin was a chimney. This was built by laying across an extra log some three feet or so from the end wall, and then building upward to and beyond the roof with a mixture of sticks and clay. A thick layer of clay was also plastered at the back of the chimney to keep the fire from the logs of the wall. A fireplace stretching the width of the cabin was needed to heat these draughty shelters in a cold winter. Although clay was used to block up the gaps between the logs, most cabins as the wood dried out were left with a variety of cracks and holes.

In the early days, when Indian attack was still to be feared, there was only one narrow door and no windows; but in more settled times a cabin might have a door at each side of the house and a small window cut into the

The trapper's return. *Port-Folio*, January–June 1810. (The New York Public Library)

An American log-house. From Collot, *Voyage dans l'Amérique*, 1826. (The New York Public Library)

logs. As there was usually no window glass, light was admitted through some substitute, sometimes a newspaper, well greased with hog's lard.

Inside, in the first winter, conditions were of the utmost simplicity: four walls, a dirt floor, a few simple utensils, and blankets, skins, or leaves for beds. The more enterprising settlers quickly added improvements. A floor was constructed of hewn puncheons, some two or three inches thick, placed across sleepers a foot or so above the ground. These frequently shrank to leave sizable gaps in the floor. When famous pioneer physician Daniel Drake settled in Kentucky as a boy in 1788, his family spent the first winter stepping from sleeper to sleeper across the floor, as there had not yet been time to split and lay the puncheons.

When the family had more time they were likely to build a loft within the cabin, reached by a ladder. This loft was often used by the children for sleeping, all in one big bed; the bedtick was filled with dried leaves, or later perhaps with feathers, or even, along the lower Mississippi, with dried Spanish moss. The parents used a similar rough bed on the ground floor, and visitors slept on the floor in front of the fire, wrapped in blankets or skins.[5]

Shelves were made by driving pins into the logs and laying clapboards across. On these, if the family had any pretensions at all, could be displayed a few pieces of pewter carried across the mountains. In the early days the pioneers carved wooden bowls, trenchers, and even spoons for daily use. They were also likely to have a broad slab of wood as a table, a few split-bottom chairs, or more likely several three-legged stools, which were better suited to the uneven floor. The family clothes were either hung around the walls or suspended on a long pole. On pegs in the wall, or on hooks over the door, was a rifle; "in the choice of which," wrote a traveler, "they are even more particular than in selecting a wife." [6] They also brought an axe, and probably a scythe which in the years of danger from the Indians were kept under the bed at night.

In the earliest days of settlement considerable ingenuity had to be exercised to obtain the simplest objects. Containers of all kinds were scarce. In place of barrels a section of a hollow tree could be used, with a puncheon fitted into one end. Boxes were sometimes made of bark. The simplest were of hickory bark; a more delicate article was made of slippery elm bark. This was shaved smooth, turned inside out, and sewn together; a bottom and lid were made of the same bark dried flat. These could be decorated while the bark was still green.[7]

Around the hearth were the cooking utensils: the pot, Dutch oven, frying pan, and perhaps a tea kettle. The beginnings were primitive, but the cabin could be made comfortable. One settler later wrote happily of his boyhood mornings with a "hickory forestick resting on stone andirons, with a Johnny-cake on a clean ash board, set before it to bake, a frying pan with a long handle resting on a split bottomed turner's chair, sending out its peculiar music, and the tea kettle swung from a wooden 'lug pole,' with myself setting the table, or turning the meat, or watching the Johnny cake." [8]

If prosperity increased, rooms could be added, although often at first only a storehouse; eventually the more successful built two-story frame houses to replace the old log cabins. With greater prosperity came variety, and there was far greater divergence in the homes. Also, of course, there were regional variations, even on a quite primitive level. In the lower Mississippi Valley there was often a porch all the way around the house for coolness. The typical dwelling of the trans-Appalachian frontier was the log cabin. Only as the society and economy developed was there the opportunity to move into a frame or a brick home.

While sheltering his family the settler also faced the task of clearing the land to plant crops. The great forest that stretched across the eastern half of the Mississippi Valley gave the settler shelter, fuel, and material for all manner of articles. It also posed a huge labor problem. To some extent the methods the settler used to clear his land depended upon the size and type of the timber and the proximity of neighbors. If possible, he cut down the trees and expanded the cleared area little by little each year. The logs that were not needed for the cabin or fencing were burned along with the underbrush. Often the gathering together of the logs for burning and the raising of the cabin itself was the occasion of what was usually called "a frolic." The neighbors gathered, whiskey flowed freely, and large quantities of timber were consumed in the roaring fire.

"Plan of an American New Cleared Farm." From Campbell, *Travels,* 1793. (The New York Public Library)

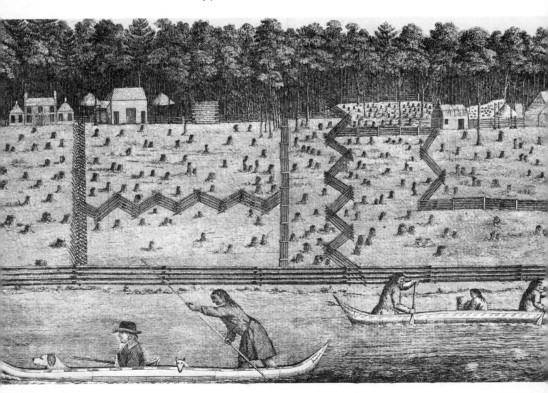

Usually, however, there were trees too large to be chopped down, and not all settlers were men of towering physique and iron wrists; there were also those who were called "the weak-handed." For at least a portion of the trees on their land most settlers had to resort to girdling; a deep notch was cut around the trunks to kill them. Some trees, like the beech, were hard to kill. Even if the settler had to girdle most of the trees in the area of his cabin, he still burned all the underbrush and the small trees and bushes.

The settler planted his crop of Indian corn among the stumps and girdled trees of his first tiny clearing. The seeds usually flourished in the fertile humus. Fortunately, in view of the many tree stumps and the root-laden soil, the rich virgin land did not need deep plowing. A primitive plow and a hoe could serve to produce a crop of thirty to fifty bushels an acre. Corn formed an essential item of diet, and all the animals could be fed on it. There was little variety in the early years, but the settlers usually found room for a small turnip patch. The New Englanders in southeastern Ohio added pumpkins, and the Kentuckians planted watermelons and muskmelons. The main danger to these crops, particularly the corn, was from the innumerable squirrels and crows. Squirrels were a menace throughout the Ohio Valley, and small boys passed many summer days banging kettles and shouting to protect the essential crop.

As soon as the first farmers entered a region, domestic animals were introduced in small numbers; when his means allowed, a pioneer would have a cow, a few hogs, and possibly a horse. When possible these animals foraged in the woods, and at first there was usually food available. South of the Ohio cattle in the early years thrived on the large, thick canebreaks, but as cultivation increased and more cattle came in these canebreaks completely disappeared. Most farmers prepared a small meadow for hay by planting timothy seed. In late winter, if the fodder had run out, the stock had to be allowed to feed from the bark and twigs of trees. Sheep were uncommon in the Ohio Valley in the early years, and those that were there suffered from the attacks of the wolves that still infested the region.

The development of a variety of crops depended on the nature of the particular region and the availability of a market, although a new area presented certain unusual difficulties in the early years of settlement. Much of the virgin soil proved too rich for wheat until successive crops of corn had been grown on it, but after that wheat soon became an important crop for the farmers of Ohio. Farther south tobacco and cotton were soon planted by farmers anxious to raise a cash crop. More general in the Ohio Valley in the early years was a flax patch. In Kentucky hemp became an important cash crop.[9]

Orchards took time to develop; at first by far the most common cultivated fruit was the peach. It had the great advantage that it began to bear plentifully in three years. A traveler commented in 1807 that "there is scarcely a settlement between Pittsburgh and the Falls of the Ohio, that has

A new method of reaping. From *Universal Asylum*, September 1788. (The New York Public Library)

not one or more orchards of them." [10] Great quantities of peaches were made into peach brandy. Apple, pear, and cherry trees were not as common in the early years. They gradually became important in the early nineteenth century. The apples were often used to produce cider.

A vital problem that the early settlers had to contend with even in the raising of corn was the shortage of mills. Until a mill had been built within traveling distance the pioneer had to depend on his own resources to grind his corn. The most primitive and arduous method was by mortar and pestle. The mortar was made in a section of a tree trunk about four feet in height by burning a cavity into its flat top. In this was placed the corn, where it was pounded with a pestle made of an iron wedge in a wooden handle. A little boiling water and lye was added, and the hulls floated to the top, leaving the hominy for bread-making. This method produced little hominy with considerable effort.[11]

More efficient than the mortar and pestle was the hand mill. This depended on the operator revolving the upper millstone by means of a rod run upward from a hole in the stone through a board. The corn was poured through a large opening at the center of the stone. This produced more than the hominy block but again required considerable effort for little result. In spite of this, the earliest settlers depended on these methods of grinding their corn, because even when the first public mills came in it was often necessary to travel a considerable distance and then to wait in line to have the corn ground. Often the charge for grinding was very high; the farmer had to pay the miller one-half of what he brought in order to get the other half ground.[12]

The early mills were often inefficient, and many operated only sporadically. Although water mills were preferred, they were frequently not working owing to lack of water at certain seasons of the year. To avoid this difficulty, settlers on the Ohio made use of "floating mills." These were erected on two boats anchored in the current of the river. The boats were placed about eight feet apart and fastened together by beams. In the center was a water wheel, which was turned by the current. One built at Belpre, Ohio, in 1791 was fastened by a chain cable to an anchor made of timber and filled with stones. In time of Indian troubles it could be anchored out in the river and protected from destruction by the Indians. Although less effective than permanent water-driven mills, they were far more certain. The alternative to a floating mill was to go to a horse mill, which required two horses to turn it. These were used throughout the West when the water was too low to drive the permanent water mills.[13]

Not until an area had passed out of the hominy block and hand mill stage could farming progress much beyond the barest subsistence level. Only when sawmills came in could planks be provided to enable the settlers to leave their log cabins and move into frame houses. In the earliest days the sawmill was combined with the gristmill to make the fullest use of the available resources.[14]

However much effort the pioneer was expending in building his cabin and clearing his land, his ever-present task was to provide food for his family. How he did this depended very much on whether he was in the first or later waves of settlers who streamed into the forests of the West and on whether the pioneer was one who constantly moved on or one who, however new the land, viewed himself as a farmer establishing a permanent home. While many of the pioneers on the edge of the frontier used wild game for much of their sustenance, some settlers, even among those moving on to virgin lands, who were not good hunters obtained their game from others and had to live primarily from their farming.

The first wave of settlers in most areas of the West combined hunting and farming. They depended on the wild game available in the country to sustain them until their farms became productive. The first settlers in the Ohio Valley after the Revolution were still able to find buffalo and use the meat; but the great majority of the new settlers made use of deer, turkey, bear, and even opossum. They also killed elk, raccoon, wild ducks, and squirrels, and in times of scarcity anything else they could find. Venison was a staple of the earliest settlers. Bear was often prepared as bacon. The fat was taken out; the meat was salted and then smoked. Bear oil was also of great value as a substitute for butter and hog's lard. Often turkey and venison were cooked in it to give them more fat. Wild turkeys were seen in countless numbers. They were at their best around Christmas, and it was said that they were so fat that when they fell from the tree after being shot their skins often burst. When shot in large numbers after a turkey hunt, they were cut in two, salted in troughs, and then hung up to dry. Later they could be stewed or fried in bear's oil, and such was the shortage of grain on the very edge of the frontier that turkey was talked of as a substitute for bread. Pioneers often cloyed on wild game in the first years of settlement.[15]

One major complication in depending on wild game was the great shortage of salt in the early West, both for salting down the meat and even for flavoring fresh meat. At first the settlers were supplied from the salt licks, or on salt brought over the Appalachians on packhorses. At the famous Kentucky Blue Licks 800 gallons of water had to be boiled down to obtain a bushel of salt. Kentucky settlers used to travel there from a considerable distance to barter corn or hay for it. In the Marietta region in the mid-1790s salt ranged from $5 to $8 a bushel; on occasion meat was cured with strong hickory ashes because of the scarcity and high price of salt.[16]

Not all the early settlers had an abundance of game. There were inept hunters on the frontier as in the rest of the country, and not all pioneers were eagle-eyed riflemen. In western Pennsylvania soon after the Revolution rifles were scarce among some of the new settlers, who were more accustomed to the musket.[17] The Ohio Company pioneers along the Ohio also had difficulties. In 1789 wild animals were scarce in the neighborhood of their settlements, and the new settlers were not skilled hunters. Although in the midst of the wilderness, pioneers at Belpre, Ohio, secured their game from an older settlement on the Virginia shore at Bellville, inhabited by people brought up in the woods. There was ample fish in the Ohio River, but salt was so scarce and expensive that it was difficult to cure it; the fish had to be eaten at once. The first years for the Ohio Company pioneers north of the Ohio brought hardship, as there were yet few hogs or cattle to offset the difficulties in securing game.[18]

Wild game was only a part, although a vital one for the first settlers, of the natural resources which were used for food. The early pioneers wasted little that had been provided for them by nature. The sugar maple was of great use to the settler, and he liked to have a grove near his cabin. When well established, if he had no maples on his land, he would rent a grove in the vicinity, in order to lay in a good supply of maple syrup and sugar. The tapping was carried out in late winter and early spring, when the trees were notched with an axe and the sap run off into troughs and then boiled.[19]

In the early years the settlers also sought nuts and wild fruit to fill a need until the peach trees matured. Most used were walnuts and hickory nuts. These were gathered by the children in the fall and eaten on the long winter nights, along with turnips, which were always one of the first crops planted. Pioneers often reminisced in later life of winter evenings spent cracking nuts and scraping turnips by the light of a fire made brighter by pieces of hickory bark, to save candles. One Quaker remembered that

> The evening of the first winter did not pass off as pleasantly as evenings afterward. We had raised no tobacco to stem and twist, no corn to shell, no turnips to scrape; we had no tow to spin into rope-yarn, nor straw to plait for hats, and we had come so late we could get but few walnuts to crack. We had however, the Bible, George Fox's Journal, Barkeley's Apology, and a number of books . . . soon after added a borrowed copy of the Pilgrim's Progress. [20]

The woods had a variety of minor fruits that could be made use of: the children sought out pawpaws, hackberries, plums, and grapes, and crabapples were collected to be made into preserves. When food was in short supply or monotonous in the late winter, the settlers waited anxiously for spring. As soon as possible out they went to collect the tops of nettles (hopefully to boil them with any salt meat that was left), celandine, and particularly purslane. Even after the really hard times were over, settlers still went out in the spring to collect "greens" to accompany the dinner; earlier these had sometimes been the dinner itself. The woods even provided tea to drink, after a fashion; bohea, sage, cross-vine, spice, and sassafras all were used by the pioneers.

Apart from the game, the fruits, and the greens, the settlers had to depend on what they brought with them to tide them over until their first crops came in. Some settlers who could afford it brought flour and lard; others who came in later might be fortunate enough to buy some supplies from neighbors who were already established. Their main dependence, however, was on their first corn crop, and there was heartbreak if anything happened to it. In much of the Ohio Valley in the late summer of 1789 a frost ruined the young corn on which the hopes of the newcomers rested; it meant a long, hungry winter.[21]

Corn, however, was not merely the first crop, it was also a basic part of the pioneer diet. At first it was used as a substitute for wheat bread; "Johnnycakes" made of corn meal were baked by the fire to appease children and adults alike. A very common breakfast, as well as a basic diet for young children, was "mush and milk." The Indian corn was coarsely pounded, boiled for four or five hours, mixed with milk, and served in a huge bowl in the center of the table. Corn was also boiled with meat and beans. With meat it dominated the frontier diet, whether as Johnnycake, mush, or hominy, and when parched, it was even mixed with water and drunk, called by some men of liberal imagination a substitute for coffee. Perhaps most memorable of all to the pioneers were the young roasting ears, eaten at all meals, when the corn was in the milk. Corn was vital in the life of the pioneers.[22]

The pumpkin was also an important part of the diet of the Ohio Valley settlers in their early years, particularly in southeastern Ohio. It was said of the Yankees of that section that "they lived entirely on pumpkins, molasses, fat meat, and bohea tea." [23] The pumpkin was most frequently made into pie, but its juice was sometimes boiled down to make a sort of molasses, and in times of shortages of meal it was mixed in to make pumpkin bread. In times of scarcity this was often more pumpkin than bread.

Even when the people were too poor to have many animals for meat, they tried to have a cow to provide milk. Some travelers viewed this with alarm. It was said of Mississippi Territory in 1808 that "Milk is used to excess, which I have reason to think is an additional cause of the prevalence of bilious disorders." [24] Another traveler some nine miles east of Nashville, Tennessee, in 1797, commented that he was given for supper "nothing but some Indian bread and butter, and some milk, which is a standing dish in all these new countries." [25]

With the increase in livestock, pork soon became the staple meat. Hogs were easy to keep on the frontier; they could grub in the surrounding forest and were fed on the remnants of corn and other crops. The frontiersman killed his hogs at the end of the year, chopped some of the meat for sausages, prepared bacon, carefully kept the fat, and salted down enough pork for the rest of the year. With the fat from the hogs the frontiersmen were even able to vary their diet by deep-frying doughnuts and crullers in the fresh lard.

The frontiersmen soon became accustomed to a diet of salt pork and were prepared to eat it at any meal. If travelers calling at the house of a frontier farmer in the early years of settlement were given more than mush and milk, it was usually a piece of salt bacon. Sometimes the bacon was fried at breakfast; often it was boiled, usually with some greens or with corn, and served with corn bread. Mutton was not a popular meat among the frontiersmen, and beef was much less common than pork.[26] As prosperity increased, fowl were served quite often to guests and in western taverns. At Columbia, Ohio, in 1797 one visitor was given boiled chicken, buckwheat cakes, tea, and coffee for his breakfast, and it is obvious he was being given a special treat. Coffee was very rare in the early Ohio Valley, and even store tea rather than some wild substitute was a delicacy to be husbanded with care. In later years the visitor could expect more abundant fare. At a good inn in Ohio in 1807 a traveler sat down to "good coffee, roast fowls, chicken pie, potatoes, bread and butter, and cucumbers both sliced and pickled, all not only good, but delicate." [27]

The cucumber patch was a common sight in western settlements, and although some visitors accused the westerners of living exclusively on salt pork and whiskey, they had quite a number of vegetables once they passed the half-hunting economy. Apart from the ever-present corn and turnips, there were pumpkins, potatoes, cucumbers, peas, and beans, as well as wild greens in the spring.[28]

Although the great mass of settlers who went into western Pennsylvania, western New York, Ohio, Kentucky, and Tennessee lived on similar diets, there tended to be differences in food along the Mississippi, particularly among the pioneers of French and Spanish extraction. In the 1790s the French in what was to become Missouri made far greater use of vegetables than was usual among the Americans: "Instead of roast and fried, they had soups and fricassees, and gumbos, . . . and a variety of other dishes." [29] The emphasis on vegetables and soups was general among the French Creoles all the way down the Mississippi. Gumbo was already a favorite among these settlers, and a large bowl of it was placed in the center of the table in the place of the bowl of mush of the inhabitants of Kentucky or Ohio. A basic gumbo was made by boiling okra until it was tender and seasoning it with a small piece of fat bacon. Strangers found this "ropy and slimy" and difficult to eat, but in centers like New Orleans gumbo became an elaborate soup of numerous ingredients, including shrimp.[30]

To the typical pioneer who plodded slowly through the Cumberland Gap or floated down the Ohio, feeding his family was at first a time-consuming task, but the richness of the soil and the abundance of wildlife meant that early worries usually passed into a time of rude-plenty and greater variety. The pioneers were not delicate eaters. In 1784 a few men on their way into Tennessee after crossing the Holston "borrowed a pott & cooked the hens which had been flung away by the old Gentln, the stench being very great from the hens, but however we made our Brackfast with the hens with a few slices of Bacon & half bushel of Clabber & Butter milk." [31] But by 1815 the trans-Appalachian West had been transformed. In a center like Cincinnati there were four markets a week, providing beef, veal, pork, mutton, and fine poultry. There was also fish, venison in season, and still occasionally bear meat. Butter and cheese were sent to the market from the farms of the region, but such was the urban development that the supply was usually not equal to the demand. Vegetables were in abundance, as well as a variety of fruits: apples, peaches, pears, cherries, plums, straw-berries, melons, and numerous others.[32] Farther west, other pioneers were at this time waiting anxiously for their first crop.

While the pioneers soon achieved variety in their food, the accounts of their drinking have a remarkable similarity. It was generally agreed by travelers that the frontiersmen were almost universally consumers of hard liquor; the main disagreement among contemporary observers was whether the frontiersmen constantly drank to excess or whether their drinking habits were merely normal in a hard-drinking age. The main drinks of the fron-tiersmen were peach brandy and corn whiskey; although rye was also used. Peach brandy was an especially popular drink among the early frontiersmen; there was an abundance of peaches and not as many uses for them as for corn.

It is necessary in writing of drinking on the frontier to distinguish between those settlers who were on the very cutting edge of the frontier—the first wave of restless seminomads ready to move on as game diminished—and the later waves of settlement—the farmers, the permanent settlers. Undoubtedly those on the edge of the frontier, living in semi-isolation, untrammeled by social pressures or even moderate religious influence, and engaged in backbreaking work, often drank to excess. Yet throughout the East and Europe this was an age of hard drinking, and the scenes of drunkenness and degradation in the slums of the larger towns would have shocked most frontier dwellers. Once settlers came into western areas to establish permanent farms and build villages and churches, there was still hard drinking, as there was in the rest of America and Europe, but there was not general drunkenness.

For most frontiersmen throughout this period hard liquor was regarded as a necessary and useful aid to living. "A house could not be raised, a field of wheat cut down, nor could there be a log rolling, a husking, a quilting, a wedding, or a funeral without the aid of alcohol." [33] Most churches did not interfere with drinking. Only the Methodists believed in temperance, and even the famous Bishop Francis Asbury of that church believed in the medicinal use of wine. For the rest of the population, even among churchgoers, there was nothing wrong in the general use of alcohol. Whiskey was always offered when a neighbor came in, and even the women offered their visitors hard liquor, perhaps mixed with a little sugar, milk, and spices. Although it was usual to drink the liquor straight, it was embellished at times; even by the men: Travelers were sometimes offered a bowl of "toddy," made of sugar, water, whiskey, and peach juice, and when traveler John

Making cherry bounce, 1806. From Lewis Miller, *Sketches and Chronicles.* (Historical Society of York County, Pa.)

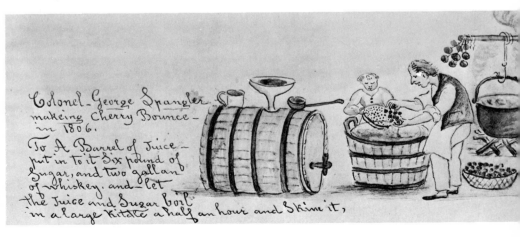

Pope was on the Mississippi on St. Patrick's Day in 1791 the Irishmen in his party "purloined all our Brandy, sugar, and eggs to make a tub of Egg-Nog." [34] On the lower Mississippi in the first decade of the nineteenth century, whiskey, cider, and bottled beer were imported from the Ohio, but the inhabitants also made their own "taffia" out of sugar cane, and imported wines into New Orleans. [35]

Water was not generally favored as a beverage in the early West; in some areas partly because of the difficulty of obtaining a palatable supply. In many parts of Kentucky the inhabitants suffered from a water shortage in summer when the springs ran dry. Those in the vicinity of the principal rivers usually used the river water throughout the year. One traveler on the Ohio in 1807 thought the river water tasted as good as the best brook water, but that it was "thick and turbid, and the thousands of dead squirrels putrefying on its surface and its shores, contribute very little to render it more agreeable." [36] The water had to be left to settle before it could, be used. Settlers on the lower Mississippi also used the river water for all purposes, and there it was said that the water would deposit a sediment a half-inch deep in a half-pint tumbler of water. This did, however, have its compensations, as the waters of the Mississippi were reputed to be a powerful specific against sterility and the itch. [37]

An irregular water supply not only harassed the frontiersman who had his stock to water, it threw yet another burden on his already overworked wife, who had to carry her water from the nearest spring or pond. To supplement this supply, a trough or barrel was placed to catch rain water coming off the roof. In times of drought when a shower finally came, every usable container was lined up outside the cabin. On wash day the frontier wife could go to a nearby pond, boiling her clothes in a large kettle alongside it. Or her family could haul water to the cabin in barrels; the fire would be lit outside the cabin and the clothes boiled, often after the water had been softened with ashes.

Washing, cleaning, bringing up a horde of children, and cooking were only a small part of the task of the frontier wife. Much of the food she cooked and served first had to go through preliminary stages of preparation —whether it was pounding or grating corn, rendering down fat, or making cheese and butter. The typical, large frontier family provided hands for the arduous task of clearing lands, tending young crops, watering and watching stock, and splitting rails, as well as for churning butter, pounding corn, or carrying water. Candles and soap had to be made, and while the father and older boys were clearing land, the mother had to depend on any younger children and girls to help her. It was perhaps as well that it could be said on the Ohio in 1807 that "throughout this whole country, wherever you see a cabin, you see a swarm of children." [38]

The earliest settlers depended heavily upon deerskin for their clothes, although the family would have to be extremely isolated or in dire straits for the women of the family to use it. After the skin had been dressed the women cut out the garment and by means of an awl used the sinews of the deer to sew it together. A hunting shirt was ornamented with a fringe down the outside of the sleeves and around the collar and tail, and could be rubbed with deer's tallow or bear's oil to keep out the rain. Pantaloons too were made of buckskin, although tow linen was preferred if available. Fitted to the leg from the ankle was a pair of buckskin leggings. These were fastened by a strap to the pantaloons. As in the case of the hunting shirt, the leggings were usually ornamented with a fringe along the outer seam. Buckskin moccasins usually had dry oak leaves in them in place of stockings. For the head there could be a coonskin cap.

As soon as possible the frontier family raised the crops that would enable the mother of the family to manufacture clothes, for "store-bought" clothes were a rare treat. Flax was generally grown; south of the Ohio there was usually a cotton patch, and sheep were slowly introduced throughout the Ohio Valley. The flax had to be water-rotted and broken by hand, and the fibre prepared in "knots" for the distaff and then spun. After it had been woven, it was bleached by being daily stretched out in the sun and brought in at night. The seeds of the cotton were picked out by hand before it was carded, spun, and woven into cloth. After the sheep were sheared, there was the tedious job of picking out all the burrs and debris in the wool before it was carded and spun. Every cabin had its spinning wheel, and many had a loom. If the clothing was to be colored, the frontier housewife dealt with this task as well. The most common color was the dull yellow-brown butternut, which was obtained by using the inner bark of the white walnut. Black could be obtained from the hulls of the black walnut. The dyes for blue and red had to be bought from the store in the form of indigo and madder.

In the early days of settlement in Kentucky, or elsewhere on the frontier, a woman might well dress in a linen chemise, a short gown, and a petticoat that ended a little below the calf, and not wear shoes or stockings in summer. As soon as possible a few "boughten" clothes were obtained for Sunday morning wear; a length of fustian or calico. The frontier wife could then go to meeting in a calico dress and possibly a black silk bonnet, and her son in a new fustian jacket. A common sight in summer on Sunday morning was the girls carrying their shoes and stockings to and from the meeting house. But, though all but the poorest families would try to brighten their lives with some bought article, clothing the family was for the most part yet another of the tasks of the frontier wife, tasks undertaken while year after year pregnant.[39]

Amid all the other hardships, a frontier woman lived with ever-present fear for her health and the health of her family. The first settlers were isolated in their tiny clearings in the forest, at times under attack from the Indians. Pregnancy itself posed its terrors when there was no doctor or midwife, and the nearest woman might be several miles away. Certain diseases were general throughout the Ohio and Mississippi valleys. Undoubtedly the most complained of were a variety of fevers and agues, some of them malarial in origin. Mosquitoes abounded, breeding in the numerous undrained swamps and marshes, but the settlers blamed their problems on "bad air." The fevers were not usually fatal, but left the frontiersmen debilitated and susceptible to other diseases. In the Mississippi Territory, and generally in the lower Mississippi country, the months from July to October were all unhealthy; intermittent fevers, with or without ague, prevailed throughout the area. New Orleans was particularly dangerous to new settlers, for along with malaria, the town had periodic epidemics of yellow fever, which caused great mortality. American Governor Claiborne lost his wife and daughter on the same day.[40]

Apart from the fevers, exposure to cold and damp made muscular and rheumatic pains the regular lot of the frontiersmen. In the Ohio Valley a popular remedy for this, and a variety of other diseases, was "Seneca Oil" from western Pennsylvania. This was actually part of the natural oil deposit of western Pennsylvania which rose to the top of the springs. It was fairly innocuous when rubbed on rheumatic joints, but probably less so when taken internally. Troops on their way to the western posts bathed their rheumatic joints in Seneca oil floating on the surface of the springs and from drinking the water below found that it acted as "a gentle cathartic." [41]

The frontier children suffered of course from all the usual childhood diseases. There were also more serious epidemics in the early years of settlement. In 1792 the children of the Ohio Valley suffered from a severe attack of scarlet fever (usually called "putrid sore throat"). It was particularly destructive in parts of the Ohio Company settlements in southeast Ohio, and it was said that "five or six in some cases died out of a single family." [42] Smallpox was also a great danger in the eighteenth century, and many submitted to the quite serious discomforts of innoculation in order to protect themselves against the natural attack of the disease. The discovery of vaccination promised an end to this scourge; vaccination became quite common in the West from 1802.[43]

For the most part, however, the frontier mother had to contend not with the fatal epidemics, but with the common round of childhood and adult diseases and accidents under primitive conditions. One traveler across southern Kentucky in 1796 found that "in all the Houses the children were suffering from Hooping Cough," [44] and pneumonia was a threat in draughty, damp cabins. Even if doctors were available, most of them placed great belief in bleeding as a means of cure, and in some cases those on the frontier might well have owed their lives to their distance from medical help.

The typical frontiersmen, both men and women, worked long hours under conditions of extreme hardship to shape new lives in the wilderness in which they had settled. For the women it was often a short life; they died prematurely aged, worn out by childbearing and work. Yet for most it was not a depressing existence. They lived under conditions of political and religious freedom that were for the most part unknown in Europe. They knew that with work they stood an excellent chance of at least moderate prosperity. Although the great majority had little leisure, they took every opportunity to ease their work with enjoyment, and where possible turned their work itself into a general social occasion.

Even in a new settlement there would be the opportunity of gathering the neighbors for a log-rolling and cabin-raising, and the same festivities took place later when more land was cleared or a barn put up. The men from the neighboring cabins gathered to do the work, passing the whiskey freely, while the women prepared the meal. After the work there would be more drinking, running, jumping, and fighting. Corn-husking was always the occasion of a social gathering. The ears were heaped in a long pile, and "the neighbors notified, rather than invited, for it was an affair of mutual assistance." [45] In later years when wheat was grown, the harvest usually provided the same type of "frolic." The women also had their own particular gatherings, the quiltings and the sewing bees, to help make light of their domestic tasks.

A wedding usually brought neighbors from miles around. One observer commented that there "were scenes of carousal, and of mirth and merriment of no very chastened character." [46] If possible a fiddler played for the dancing, there was much drinking, and the men as on most of these occasions ran races, wrestled, shot at a mark, and threw tomahawks. The merriment also continued for a second day, for the "infare," in which the celebrations were repeated at the cabin of the groom's father.

But the settlers really did not need an obvious occasion such as a wedding to meet and enjoy themselves. Their daily work was lonely and hard, and when possible they gathered socially. As areas became more settled, even hunting sometimes became a social affair. To help rid the country of squirrels, parties shot in competition and ended with a gathering at one of the cabins. In a new country with much to be done the line between work and play was not firmly drawn, for if it had been, the frontiersmen would have blanched before the prospect of days of unremitting toil; of days devoted entirely to carving farms and homes out of a forest. [47]

The typical inhabitant of the trans-Appalachian West in the years before 1815 was not a land speculator, a carousing Mississippi boatman, or a fervent frontier preacher. He was a farmer living with his family in a log cabin, gradually enlarging his clearing in the forest, finding his pleasures in gatherings of his neighbors for mixed work and enjoyment. Yet as settlement increased, the world of these farmers was broadening. Some traveled for miles through the forest to join with thousands of others in fervent religious experience. Many sent off their children each day for a few months to learn to read and write in a log-cabin school. Others went to trade at the local county seat, or even as far as to a town where there were newspaper offices and books for sale. They might hear of, even if they could not use, a new circulating library. They might even see, if they did not enter, a new theater. The frontier farmer in his lonely clearing was never, as settlement increased, confined to his purely local environment, and the society he lived in became increasingly complex as the population became more numerous and the prosperity increased.

◁ **7** ▷

The Development
of Frontier Society

*S*ince travelers first described the settlers who pushed into the West in the years after the Revolution, there has been considerable difference in how they have been depicted. To some, the frontiersmen have always been illiterate backwoodsmen, gouging eyes and biting off ears, losing their religious beliefs, scoffing at learning, and praising above all else a tough, individual reliance on axe and gun. To others, the pioneers have been heralds of civilization, carrying Bibles across the mountains, swept by deeply felt, emotional religious experiences—men who tried desperately to create schools in the wilderness, who supported subscription libraries and eagerly bought the books that were transported painfully across the mountains.

One major source of confusion has been that the writers have often not been describing the same people. The pioneers who settled on the very edge of the frontier, dressed in buckskin, spent much of their time hunting, and were ready to move on as more settlers came in. They were very different from the moderately prosperous farmers who in the years after 1803 bought already improved farms in Ohio. Moreover, a traveler down the Ohio River who visited Pittsburgh, Cincinnati, Louisville, Natchez, and New Orleans

126

was seeing a very different frontier from that known by the mass of the settlers in their cabins in the woods.

This confusion has brought about overwriting on the violent nature of frontier society. There was a rough, crude violence on the frontier, in rural areas as well as in towns. But this violence was far more concentrated in the newly settled edge of the frontier and among the boatmen and riffraff who hung about the river towns than it was on the farms of longer-settled areas.

There is little doubt that the edge of the frontier not only attracted the Daniel Boones of American folklore but also the lawbreakers and misfits of eastern society, who were lured by the lack of civil order and legal procedure. In the early 1790s "the barrens" between the Green and Cumberland rivers in Kentucky had become a refuge for lawbreakers, and as more honest citizens moved in they had to act as "regulators" to throw the ruffians out. In 1799 it was commented that the moral character of the inhabitants of Knoxville, Tennessee, had much improved in recent years "since bad people have moved more to the border." After the Revolution, fugitives from justice in Georgia and the Carolinas moved into the very isolated settlements north of Mobile, in what is now the state of Alabama.[1] The combination of semi-nomadic hunters and lawless fugitives was obviously well designed to create turbulence and violence in the opening of any new frontier region.

Similar special circumstances existed in the case of the frontier towns, which in regard to population were often no more than villages. The merchants formed the backbone of the frontier towns, but these towns also attracted a fringe of hangers-on—those discontented with life on the farm, minor lawbreakers, and gamblers. This was particularly the case in the river towns, where the usual drifters were augmented by the boatmen who took goods downriver to Natchez or New Orleans. In 1814 the boatmen were described as "a set of men as much corrupted perhaps, as any in the country."[2] After the long voyage down the river through the wilderness from Louisville to Natchez they were ready for rough entertainment; this was readily provided. That part of Natchez immediately on the riverfront was, in miniature, reminiscent of docklands throughout the world: "Here is the bold-faced strumpet, full of blasphemies, who looks upon the virtuous part of her sex with contempt and hatred; every house is a grocery, containing gambling, music and dancing, fornicators &c."[3] Another traveler said of Natchez in 1812 "for the size of it, there is not, perhaps, in the world a more dissipated place."[4]

At Louisville in 1785 a boat struck a rock and sank in attempting to shoot the falls. The survivors scrambled onto some small islands but could not reach the shore. The Louisville residents were told what had happened by other travelers but "the good people of this town diverted themselves at cards (a very favorite amusement here) while their ears were assailed with the cries of the unhappy sufferers, which seemed to create no other emotions than some ill natured reflection on their folly." Not until the next morning were some men persuaded to go and help the survivors to shore, and one of the men who went was drunk.[5] As late as 1806 it was said that the inhabitants of Louisville were universally addicted to gambling and drinking, and that the billiard rooms were crowded from morning to night. Billiard tables, with the opportunity for gambling, were common in the frontier towns. Even "Smith Town," at the mouth of the Cumberland on the Ohio, which consisted of only a handful of cabins inhabited mainly by unemployed boatmen and runaway boys, had its billiard table in 1807.[6] Those traits of violence that existed in all frontier society were epitomized and exaggerated in the river towns, and these were the towns most frequently seen by travelers.

In the rural areas the rougher aspects of frontier life were more obvious in the villages and county seats. On Saturdays the rural population flocked in for the meetings of the local courts, militia musters, barter, gossip, and drinking. The taverns were crowded; there was a good deal of gambling; and a variety of running, jumping, and wrestling competitions were constantly waged among the men. Some of these deteriorated into brutal brawls, particularly among those who had drunk too much. It was on these occasions that the oft-quoted incidents of eye-gouging and maiming occasionally occurred. Pioneer physician Daniel Drake, who was certainly a sympathetic observer of the frontier life in which he had participated, wrote at a later date of pitched battles between two bullies who "would lie on the ground scratching, pulling hair, choking, gouging out each other's eyes, and biting off each other's noses in the manner of bull-dogs."[7]

Other observers wrote similar descriptions. When one traveler wrote of the frontiersmen that their "hands, teeth, knees, head and feet are their weapons, not only boxing with their fists . . . but also tearing, kicking, scratching, biting, gouging each others eyes out by a dexterous use of a thumb and finger, and doing their utmost to kill each other," the frontier editor who published the work in 1810 did not deny that this happened but said that this might better have been applied fifteen or twenty years before, and that such happenings were particular cases, not of general application.[8] What has sometimes been forgotten by later writers, and was usually ignored by travelers at the time, is that such violence and brutality could easily have been matched in the filthy alleys and courts of London at the same period. It was a callous age, as yet little touched by the great humanitarian reformers.

As the hunters and lawbreakers were succeeded by farmers establishing permanent homes and as rough, shantytowns became settled communities, the violent tenor of life was softened. Some of the lawbreakers and thugs were still there, but there were also many law-abiding citizens who no longer allowed obvious violence to go unpunished. It was written by a visitor in 1811 that "in Kentucky, and, indeed, in the western country, there are a vast majority of civil, discreet, well-disposed people, who will hold the lawless and disobedient in check, and in time correct the morals of the whole." [9] The last was too hopeful, but the first was becoming increasingly true. There were still many in 1815 who despaired of the morals and character of the westerners, but the worst critics were usually clergymen and the occasional, jaundiced foreign observer. Some always saw the squalor rather than the hope of western life, and echoed what was written by a returned clergyman in 1803: "once more I have escaped from filth, fleas, rattlesnakes, hills, mountains, rocks, and rivers: farewell, western world, for a while!" [10]

The amelioration of western society in the first decades of the nineteenth century is hard to gauge. Listings of churches, libraries, and schools cannot measure the full impact of these institutions on contemporary western society. At times it seems likely that the number of frontiersmen who were deeply religious, and who sought books and education has been exaggerated, simply because those who felt these desires have left a record of their activities while the hundreds of thousands who were content to concentrate on material ends, clear their lands, and obtain only a rough, rural enjoyment have left little mark. These were the numberless settlers who were not religious enthusiasts, did not subscribe to libraries, and did not buy books. To achieve material well-being in the wilderness was in itself a hard enough task, and those who wanted to do more—who wanted a cultivated society or a society dedicated to God—faced immense difficulties.

Organized religion in America had undergone profound shocks in the eighteenth century. The impact of rationalistic and deistic thought from Europe had been great. These influences had weakened the traditional religious emphasis of society, and many of the American leaders had thrown off the formal bonds of religion. It was no surprise that many of their countrymen had chosen to do likewise. The decline of religious fervor had been accelerated by the Revolution. The democratic ideas generated by that conflict had tended to throw all hierarchies, including religious ones, into disrepute, particularly in those areas where church leaders had been equated with a ruling class.[11] This mode of thinking inevitably had its influence in the West, and as late as 1799 it was asserted that in Nashville and the surrounding region deism and irreligion were rampant, especially among the ruling classes.[12]

The Episcopalians, with their strong ties to England, had been especially hard-hit by the Revolution. Their church's lack of popularity was marked even in the East, and in the West it made little impression in the years before 1815. It had a rigid organization and formalism which ill-fitted it for the extraordinary measures needed to carry the message of the church into the frontier regions. In 1820 there were no Episcopalian ministers in Indiana, Illinois, or Tennessee and only ten in Ohio and Kentucky.[13]

Also comparatively weak on the frontier in the years before 1815 were the Roman Catholics. Such strength as they had was primarily in the former

Spanish and French settlements of Louisiana and Illinois. Even in those areas there were often complaints of the lack of religious enthusiasm.[14] When in the 1790s priests were sent to serve the long-neglected French communities along the Wabash and upper Mississippi, they discovered that negligence had produced considerable laxity. The priest who went to Vincennes in December 1792 found that only twelve inhabitants would take communion during the Christmas season, and the log church was practically a ruin. Kentucky was the main western area to gain a new immigration of Catholics in this period. They began to move in from Maryland in the 1780s, and by 1815 Kentucky had some 10,000 Catholics and ten priests.[15]

The largest and most influential of the religious groups in northeastern colonial America had been the Congregationalists. At the end of the eighteenth century, in spite of revivals, they were under attack from rationalistic and deistic ideas. Although they managed to revive their influence in New England, the Congregationalists were unable to adjust themselves sufficiently to frontier conditions to make a real impact in the West. Their most important frontier influence was in northern New England.[16]

In Vermont the Congregationalists had seventy-four churches by 1800. Their Connecticut Missionary Society, which was founded in 1798, concentrated much of its work on this New England frontier, and soon after 1800 was helped by revivals which brought considerable religious excitement in Vermont. But the Congregationalists had competition. The Baptists made considerable inroads; some Methodist missionaries came into the state; and new sects—the Christians and the Universalists—won converts. As in all frontier areas, the task of overcoming indifference and even outright opposition was a difficult one. A minister asserted in 1789 that about "one quarter of ye inhabitants & almost all ye men of learning [are] diests in ye state." He thought that about half of the families "would chuse to have no Sabbath no ministers—no religion—no heaven—no hell—no morality." [17]

On the rest of the frontier in this period the only major effort of the Congregationalists was in western New York, where so many of the settlers were from New England.[18] Even in Ohio, where the foundation of Marietta in 1788 seemed promising for the Congregationalists, they were unable to make any marked impact. Not until 1796 was a church founded at Marietta, and it was another five years before one was established in the Western Reserve. The Congregationalists lacked the centralized organization of the Presbyterians and Methodists and the willingness of the Baptists to depend on local farmer-preachers. As a result of their failure to establish churches beyond the Appalachians, the Congregationalists in 1801 agreed to a plan of union with the Presbyterians that eventually gave the latter great strength in the Ohio Valley. The plan of union was intended primarily for frontier activity. It empowered Congregational and Presbyterian settlers to form themselves into one congregation, and call a minister from either denomination, organizing their local church as they saw fit. In the West, including western New York, the effect of the union was usually to bring the association under the control of the Presbyteries. Not until the time of Jackson did Congregational churches again begin to be established in any numbers in the West.[19]

The Episcopalians and Congregationalists failed in the West in this period because they did not adapt themselves to meet the needs of westerners. The task any religious group faced on the frontier was a difficult one. The first settlers were poor and isolated. Many were going to move on in a few years and were not interested in creating permanent institutions in a temporary resting place. Even later settlers at first had to concentrate on feeding and clothing their families rather than on founding, endowing, and supporting churches; the population needed to support a church was likely to be scattered over a wide area. Any religious group that thought in terms of a substantial building and a paid, educated clergy as the center of a community was doomed to disappointment in prevailing western conditions.

Yet the situation of the westerners did have certain advantages for enterprising religious groups. In the same way that the pioneers sought relief from their lonely, hard-working lives in all possible types of local social gatherings, they could be expected to respond favorably to religious inspiration if it excited them and took them out of their daily drudgery. The early settlers were not highly educated, and they were certainly not responsive to a highly sophisticated religion. Many of them were prepared to respond to a simple, direct emotional appeal—to a religion that enlivened their life on earth and promised a rich reward in the world to come.

Revivalism first swept powerfully through the backcountry of the American colonies in the 1730s, and there had been sporadic renewals of enthusiasm since that time. In the decade after the Revolution there were signs of a Presbyterian revival first in Virginia and then in North Carolina, but at the end of the eighteenth and the beginning of the nineteenth century a far more general religious revival gained adherents in all parts of the country, particularly in the western regions. Those who resented the growth of irreligion and had no sympathy with the intellectual deism of many of the elite were now able to express their fervor in an emotional outburst.[20]

The leading figure of the trans-Appalachian revival was James McGready. McGready, a Presbyterian, had lived his youth in North Carolina and had been involved in religious revivals of the early 1790s. In 1796 he moved to Tennessee, and soon after that into Logan County in southern Kentucky—an area of the state that had only recently received any large influx of settlers. There soon were signs that McGready was sparking a revival in his region, and in the summer of 1799 excitement soared, at the time that similar manifestations were being experienced in New England. It was soon obvious that the revival in the trans-Appalachian West was more

A Methodist camp-meeting, 1808. From Lewis Miller, *Sketches and Chronicles.* (Historical Society of York County, Pa.)

emotional and abandoned than that of the East, and that the western revival was developing its own unique features, well-suited to a frontier environment.[21]

The most distinctive feature of the western revival was the camp meeting. This well served the needs of a scattered population with too few ministers. Frontiersmen came from miles around to hear the revival message preached by a variety of ministers to a great throng of people. The distances were great and the roads bad; when frontiersmen attended these religious gatherings, they often came prepared to spend several nights, at first only in primitive camps, but later in more elaborate settings. Something like the camp meeting had been attempted since Revolutionary days, but it was only in the West after 1800 that these gatherings became an established institution. When in the summer of 1801 excitement reached its peak in Kentucky, a vast concourse attended the August meeting at Cane Ridge; estimates of the attendance ran as high as 25,000. One worshiper counted seven ministers all preaching at one time, some on stumps, others in wagons, and one on a fallen tree. The crowd was singing, praying, shouting, and "the noise was like the roar of Niagara." [22] The revival now spread rapidly through Tennessee, the Old Northwest, and the western regions of the older states. In many places the fervor continued until 1805 and sporadically even after that date.[23]

The camp meeting undoubtedly provided a liveliness and excitement lacking in the lives of the frontier settlers. They left their small isolated farms—the drudgery and the boredom—and suddenly found themselves in a crowd larger than any in the western towns they could visit, listening to an array of stirring speakers who conjured them out of their wilderness surroundings and promised heaven. The impact of the vast crowds, of the religious fervor, of the emotion-packed atmosphere brought not only excitement but also strange aberrations. The most common of these was "the jerks," which apparently first became prevalent near Knoxville in 1803. In this "hundreds of men and women would commence jerking backward and forward with great rapidity and violence so that their bodies would bend so as to bring their heads near to the floor, and the hair of the women would crack like the lash of a driver's whip." [24] Some preachers condemned the jerks, but others argued that they were sent by God to convince those who undervalued His powers.

The excesses did not end with the jerks. Others started barking like dogs, laughed uncontrollably, and ran, jumped, and danced through the mob. Some fell into trances, saw visions, and prophesied. Potential converts screamed, laughed, and wept with joy. The atmosphere was highly charged, and though the old saw that "more souls were made than saved" is unjust, there is no doubt that the social attractions of the camp meeting greatly helped the success of the western revival.[25]

The main emphasis of the revival was on salvation, on the mercy of God.

A Philadelphia Anabaptist immersion in a storm. Watercolor by P. P. Svinin. (The Metropolitan Museum of Art, Rogers Fund, 1942)

A favorite hymn began with the line "Thy mercy, my God, is the theme of my song," and continued later with the confident assertion that "Thy mercy in Jesus exempts me from hell." [26] This emphasis, and the wild emotionalism, soon made it obvious that although revivalism was not confined to one religion, the Methodists, and to some extent the Baptists, were in a better position to take advantage of it than other religious groups. The Presbyterians also shared quite widely in the revival, but the difficulty of reconciling the optimism of the revival regarding universal salvation with established Presbyterian doctrine was soon to produce deep divisions among the members of that church.

The initial advantage possessed by the Methodist Church was that it subscribed to the Arminian doctrine of free will. This idea of salvation proved far more palatable to the frontiersmen than the more pessimistic Calvinistic doctrine. To this initial advantage of doctrine, the Methodists added a strong central organization and a most efficient missionary structure, well fitted to frontier needs. The essence of the system was the mobility of its ministers. These ministers served a scattered frontier population by becoming "circuit riders"; they were given a certain section of territory through which they rode, preaching to congregations which gathered to meet them on their route. Not even a church building was needed, although a district might provide this when there were enough Methodist adherents. A courthouse, private dwelling, or even the open air could serve for the visiting preacher. In this way a Methodist minister could visit sections of the country recently settled, where no church of any type had yet been established. As the only sect available to the settlers, the Methodists had an excellent chance of winning converts from other religions and then could serve small, new congregations through the circuit system.

Moreover, unlike those religions that insisted on a well-educated ministry and had difficulty in finding enough ministers to meet the needs of a constantly expanding frontier, the Methodists were happy to accept the uneducated who had the call to preach. One western circuit rider later wrote that many of the Methodist ministers "had little or no education; no books, and no time to read or study them if we could have had them." [27] They carried a pocket Bible, a hymn book, and a Methodist "Discipline." Some of course began to study after they entered the ministry; a few drifted away again. One of the first circuit riders sent out to Kentucky in the 1780s left the church, kept a grog shop, attacked the Methodists, but in later years once again entered the ministry. The great majority neither became scholars nor slid away but served the church faithfully until they died, sometimes prematurely aged through the hardship of their lives.[28]

Before the end of the Revolution a Methodist circuit rider had crossed the mountains into western North Carolina, and in 1783 the Holston circuit was established in what is now eastern Tennessee. Although Methodist ministers also moved into the Ohio Valley and onto the northern New England frontier to serve the newly settled regions, there were few church members before 1800. In that year Methodist church membership was some 1800 in Kentucky, 700 in Tennessee, and less than 300 northwest of the Ohio. These figures are, however, somewhat deceptive as the preachers reached many more than the church members. When Bishop Francis Asbury preached at Nashville for the first time in October 1800, he estimated his audience at not less than 1000.[29]

After 1800 the Methodists began to reap rewards from the great revival. By 1812 they numbered nearly 19,000 in Kentucky and Tennessee. This represented a huge percentage increase in church mmbership, but it is less impressive when compared to a total population for the two states of 700,000. Ohio had more than 8000 Methodists by 1810, and outside of the Western Reserve (where the Presbyterians predominated), they outnumbered other sects. Moreover, the Methodists continued to send ministers to distant frontiers. By 1815 circuit riders were in Indiana, Illinois, and Mississippi territories, and even in Louisiana. The Methodists in the United States increased from 8504 in 1780 to 174,560 in 1810. In that period they were in the vanguard of religious activity among the frontiersmen. Their adherents did not form a large proportion of the total population, but many more heard their ministers and were influenced by their advocacy of temperance, and modesty in dress, action, and behavior.[30]

The main competition to the Methodists on the frontier in these years was provided by the Baptists, who in spite of schisms, were particularly strong south of the Ohio. Although many Baptists were originally Calvinists, they were willing to modify the doctrine of predestination. On the frontier the church members held a variety of views. Perhaps most important of all for their success in newly settled areas, they did not depend upon a trained ministry. To fill the need for ministers, they drew upon the pioneer farmers themselves. When a member of a congregation felt the call to preach, he could be licensed and eventually ordained if he took charge of an actual congregation. This local system of preachers served the Baptists well. It gave them a numerical superiority over other denominations, cost less, and ensured a church that sprang from at least one segment of the frontier population rather than being imposed from the East.[31]

The Baptists were most successful in Kentucky and Tennessee, where they already had ministers during the Revolution. There was a Baptist association in central Kentucky by 1785, and by 1812 there were 22,694 church members in that state, and 11,325 in Tennessee. On the rest of the frontier the Baptists were not numerous in these years, although in Vermont the Freewill Baptists, who broke off from the Calvinist Baptists in the Revolution, won many converts. Northwest of the Ohio the Baptists were not as successful as the Methodists, but their ministers were in Indiana and Illinois by the late 1790s. By 1815 there were also Baptist ministers in Missouri and Mississippi territories.[32]

The Presbyterians were able to compete successfully with the Congregationalists in this period, but had considerable difficulty in deciding how far the church should go in adapting itself to frontier conditions and desires. Doctrinal arguments caused severe schisms within the church; many on the frontier were not prepared to accept an uncompromising Calvinism. Moreover, in spite of the great need for ministers in the newly opened regions, the church continued to insist on a trained ministry. This insistence meant that the Presbyterians had great difficulty in providing ministers for the rapidly growing population across the Appalachians.

The Presbyterians were strongest in western Pennsylvania. Their ministers had entered this region even before the Revolution. By 1802 there were three presbyteries organized under the new synod of Pittsburgh. Northwest of the Ohio they were slower in getting established. Not until 1815 was there sufficient strength for organization of the synod of Ohio. In Indiana there was only a handful of Presbyterian ministers by 1815, and they were "obliged to provide principally for their own support, by keeping school through the week, or by manual labor." [33] This was usually the case throughout the West. In the villages, where the ministers were mainly established, they taught school; in the country they farmed; and sometimes they combined religion with medicine.[34]

Presbyterian ministers were in both Kentucky and Tennessee at an early date, but they experienced considerable difficulty in meeting the challenge of the Methodists and the Baptists. The Great Revival for a time seemed to benefit the Presbyterians, but it soon helped to bring about major schisms in the church south of the Ohio. The Presbyterians who were at the center of the revival movement in Logan County, Kentucky, soon discovered that the Presbyterian leaders would not accept its more extreme features. The Cumberland presbytery of southern Kentucky and Tennessee was willing to license uneducated ministers who had experienced the call to preach during the revival. This view that education was not necessary for a minister was unacceptable to the main body of the church, and the Cumberland presbytery was dissolved. Some of these Presbyterians now joined different sects, others eventually formed themselves into an independent Cumberland presbytery. They adopted the doctrines of the Presbyterian Church with the major exceptions that they threw out the strict Calvinistic idea of predestination and the requirement that a candidate should be educated before being licensed to preach. Many of the new splinter groups differed little from the Methodists.[35]

The Presbyterians also ran into trouble in Bourbon County, Kentucky, where the "New Lights" broke off from the church in the fall of 1803 when five Presbyterian ministers were expelled by the synod of Kentucky for teaching error. The New Lights believed that the Great Revival was the beginning of the millenium. They renounced all confessions of faith and catechisms except the Bible and finished up by attacking synods, presbyteries, and predestination. The New Lights did not gain major support, but in 1813 there were six New Light preachers in Indiana and only one Presbyterian. Eventually, in the 1830s the New Lights, then called the "Christians," united with the Campbellites to form the Church of the Disciples. The Campbellites represented yet another split from the Presbyterians; the movement started in western Pennsylvania in 1808.[36]

The Presbyterians viewed the Great Revival with mixed feelings. It had brought a new enthusiasm, but it had also brought a sharp challenge to long-entrenched doctrines which the frontiersmen were not prepared to accept. After the expulsion of the Cumberland presbytery, some Presbyterians even joined the eccentric Shakers, who were given their name because of their coordinated marching, swaying, dancing, and singing. The Shakers won converts in the West in the enthusiasm of the revival, but their belief in celibacy aroused hostility among the frontiersmen. Their Union Village in southern Ohio was attacked by mobs in the years directly preceding the War of 1812, and the Ohio legislature passed a law in 1811 levying a fine on anyone who enticed a man away from his wife and family to join the Shakers.[37]

For all the enthusiasm of the revival and the assertions of dramatic growth, church members were a small proportion of the settlers. One reasonable estimate places church membership in the Old Northwest in 1810 as only some 7 percent of the total population.[38] While there is no doubt that the effects of the church's emphasis upon morality and decent behavior extended far beyond that small percentage, there also seems little reason to doubt that in the early years many frontiersmen were untouched by religion. It was only as population increased, permanent settlers multiplied, and new churches arose to serve them, that religious precepts exerted a wider influence. Indeed, it seems likely that one of the impelling factors of the frontier movement was a revolt against an ordered, carefully controlled society, represented in part by the role of the church. The West undoubtedly was more likely to attract those who were in some way dissatisfied with the prevailing social order than those who were its very pillars. The late eighteenth century had brought not only a struggle for freedom from England but also a struggle for freedom from religious orthodoxy. This had been represented partly by the magnificent victories for religious freedom in the 1780s and partly by an actual irreligious feeling. Certainly the West had more than its proportionate share of those who wanted to escape from religious orthodoxy. In the Ohio constitutional convention of 1802 a clause was inserted in the constitution that there would be no requirement of a religious test for the holding of office. An attempt to eliminate this clause and substitute a provision that no person who denied there was a God or a future state of rewards and punishments could hold office was defeated by a vote of thirty to three.[39]

Yet in certain respects, westerners were not prepared to throw off all the benefits of an organized religion. A favorite phrase of western petitioners

American Friends going to meeting in summer. From Sutcliff, *Travels*, 1815. (The New-York Historical Society)

was that religion and morality were essential for the maintenance of a sound government, and the West also showed a tendency to attempt to legislate morality and enforce the Puritan Sunday.[40] The Ohio Assembly in 1804–1805 tried to prohibit quarreling, shooting, or common labor on the Sabbath and also banned gambling and provided a fine for swearing by the name of God, Jesus Christ, or the Holy Ghost. Such efforts had little effect. A clergyman traveling through southeastern Ohio in 1812 stated that the "people are loose in morals: the profanation of the Lord's day, swearing and drunkenness, together with horse-racing and gambling, are very common." [41] Another clergyman who in 1811 went to preach in Newark, Ohio, a town "notorious for its wickedness," hid his horse in the bushes because he was afraid the inhabitants would shave it or cut his saddle. One can sympathize with Methodist Bishop Asbury's comment on his visit to Steubenville in 1803 that "I feel the power of Satan in these little, wicked, western trading towns." [42]

In general, however, it was on the new areas of the frontier that the vices attacked by the clergymen were most common. The expansion of church activity as the West became more settled helped to soften the rough violence of western society. Although in this way religion helped to recreate a traditional society in the West, religious belief itself had been modified as it developed in western society. It was not the traditional Episcopalians and Congregationalists who won the successes in the West but the Methodists and Baptists. The Presbyterians who tried to maintain their old traditions in the frontier region found themselves rent by schisms. Rather than merely accepting the old churches and the old beliefs, the westerners created the religion they wanted: an optimistic religion in which the primary appeal was to emotion rather than reason, in which faith was more important than doctrine, and in which the ministers preached salvation not damnation.

The establishment of an efficient system of education in the West proved more difficult than the expansion of religion. While an educated ministry could be replaced by inspired, semiliterate preachers, inspiration was not enough to teach reading, writing, and arithmetic. To build schools and to

American Friends going to meeting in a settled frost. From Sutcliff, *Travels,* 1815. (The New-York Historical Society)

Lutheran school-house, 1805. From Lewis Miller, *Sketches and Chronicles*. (Historical Society of York County, Pa.)

hire schoolmasters the West needed money, time, and sufficient population. By great efforts and cooperation many on the frontier obtained an elementary education in this period, but there was hardly time to go beyond this. Often the laws and methods of support were on the books with little achievement in practice. The settlers of northern New England and the Old Northwest frequently brought with them a tradition of respect for education, but their efforts inevitably were restricted by the nature of the society in which they lived. Children were needed to help in winning a farm from the wilderness. Shelter and food had to come before a complete education.

While settlements were still widely scattered, the frontiersmen found it extremely difficult to organize schools. Many young children learned to read and write from their mothers or neighbors. As soon as a small village had been founded, or a number of families settled close together, the settlers often banded together to pay a schoolmaster. Sometimes this was a local preacher, or often at first a local resident who combined teaching with other work. One teacher in central Ohio in 1811 combined teaching with keeping a tavern and farming a small piece of land. If the teacher regarded teaching as a profession, there was a risk that he had come out West because he drank too much, was incompetent, or had been concerned in some scandal back home. It was said of Ohio in 1812 that "the instructors, at least many of them, need to be instructed themselves, not only in knowledge, but also in manners and morals." [43]

The settlers from New England were usually particularly determined to establish schools. At Belpre, Ohio, a lady was employed as early as the summer of 1789 to teach the small children, and in the winter a male teacher was employed for the larger boys and young women. In the Holland purchase in New York in 1811 a traveler commented that education was usually supported by settlers of the area, and that whenever ten families were settled near each other they would associate and obtain a schoolmaster. [44]

At first the children were likely to be taught in someone's home until the neighbors got together to raise a cabin for a school. The cabin resembled the one they lived in, with its huge fireplace, puncheon floor, and light let in through a small window of greased paper. These elementary schools offered reading, writing, and a little arithmetic. The basic book was usually "Dilworth's Spelling Book," a work long used in England and America. The children usually recited their lessons aloud, and there was a strong religious, moralistic content; the first line of lesson I in Dilworth was "Hold in the Lord, and mind his Word." It was quite common for the children to be taken out of the school for months at a time. Clearing of land, corn-planting, sugar-making, and other tasks often required the presence of the pupils at home. No doubt most of them were glad of the break, for discipline was strict, and the rod used regularly. Frontier informality did not extend into the classroom; at one Kentucky rural school in the 1790s the boys took off their hats and bowed on entering the school, and the girls curtsied. [45]

The development of a program beyond the elementary level was slow in the early days, because of the lack of both money and competent teachers. Before 1815 it was usually only possible for academies to develop in the towns and larger villages. Where academies did exist the emphasis was strongly on a traditional education in Latin and Greek. More was sometimes promised but seldom provided.

When in 1801 trustees who had been chosen by subscribers to establish the Jefferson Academy at Vincennes petitioned the government for support in the form of land, they said they had already engaged masters in the classics, belles-lettres, mathematics, English, and French. Eleven years later one Vincennes resident wrote "there is no other resource here but a certain latin school, where a few scraps are taught, good or bad, no body here knows." [46]

Much of the education acquired in the West before 1815 had to be paid for, although provision had been made for a system of public schools. The basic advantage in the Old Northwest was the reservation of section sixteen in each township for the support of schools. This provision was included in most of the later acts calling for the sale and survey of land. After 1801 the Ohio legislature gradually made provision for the lease of the sections that had been reserved for schools in the Ohio and Miami purchases, and in 1805 it established a board of trustees in each township to arrange for the lease of the school lands. These efforts only came to fruition after the War of 1812. Mississippi Territory also had section sixteen reserved for the support of education but was able to achieve nothing in this period as the federal government had not given the territorial legislature the power to dispose of or lease these lands for the support of education.[47]

In other states the legislatures attempted to provide for public education. In Vermont, township grants included some land for the support of education, and the Vermont constitution directed that a school system be established. As early as 1782 a law authorized the setting up of local boards of trustees to administer school lands and provide for the maintenance of school systems, usually through a tax on the inhabitants of a local district. But little was accomplished before 1815.[48] The Kentucky assembly in 1798 attempted to provide for the establishment of county academies by granting 6000 acres for the support of each one, as well as lotteries to help them with the expenses of getting established, but once again little was done. Private academies remained the norm in Kentucky. Tennessee had the advantage that Congress had appropriated 100,000 acres for the purpose of establishing academies in each county, and a good many were in operation by 1815.[49] Yet for the most part there was more ambition than accomplishment in the realm of public education at the high school level in the West before 1815.

The legislatures of many western states also hoped for universities as well as schools and academies, although once again the desire exceeded the performance. In 1785 Transylvania Seminary, supported by land grants from Virginia, was opened in Danville, Kentucky, and after moving to Lexington was given a new charter in 1798 as Transylvania University. This was to become a famous western institution in the years after 1815, but at that date it was still really an academy, not a university.[50]

In Ohio two townships had been included in the Ohio Company purchase for the support of a university, and in 1802 and 1804 the Ohio legislature granted charters for a university at the new town of Athens. Ohio University finally began operation in 1808–1809, and in 1815 two students were granted degrees. It was a small beginning, but only twenty-five years before, Ohio had hardly been touched by American settlers. Tennessee had a college at Nashville, endowed by the United States with 50,000 acres, and by 1812 it had about fifty students. The college at Knoxville was slower to start, but eastern Tennessee did have small colleges in Washington and Green counties which produced ministers, lawyers, and physicians for the new state of Tennessee. In a similar manner colleges at Cannonsburgh and Washington in western Pennsylvania provided clergy for the region.[51]

By 1815 a good deal had been done to provide the older settled areas of the trans-Appalachian West with educational opportunities. In Ohio, Kentucky, and Tennessee elementary schools were to be found in most districts, and academies, in the larger settlements; and there were occasional opportunities for higher education. For the most part, however, the children of these states attended school only long enough to gain the rudiments of reading and writing. Farther to the west in the territories of Indiana, Illinois, Mississippi, and Missouri even this was often lacking. In most cases the concentration of population needed to support schools was lacking, and settlers were still deeply involved in the task of clearing the wilderness. In Mississippi Territory it was said in 1808 that because of the usefulness of the children in gathering the cotton crop most of the inhabitants could not afford to spare their labor, and education was almost totally neglected.[52]

Yet even in the territories educational ambitions ran high. The Indiana territorial legislature incorporated a university in 1806, and the trustees petitioned Congress for support in the following year. The trustees, probably much influenced by the Burr conspiracy, argued that "the only safeguard and secure shield, against the dark Cunning of individuals and of foreign governments, is the blaze of science which will reach the mind of the plowboy, as well as the most wealthy citizen." They wanted to secure "domestick happiness" for the citizens, "and stamp the principles of our government upon their plastick minds." Although the institution opened in 1810, it was really only a grammar school, teaching "the rudiments of the languages," geography, and mathematics.[53]

The westerners made determined efforts to bring education into the West in these years. They had ambitious plans for a public education culminating in universities, and often argued the benefits of education in Jeffersonian terms. For the most part, however, their children did not receive an extensive formal education, although they did generally learn to read and write once permanent settlers came in large numbers into any area. There were no radical innovations in this education; usually it consisted only of obtaining the rudiments of learning. When it went beyond this, it followed traditional lines.

"Every man, woman, and child, almost," wrote one traveler in Ohio in 1811, "read the newspapers." [54] Even allowing for exaggeration, this indicates not only a degree of literacy among the settlers but also an eagerness for the printed word. Although there are few indications that the hunters and squatters on the edge of the American frontier had any passionate interest in reading matter, the settlers who followed clearly desired more than a wilderness life. These were not transients. Many longed for news of the world outside their narrow bounds. They came to the frontier not to discard the society they had known but rather to enhance their own position within it.

Newspapers were founded with surprising frequency in the early history of western expansion. It was a very tiny town that could not boast its local newspaper, albeit with a very small circulation. In the early days publication was complicated by the shortage of paper. Until paper mills were opened, paper was imported down the Ohio, and newspapers sometimes had to suspend issues owing to the nonarrival of their supply. The introduction of western mills gradually solved this problem. There was a small one at Georgetown, Kentucky, by 1793, and two in the valley of the Little Miami in southwestern Ohio by 1811.[55]

The first newspaper of the trans-Appalachian West, the Pittsburgh *Gazette*, was established in 1786. At first a weekly, it became the most influential paper of the western Pennsylvania and eastern Ohio region. Other papers soon were founded in the surrounding territory and in Pittsburgh itself, and only one year after the first Pittsburgh newspaper was issued the Kentucky *Gazette* began publication in Lexington. John Bradford was the founder of the *Gazette*, and with his sons he long held a dominant position in Kentucky newspaper publishing. By 1810 Lexington had five newspapers, and there were numerous papers in other Kentucky towns; some thirty-two had been founded in Kentucky by 1810, although several of them had already ceased publication. Tennessee and Ohio had similar developments to Kentucky. The Knoxville *Gazette* was established in 1791, and at Cincinnati *The Centinel of the North-western Territory* was founded in 1793. Both states soon acquired others newspapers. Even sparsely populated Indiana had a newspaper by 1804 when the Indiana *Gazette* was established at Vincennes; it became more famous from 1807 under its name of the *Western Sun*.[56]

These early newspapers were not elaborate publications. They often contained a reprinting of out-of-date national news, a selection of local advertisements, and the occasional publication of a local poet. The papers were small, usually four pages, and at first appeared weekly. The standard for the most part was not high, although newspapers such the Pittsburgh and Kentucky *Gazettes* and *Liberty Hall* (founded in Cincinnati in 1804) managed to reach and possibly influence a greater population than existed in their immediate area. The number of printed copies was few—*Liberty Hall* printed 2000 copies a week by 1813—but a western newspaper reached far more readers than its subscribers or printed copies.[57] Once the early days of isolation had passed, most westerners had access to the news. It was out of date, but it was similar to that presented in the rest of the nation.

Even with the scattered nature of the western population, its inevitable concentration on food and shelter, and the difficulties of transportation, an attempt was soon made to provide a variety of books. The small western towns were the center of this effort. Before the West was able to support specialist booksellers, the general stores and the newspaper offices attempted to provide a selection of books for their customers. Moreover, the newspaper almanacs were popular, and the Kentucky *Almanack* was issued from the offices of the Kentucky *Gazette* by 1790. Actual book printing soon followed.[58]

The book trade expanded considerably after 1800. In 1802 Zadoc Cramer, who had established himself as an editor, began to issue not only his Pittsburgh *Almanac* but also the first edition of the more famous *Navigator*. This was constantly reprinted in the following years and was the standard guidebook and reference work for the traveler down the Ohio. Cramer published weightier works in subsequent years, and by 1815 Pittsburgh was flourishing as a western book center.[59]

Kentucky also proved active in the book trade after 1800. In the winter of 1802–1803, Joseph Charless, a printer who had come to Pennsylvania from Ireland, traveled west to Lexington. He took with him his printing press, sent over $500 worth of books, and brought with him an additional $4000 in books and stationery. In order to pay for the trip west he sold some $800 worth of books en route. Although Charless' newspaper failed, he opened a bookstore and wrote in February 1803 that "classics has a great sale here. I could sell since I arrived some dozn of Virgels, Pantheons, Horrace, Ovid &c &c." He also commented that Bibles, and religious books of every description, particularly by new authors, were in great demand. Charless in the following years not only sold books in Lexington but also peddled books in the surrounding areas; sometimes leaving books in different towns to be sold on commission. In the summer of 1805 he drove a wagon loaded with books through Ohio and Indiana Territory; and he later took a wagon load of schoolbooks to Nashville and bartered them for cotton.[60]

In order to meet the demand for books there was at an early date a movement for the establishment of libraries. It proved a difficult process to raise the money and secure the books, but circulating libraries began in the mid-1790s. At Lexington $500 was raised to establish a circulating library in 1795, and books were bought in Philadelphia. The library had 750 volumes by 1801. Belpre, near Marietta, had a library of 80 books by 1796, although it was not until 1814 that a library was successfully established at Cincinnati. In 1804 the well-known "Coonskin Library" was established near Marietta; shares in the library were paid for in coonskins because of the shortage of currency, and the library originally consisted of fifty-one volumes. By 1815 the major western centers possessed small circulating libraries.[61]

While the western towns were often attacked by clergymen as sinks of iniquity, there is little doubt that they did a great deal to transplant into the West the culture that was known in the East. They published the first newspapers, sold the first books, started the first libraries, and even pioneered in bringing the first glimmerings of theatrical activity to the West. There was amateur theater at Lexington in Kentucky before 1800 and other amateur activity continued throughout the first decades of the nineteenth century in the main towns of Kentucky and Ohio. By 1810 the practice was so well established that a professional company visited the West, established itself in Lexington, and toured through Cincinnati, Frankfort, and Louisville. In 1812 Pittsburgh built a theater seating more than 400, and in 1815 the Pittsburgh company went on tour down the Ohio River.[62]

The larger western towns by the end of the first decade of the nineteenth century could offer a variety of experience unknown in the rural areas. Lexington in 1811 had a theater, a public library (with a youth library attached), two bookstores, and three newspapers. As early as 1807 it had a coffee house with forty-two files of different newspapers from all over the United States. Frankfort by 1814 had a theater, three printing offices, a bookstore, a library, and a book binder.[63] Cincinnati and Pittsburgh flourished in the same manner. Although the smaller towns could not offer as much, they did provide variety in contrast to the surrounding countryside. The situation was much different in those areas of the West just beginning the process of settlement. "The people are considerably dispersed," it was written of the district of Mobile in what is now Alabama, "and have enjoyed but few opportunities for mental improvement. We have no colleges—no permanent schools—no regular places of worship—no literary institutions—no towns; no good houses, and but few comfortable ones." [64]

In the transformation of the West from wilderness to civilized society the towns were able to provide in microcosm a transplanting of traditional culture. This could not emerge immediately on settlement, but it came as soon as the increase of population in the rural areas brought to the towns the prosperity and the population needed for pursuing more varied pleasures than drinking, card-playing, and fighting.

There were determined efforts in the West in the years after 1783 to establish the patterns of life that had been known in the East, or the patterns of life that had been hoped for and envied. Some of the attempts at preventing any radical departure of ways in the West came from outside, through the organized efforts of the churches, which had no desire to see the frontiersmen throw off their religion while creating a new life. In some ways this attempt to retain the allegiance of the westerners to old ways, or perhaps in some cases to regain those who had already drifted away in the eighteenth century, failed. Church membership represented only a small proportion of the total population, and the churches which were most successful were those prepared to modify their views to satisfy the spiritual and emotional demands of the westerners. The religious groups undoubtedly helped to set a moral standard in the West in these years, but in spite of the revivals the frontier was not an ardent religious society.

Others who attempted to prevent westerners from drifting too far from accepted cultural standards and values of eastern and European civilization were actually within the West, and as in most societies undoubtedly represented a minority. These were the men who established libraries and schools, and who tried to set cultural standards for the new areas. They did not change the lives of the majority of the population in the years before 1815, but they tried to ensure that certain values remained as ideals. The majority of frontiersmen in these years before 1815 were not enthusiastic church members, did not attend an academy or college, did not borrow books from a circulating library, and certainly did not attend a theater. Most of them were far too busy working and were too isolated to be warmed even by the dim glimmers of a more varied life that were visible in the small urban communities. They were more worried about living, farming, and finding a market for their crops than for greater refinements. Most of them were neither eye-gougers nor active proponents of an old cultural tradition. Yet the society that was being shaped for them, by leaders and churches from without and by a fairly small group of leaders within, echoed in its significant features that which they had known in the East, and that which their forefathers had known in Europe.

◁ 8 ▷

The Growth of Frontier Prosperity

A s settlers advanced onto the frontier, most thought not only of survival but also of agricultural prosperity. To achieve this they had to tame the land, develop cash crops, and raise livestock while attempting to find a market. On most areas of the frontier in these years, the initial task was simplified by the fertility of the soil and sufficient rainfall, but the process of growing ample crops was slowed by the task of clearing the forest cover. In expanding his farm the frontier farmer often encountered a labor shortage that was only partially solved by large families and neighborhood cooperation. In most cases he at first did not have sufficient capital to hire additional men. Moreover, frontiersmen usually wanted to own their own lands, not hire themselves out as farm laborers. Even south of the Ohio where slavery existed, the typical farmer did not have the money in the early years of immigration to buy slaves to clear and till his land, although richer settlers often based their plans on the use of slave labor.

On the frontier of northern New England the usual problems of a frontier farmer were increased by a climate that severely restricted the growing season and by a soil that lacked fertility. The inadequacies of the soil were at first obscured by the forest deposit, but by the end of the first decade of the nineteenth century many farmers were disillusioned. Vermont farmers usually did not specialize, although wheat became at an early date the most prominent of the crops and the one that presented the best possibility for marketing. They also tried other grain crops, including corn, as well as beans, peas, and flax. Livestock was an important element in the economy, and horsebreeding was soon to give Vermont a reputation similar to that of Kentucky.[1]

Across western New York, western Pennsylvania, and throughout the Old Northwest, although there were regional variations, the general agricultural development before 1815 was very similar. In the early years corn was the staple, but it was too bulky for profit as a cash crop; it could not be transported economically. Surplus corn was used to feed the livestock or to make whiskey. Frontier farmers needed either a crop that produced a high yield for weight, or a source of profit that could walk to market. Before 1815 wheat offered the northern farmers one of their best opportunities for trade, as it could be exported profitably as flour. Certain areas soon became renowned for their wheat production, particularly the Genesee Valley, the Monongahela River region, and the Pickaway Plains in Ohio.

Livestock provided another essential element in the northern economy. Cattle and hogs were important in the longer-settled frontier areas by 1800 and had the advantage that they could not only be sent downriver to New Orleans as beef and pork but could also be driven eastward on the hoof. By 1810 certain areas, such as the Western Reserve, had become important producers of dairy produce. Sheep were also becoming of increasing importance to northern farmers, and experiments were being made with Merino sheep for their wool.[2]

On the edges of the frontier in the Old Northwest—Indiana and Illinois —farming was still little removed from the subsistence level in 1815. There were some attempts to move beyond the ubiquitous corn to more exotic crops, notably the effort by French Swiss to introduce wine-making at Vevay, Indiana, on the Ohio; but by 1810, eight years after settlement, the colony was only producing some 2400 gallons of red and 120 gallons of white wine a year.[3]

The first settlers of Kentucky and Tennessee often had farms similar to those of Ohio. The main crop was corn, and farming was of the subsistence type. One difference was that even in the earliest years some settlers had slaves; as settlement increased slaves became more numerous. After 1800 Kentucky produced many crops that competed with those of the North. Wheat was grown extensively in Kentucky and exported as flour. The farmers of eastern Tennessee also developed grain crops. Livestock became of great importance in Kentucky and eastern Tennessee. Cattle and hogs were numerous, as in the North, but in Kentucky particular emphasis was placed on the breeding and training of horses.

Kentucky and Tennessee also developed tobacco, hemp, and cotton.

Tobacco is prepared for market. From Tatham, *Historical and Practical Essay*, 1800. (The New York Public Library)

Transporting tobacco. From Tatham, *Historical and Practical Essay*, 1800. (The New York Public Library)

The early settlers from Virginia when seeking a cash crop naturally tended to plant tobacco; it was also considered desirable to plant tobacco on fertile land before it was used for the growing of wheat. The cultivation of tobacco began in the earliest days in Kentucky. By 1800 it was prospering in the southern and north central sections. Hemp also provided the basis of a flourishing industry.[4]

While eastern Tennessee and Kentucky developed grain crops and live-stock, western Tennessee, although cultivating tobacco from an early date, turned to cotton as its main cash crop. Eli Whitney's cotton gin was eagerly awaited, and the Tennessee legislature promised to pay Whitney 37½ cents for each gin used in the state from 1804 to 1807. By 1810 cotton production was estimated at 3,000,000 pounds, and there had been a great increase in the number of slaves in the western part of the state.[5]

In what are now Mississippi and Alabama, the main area for agriculture in the years before 1815 was in the Natchez district. After the Revolution planters had first tried tobacco and then indigo as cash crops, without success. Not until 1795 did they begin to cultivate cotton on any extensive scale. By 1800 it had become the staple crop, and in 1801 earned some $700,000 for the farmers of the Natchez region. Commercial difficulties with England and the cotton disease ("the rot") which in 1811 spread through the lower Mississippi Valley caused difficulty. But by 1815 the cotton kingdom was well established on the Mississippi, and planters were importing many of their provisions instead of growing them. Although cotton cultivation also began along the Mobile and Tombigbee and in the Tennessee River valley in what is now Alabama, it was of very minor importance before 1815.[6]

Louisiana was more developed agriculturally than any other area of the lower Mississippi Valley. During the eighteenth century the main cash crop had been indigo, but poor prices and insect damage threatened its future after the Revolution. Faced by this crisis the planters turned to the cultivation of sugar cane and cotton. In the newer, west central regions of the state they engaged in cattle grazing on a large scale; a ready market was to be found at the end of the drive to New Orleans.

The 1790s saw the real beginning of the Louisiana sugar industry. Experiments in the cultivation of sugar cane were given a boost by the revolution in Santo Domingo which brought exiled Creole sugar planters to Louisiana. Louisiana planters had already made a start under the leadership of Étienne Boré, and by 1801–1802 it was estimated that there were some seventy-five plantations occupied in the production of sugar, producing from 4,000,000 to 8,400,000 pounds annually. Cotton production also began in Louisiana in the 1790s. It flourished after 1800, extending along the Mississippi to the vicinity of Baton Rouge and spreading both into the Red River valley and the Opelousas region, where cotton planters began to supersede cattlemen.[7]

Although western lands could readily be made to yield an agricultural surplus, the difficulties of marketing severely hampered the efforts of western farmers to achieve prosperity. To some extent all the frontier regions did provide at least one important outlet of their own; that was the influx of new settlers buying supplies until they became established. It was said of the Zanesville, Ohio, region in 1811 that "at present, almost the only article of surplus produce is flour. . . . Other articles are raised in abundance, but the great influx of emigrants consumes nearly the whole." [8] The inhabitants of the growing western towns also consumed agricultural produce from the surrounding regions, but the towns were not large enough to absorb large surpluses. Pittsburgh, the largest of the western towns outside New Orleans, had only about 8000 inhabitants in 1815.[9]

Other local outlets for western produce were few, although the army proved useful in some areas. In the early 1790s when Cincinnati was the gathering place for northwestern expeditions against the Indians, the trade of the region was considerably stimulated. Even the inhabitants of the small Ohio Company settlement farther up the Ohio were, in the fall of 1794, able to load up two boats with corn to sell to a contractor for troops at Fort Washington. Yet, after Wayne's victory in 1794, the western posts were small, and it was not until the War of 1812 that the western farmers were again able to sell agricultural surpluses in large amounts to the army.[10]

The frontier inhabitants of northern New England and western New York had marketing problems different from most western areas in these years before 1815. Rather than depending on the Ohio-Mississippi river route, these northern settlers had to look mainly to the Lakes and to the St. Lawrence, or south and east to New York. The northern settlements in Vermont and the northern and western settlements in New York sent large quantities of wheat, flour, beef, pork, potash pearlash, and timber northward to Canada, via the Champlain Valley, Lake Ontario, and Lake Erie. Even in the settlements at the eastern end of Lake Ontario, around Sackets Harbor, which was not developed until after 1800, it was said in 1811 that "the quantity of wheat, flour, beef, pork, ashes, and lumber that is annually exported to Montreal would exceed belief." [11] In return the settlers received British manufactured goods, salt, and specie. This trade was hampered by the commercial warfare with England after 1807, but extensive smuggling continued. During the War of 1812 there was a considerable trade between the settlers and Canada; without it, the British army in Canada would have been in considerable difficulty for supplies.

Southern Vermont mainly exported its products to the south. Flatboats carried provisions on the Connecticut River to Hartford, Connecticut, and in southwestern Vermont goods went south to the Hudson Valley. The interior roads were bad; the country was mountainous; and the distances to profitable markets were great. The settlers of western New York also shipped their products eastward along the Mohawk and Hudson valleys, but here there was a considerable problem of shipping overland to reach the navigable rivers. Sometimes wheat and flour were sent in winter, when the lack of roads could be overcome by the use of sleighs. Yet western New York could not reach its full agricultural potential while the difficulties of communication persisted.[12]

For the settlers who had crossed the mountains into western Pennsylvania, Ohio, Kentucky, and Tennessee, a different problem existed. The Appalachian barrier made impractical the export of bulk farm produce from West to East; the main hope for direct trade eastward was in the driving of cattle, hogs, and horses across the mountains. During the entire period from 1783 to 1815 the great mass of trade carried on across the Appalachians moved from East to West. This trade mainly consisted of bringing manufactured goods, often British, from Philadelphia and Baltimore.

In the years immediately after the Revolution packhorses were still used as an important means of bringing goods to Pittsburgh, but they were rapidly being superseded by Conestoga wagons. These great wagons, drawn by four to six horses, moved westward as soon as the roads were more than mere tracks. The journey from Philadelphia to Pittsburgh took about three weeks, and the rates of transportation were very high; often as much as $4 to $6 a hundredweight. To some extent the high cost was because many of the wagons had to return empty, although they sometimes returned with pelts or ginseng. Pittsburgh was the main mart, but many goods were also sent to Wheeling, farther down the Ohio; the journey was longer but there was less likelihood of difficulties in the navigation of the Ohio because of low water.[13]

The inhabitants of western Pennsylvania shipped their goods to New Orleans rather than eastward to Philadelphia. But the unfortunate inhabitants of eastern Tennessee had little choice; for the most part they had to send their produce eastward because they had no natural connection with the Ohio-Mississippi river route, except by the Tennessee River where shallows and rocks impeded navigation. Their main natural outlet was along the Great Valley running north. Eastern Tennessee brought its manufactured goods in by land and sent out what produce it could to Baltimore, Richmond, and Philadelphia. This dependence on uneconomical land transportation was a severe handicap to eastern Tennessee in these years.[14]

The only product western farmers were able to export in any quantity to the East over the Appalachians was livestock; the inhabitants of western Pennsylvania, Ohio, Kentucky, and eastern Tennessee all drove their stock to market by this route. The trade was mostly in cattle and hogs, but drives also included Kentucky horses and, toward the end of this period, even sheep. The normal destination was Philadelphia or Baltimore, and the drives really got underway after 1800. It took six weeks or more to take the livestock from southeastern Ohio to Baltimore, but it was not always necessary to drive them the whole way.[15] One drover, who started from southeastern

Ohio with eighty-six head in July 1809, drove his cattle into Pennsylvania and sold them two or three at a time on his way east. He reached the Susquehanna River at the beginning of September, soon sold the remaining cattle, and returned home. Sometimes the cattle were not sold directly but were driven east and fattened in eastern Pennsylvania and along the banks of the Potomac. Western livestock owners sometimes went into partnership with easterners to carry out this type of trade; the western partner being responsible for raising or buying and driving the cattle and the eastern one for fattening them; profit or loss after expenses was shared equally. The main Ohio drives were to the east, but there was also cattle-driving westward across Ohio to the market along the Detroit River.[16]

The Kentuckians also dealt extensively in livestock for eastern markets. Like the Ohioans they drove cattle in large numbers to the Potomac, to be fattened for the Baltimore and Philadelphia markets, but they also exported horses. These were sold mainly in the southern states, particularly in South Carolina. This was not such an extensive business as the cattle drives, but many horses were driven east in the early part of winter.[17]

Although livestock could be driven east, the drive was long and arduous, and the eastern route was useless for the bulk of western crops. To dispose of these the westerners depended, except for internal sales, on the river route southward to New Orleans. The Ohio-Mississippi route cut through the heart of the area, and the only real block to navigation was the falls of the Ohio at modern Louisville. This obstacle was by no means insuperable. The rapids could be shot by large vessels in high water, and it was only in dry seasons that they became a major problem; it was then frequently necessary to make a portage. At an early date it was realized that a canal around the rapids would be a great aid to navigation. Although a canal company was incorporated in 1804, the canal was not constructed until more than twenty years later. Apart from the falls the main problems in navigation were the low water on the upper Ohio (except in spring and autumn) and the two or three months each year when the boats were endangered by ice. These difficulties, together with the seasonal nature of the crops, meant that there was heavy shipment down the Ohio at particular times of the year; this had a depressing effect on prices for produce at New Orleans. It was difficult to obtain news of market conditions in New Orleans in time for it to do any good.[18]

In spite of these disadvantages, and although land routes were needed to provide access to the waterways for those in the interior, the Ohio-Mississippi route was the essential lifeline by which the settlers of the trans-Appalachian West transported their produce to market. Before 1795 it was a particularly unsure lifeline, because to that date Spain did not grant United States citizens free navigation of the Mississippi. American farmers, however, already knew the value of the New Orleans market. At the end of the Revolution settlers in western Pennsylvania were sending cargoes of flour downstream to New Orleans. Spanish restrictions stopped most of this trade from 1784 to 1789, and into the early 1790s the export of produce was still on a very small scale, consisting mainly of flour, tobacco, beef, and pork. As late as 1794 less than fifty boats came down the river to New Orleans.[19]

These early efforts at shipping produce through New Orleans for the most part did not involve elaborate marketing transactions. Although conspirator James Wilkinson acted as a middleman in taking goods downriver, in many cases farmers took their own produce on the long journey, sent their sons, or acted in concert with their neighbors. In western Pennsylvania after 1790 groups of settlers sometimes acted together to build flatboats—some working, others providing materials. Each put on board his flour, bacon, and whiskey at his own risk. One of the group went as "captain," and a crew was hired for the long voyage to New Orleans.[20]

As trade increased after 1795 marketing arrangements gradually became more elaborate, and a key role was played by general merchants and exporters in the small western towns and villages. The merchants were usually engaged not only in exporting to New Orleans but also in importing from Philadelphia and Baltimore. A pivotal town in this western commerce was Pittsburgh, through which the bulk of the goods from the East came. Merchants at Pittsburgh received their manufactured goods from Philadelphia or Baltimore on nine- or twelve-month credit. Many of them were partners or the factors of Philadelphia trading houses. As Pittsburgh was also the market for the farm settlements along the Monongahela and Allegheny, the imported manufactured goods were usually exchanged for the farm produce of the country, which was then shipped down the Ohio and Mississippi to New Orleans. There the brokers of the Pittsburgh merchants would sell as much as they could for ready money to be remitted to Philadelphia and Baltimore. If not ready money, then the brokers would exchange the frontier produce for cotton or sugar and consign this to the Philadelphia and Baltimore houses.[21]

Merchants at Pittsburgh and Wheeling also engaged in a lucrative trade with the settlements down the Ohio, transporting both manufactured goods from the East and, particularly in the years after 1800, the products of local industry. In the early days traders supplied themselves at Pittsburgh and went up and down the Ohio and its tributaries in canoes with manufactured goods, haberdashery, tea, and coffee. Barter was the normal method of western trade, owing to the great scarcity of specie. So scarce was money that when a specie round dollar appeared in the West it stayed intact for only a short time before it was cut into eight equal pieces to serve as smaller change.[22]

The canoes on the Ohio were only the beginning of what gradually became an elaborate trade carried on in floating stores with a great variety of merchandise, in the manner of a village general store. The large flatboats, fitted with shelves and counters, floated downriver from settlement to settlement making small sales. After two or three months on the river in the spring or autumn, the trader would sell the farm produce he had collected to a merchant in one of the small towns and make the best deal he could for his flatboat.[23]

The type of trading operation carried on by the merchants of Pittsburgh was duplicated throughout the West, though often on a lesser scale, by the merchants in the smaller western towns. Frequently they did not allow the merchants of Pittsburgh to act without competition as middlemen in the importation of British manufactured goods from Philadelphia and Baltimore, or even New York. It was common for western merchants to go all the way to Philadelphia once a year to lay in their trading goods. As early as the fall of 1793 when the Old Northwest was still in the midst of Indian warfare one merchant from the Cincinnati region visited Philadelphia to buy goods to trade with General Anthony Wayne's army.[24]

The merchants of southwestern Ohio were helped by the demand created by Wayne's forces in the 1793–1795 period, and as settlers came into Ohio after 1794 Cincinnati became a major trading center. In 1803 the Miami Exporting Company was incorporated there with the object of exporting agricultural produce to New Orleans. As its charter permitted the issue of paper money, the original object was soon abandoned, and by 1807 it went into full operation as a bank. Although specie was still in short supply, the Miami Exporting Company proved a great help in commercial transactions. Other banks were founded in the western towns, particularly after the demise of the United States bank in 1811. By 1814 even pioneer Indiana had chartered its first two banks.[25]

In 1806 the Cincinnati area had about thirty storekeepers or merchants engaged in trading imported goods to the farmers of the region and receiving flour, pork, beef, and other provisions in exchange. Until 1815 flour continued to be the main export from Cincinnati and the Miami country. There was also considerable trade in pork, whiskey, brandy, cheese, and provisions of all kinds.[26]

In Kentucky, Lexington was the trading center of greatest importance. It was thriving in the 1790s and after 1800 became the main western town between Pittsburgh and New Orleans. "The Main street of Lexington," it was said in 1805, "has all the appearance of Market street in Philadelphia on a busy day."[27] The merchants of the town imported great quantities of goods from Philadelphia and Baltimore, and traded not only in Kentucky but also across the Ohio into Indiana Territory and even southward into Tennessee. The produce they received in exchange, they had to ship overland to Frankfort or Louisville, as Lexington, although at the center of the earliest land routes into Kentucky, was not on a navigable stream. But the Kentucky River served as the highway to the Ohio for the interior of the state and was an important artery of commerce. Louisville, at the falls of the Ohio, although not a large town in this period, engaged in considerable trade, and was the starting point for many of the Kentucky boats on their way to New Orleans.[28]

Although the Cumberland country of western Tennessee was better situated than the eastern part of the state, its channels of trade were long and difficult. The trading center of the region was Nashville, and the merchants had to import their trade goods from Philadelphia and Baltimore through Pittsburgh, down the Ohio to the mouth of the Cumberland, and then to Nashville. In spite of the difficulties, by the end of this period settlers on the Cumberland sent considerable amounts of cotton down the Cumberland, Ohio, and Mississippi to New Orleans to be exported. This was a difficult market for them, as they were competing with cotton from Mississippi Territory. And they were glad of the chance to send their cotton overland to Kentucky and by boat via the Cumberland and Ohio rivers to the state of Ohio and to Pittsburgh.[29]

The rapid development of western trade after 1795 was reflected in the great increase in the quantities of produce received at New Orleans. American shipments down the Mississippi were valued at more than $1,000,000 in 1801, and the extent to which the frontiersmen depended on the trade down the Mississippi became obvious in 1802 and 1803 when the Spanish suspension of the right of deposit brought threats of war throughout the West. Jefferson's purchase of Louisiana territory in 1803 brought an end to the danger of Spanish interference with trade on the lower Mississippi. Betwen 1803 and 1807 trade down the Mississippi grew rapidly. In 1807, over 1800 boats came downstream to New Orleans.[30]

Trade on the Mississippi was an arduous and often dangerous undertaking. The journey from Pittsburgh could take several months on a flatboat, although it was said that a barge in spring could do it in forty or fifty days; from Louisville it took as much as a month to reach New Orleans. Most of the goods were shipped by flatboat, a simple craft that usually did not hold more than fifty tons and was steered by a board on the end of a long pole. The boat had a rough shelter, but most flatboats were hardly likely to be comfortable, or even very safe. Once they had performed their task of carrying goods they were usually broken up or when possible sold on the lower Mississippi. Other types of boats existed in abundance in the Mississippi trade. Bateaux, like the flatboats, had no keel, but they were pointed rather than blunt at bow and stern. They could be rowed, sailed, or poled, and were usually covered aft. Keelboats were more elaborate and represented a bigger investment. They were often long and narrow, partly covered, and were usually rowed or poled. Also equipped with keels, but usually larger than the keelboats, were the barges, which used sails and were more to be seen in later years as trade prospered. Most of the boats on the Mississippi were flimsily made and so difficult to navigate that hidden islands, logs, and other driftwood were frequent hazards. As early as the 1780s insurance was attempted for the traffic down the Mississippi, and after 1800 companies were formed for this purpose. Still the shipping of goods was a risky proposition.[31]

The boatmen, the despair of frontier preachers, were in some respects colorful characters. Their lives were laborious and often dangerous. If they successfully navigated the long journey down the Ohio and Mississippi to Natchez, the houses immediately around the landing provided them with gambling, drinking, and prostitutes, but also bestowed a liberal proportion of fever and other diseases. Nor was the journey downstream the most difficult part of the trip; a major problem was returning home. Boatmen from western Pennsylvania often returned by ship to the east coast and then overland to their homes, but a common route was the Natchez Trace from Natchez to Nashville in Tennessee, a trip of some 500 miles. Travelers usually journeyed over the Trace in groups because it soon became the haunt of outlaws hoping to obtain the proceeds of some cargo sold in New Orleans.[32]

Some of the boatmen did not go farther south than Natchez, because after 1800 the Mississippi Territory around that settlement bought a considerable quantity of provisions from the Ohio Valley. Those who floated on between the increasingly cultivated banks finally deposited their cargoes at New Orleans, at a levee lined with a hundred or so boats from the Ohio Valley. By 1810 these carried wheat, flour, pork, whiskey, brandy, potash, beef, apples, butter, cheese, hemp, tobacco, livestock and a variety of other items, including even ice. There were also likely to be lead and furs from the Missouri and Illinois country, and cotton, sugar, and timber from the lower Mississippi.[33]

Although this Mississippi trade assumed large proportions in the first decade of the nineteenth century, it experienced severe difficulties after 1807 when already existing problems were increased because of the commercial warfare with England. In the years directly preceding the War of 1812 the Mississippi Valley suffered an agricultural depression. The real causes of this depression were connected with the inadequate communications, the lack of any real market information from New Orleans, the glutting of the market at certain times of the year, and the expense of imports. But these problems were greatly complicated by the commercial warfare with England from 1807, the American Embargo, and the British blockades.

Prices at New Orleans in the years before the War of 1812 were never as high again for western farmers as they had been in 1805. They sank gradually to 1807 and experienced a rapid decline in the embargo year of 1808. Tobacco and cotton were particularly hard hit, and by 1811 the bottom was also falling out of the hemp market. Flour was not as severely affected, as there was a market for western flour among the British troops in the Peninsula.[34] The war of 1812 put further severe restrictions on American exports, but for western farmers these difficulties were somewhat offset by the needs of the government for the western armies and by the growth in internal trade.

Commercial restriction and war did, however, have certain definite advantages for the West in the stimulation of early western industry. All over the United States, as the government attempted to change England's policy by restricting British imports, attempts were made to provide American substitutes for British goods. These attempts were not always successful, but in no area were they so necessary or desired as in the West. A great weakness in the western economy was the high expense of importing manufactured goods. This expense was a constant drain on western specie and a constant handicap in the attempt to achieve prosperity.

In the early years of settlement the western settlers depended of necessity on domestic manufactures for many commodities—producing their own furniture, clothing, and household equipment, and processing their own foodstuffs. Much of this dependence continued throughout this period.[35] Yet as the farmers achieved a surplus and were able to barter, they sought to obtain a variety of articles, luxuries as well as near necessities, for their families. As many of these articles had to come at great expense over the Appalachians, it is not surprising that before 1815 western centers had begun to use western raw materials to produce manufactured goods.

Until the years of commercial warfare after 1807, the West had very little industry; before 1800 it was practically nonexistent. One traveler through Pittsburgh in 1784 commented "the place, *I believe*, will never be very considerable," and another in 1796 thought that, in spite of the difficulty of transport from Philadelphia and Baltimore, the town had made little effort to establish manufactures. By the latter date, however, a few iron mines were being worked on the Monongahela, and coppers, cauldrons, country ovens, pots, and other utensils were being cast. There were also a few iron furnaces and forges established in Tennessee in the 1790s and some production of lime. Apart from that the only industries organized on anything but an exceedingly small scale were boatbuilding in the towns on the upper Ohio, salt-making at the various salt licks, and lead mining in what is now Missouri.[36]

With more settled conditions in the West and with population increasing rapidly, some industry began to develop in the first years of the nineteenth century. The most ambitious of these efforts was the construction of seagoing vessels on the Ohio. Marietta became the center of this enterprise and showed definite promise in the years to 1808. Probably thirty or forty vessels were built on the Ohio in these years. Shipbuilding on the river was handicapped, however, by the falls at Louisville. There were disastrous sinkings in 1807, and, contrary to most industrial activity in America, the industry was also dealt a severe blow by the Embargo of 1807–1809, which prevented American vessels from leaving for foreign ports. Only a few seagoing vessels were built after that date, although there was further activity in the 1840s.[37]

Shipbuilding also stimulated other enterprises. By 1802 there were two extensive ropewalks in Lexington, which supplied rigging for the ships built on the Ohio. At that time Lexington had little other industrial activity except for the tanneries, which were an early feature of most western towns. But by 1807 there were four ropewalks employing about sixty hands and making some 300 tons of cordage annually. Ropewalks were also later established in Ohio and Pittsburgh and provided a market for Kentucky hemp.[38]

By 1807 Lexington had a nucleus of other industrial establishments. There were three nail factories (making about sixty tons of nails a year) and two copper and tin factories. Many other enterprises, though employing a few workmen, were more shops than factories; cabinetmakers, saddlers, silversmiths, tobacco makers, hatters, and bootmakers and shoemakers fashioned their wares. More substantial was the factory making baling cloth for wool. It employed thirty-eight men and produced 36,000 yards annually. Most of the western manufacturing establishments were very small; and the dividing line between a craftsman with assistants making goods to sell in his own shop and a "manufactory" looking to a wider market was often a very narrow one. Lexington's economic progress was helped after 1802 by the chartering of the first Kentucky bank, the Kentucky Insurance Company.[39]

Pittsburgh moved forward even more rapidly than Lexington in the first six or seven years of the nineteenth century. By 1807 it had certainly passed out of the stage of being regarded as a frontier post. One observer in that year thought that the Sabbath was well-observed in Pittsburgh "considering that it is so much of a manufacturing town." [40] Pittsburgh was ideally located for such development. It had at hand the natural deposits for iron manufacturing and a readily available market. The immigrants who flocked into the town on their way west had a variety of needs, and Pittsburgh helped to supply settlers all the way down the Ohio who could easily be reached by water.

At an early date there had been small nail factories in Pittsburgh. By 1807 there were also two glassworks, two breweries, an air furnace for casting iron utensils, and a cotton factory with a mule, spinning jenny, looms, and a wool-carding machine. Smaller establishments manufactured ropes, copperware and tinware, earthenware, saddlery, and a variety of other necessities. Boatbuilding had always been of great importance, and this industry had the additional advantage that few of the many boats that left to go downstream ever returned.[41]

Pittsburgh continued to expand its industry in the years between the Embargo and the War of 1812. "In the course of my walks through the streets," wrote one traveler of Pittsburgh in 1811, "I heard every where the sound of the hammer and anvil; all was alive; everything indicated the greatest industry." [42] The cotton factories, glassworks, air furnaces, breweries, distilleries were now more numerous, and a host of other small establishments were expanding. Pittsburgh was not only supplying the surrounding country but was also exporting glass, bottles, beer, porter, saddlery, boots and shoes, tinware and copperware, stills, and cabinet work down the Ohio. By 1815 even a visiting clergyman could comment that "Pittsburg . . . has become famous in the New World—and by nature, combined with art, promises to be one of the greatest *manufacturing* towns in America." [43]

In the years after the imposing of the Embargo and the Non-Importation Act of 1807, American manufacturing was given a definite stimulus, and the West participated in this. The losses in shipbuilding were more than offset by other industrial developments. Although there was no industrial revolution, it did mean that the West began to escape from its total dependency on goods imported from the East and England. Local boosters and even travelers exaggerated the extent of industrial growth, because they were so impressed that even this much had been done in so short a time.

In the years immediately prior to the War of 1812 one of the main areas of industrial development was in the manufacture of textiles. Even outside the main centers small textile factories began to make their appearance. Western New York from Utica westward toward the Genesee River was particularly active in textile production. Utica, which had first been settled in the late 1780s, had developed as a trading town when farmers began to use it instead of Albany. It had suffered when the settlements to the west began to depend more on trade through the Lakes to Canada than on the Mohawk-Hudson route, but manufacturing began to develop in Oneida County from about 1807, helped by capital from Albany and New York. By 1811 one cotton factory was in operation as well as several woolen factories, and some establishments were in the process of being built. There were also a large number of fulling mills and ten carding machines. Cotton was being imported from New York. Throughout western New York the interest in textile manufacture was reflected in a great increase in the keeping of sheep, and it was said that "a vast quantity of woollen cloth is made through the country." [44]

Farther west the manufacturing impulse was also reaching Ohio and Kentucky. Cincinnati was still primarily concerned with commerce rather than manufacturing, but the latter was now beginning to develop. The town had sizable breweries, distilleries, and two cotton factories. Cotton was imported from Tennessee by way of the Cumberland River. At Chillicothe there were ropewalks, cotton and woolen factories, a nail factory, and several distilleries. Politician Thomas Worthington had established a ropewalk and cloth mill there in 1810; the textile mill wove wool, flax, and cotton. The flax could be obtained locally; Worthington kept the sheep that supplied the wool; but the cotton had to be imported from the South. [45]

In Kentucky, Lexington was still the main manufacturing center. As in the rest of the state the manufacture of hemp in ropewalks and in bagging factories was the most important operation; there were also cotton and woolen factories. Louisville had little manufacturing before the War of 1812, although ropes and cotton bagging were made there, as they were at Frankfort, where there was also a tobacco factory.[46]

The War of 1812 proved a considerable advantage to the internal trade and manufacturing of the Ohio Valley towns. The farmers, however, lost their foreign markets, and this was not compensated for by government demands for their produce. As the British blockade tightened around the coasts of the United States and blocked the sea connections between New Orleans and the Northeast, south-north trade turned inland up the Mississippi and Ohio valleys to Pittsburgh, then across the mountains to Philadelphia.

Although by far the largest flow of traffic had always been south along the Philadelphia-Pittsburgh-Ohio-Mississippi route, there had from an early date been some movement against that flow and some variety of internal trafficking within it. The journey up the Mississippi was an arduous one and only possible for keelboats. When a reasonable wind was blowing boats could sail against the stream, but often boats had to be manhandled to get them up river, and usually the voyage from New Orleans to Pittsburgh took at least four months.[47]

The main items that were shipped against the flow of trade were specialities of the various regions. From New Orleans, imported coffee and sugar were sent up the Ohio. Natchez sent some cotton by this route, although a far more important source of cotton for the infant industries of the Ohio Valley was Tennessee, which shipped its cotton out by way of the Cumberland River. Kentucky was able to export hemp, tobacco, and saltpetre upstream, and even Ohio sent specialities such as Western Reserve cheese to Pittsburgh markets.[48] The frontier regions on the upper Mississippi also shipped their goods to the Ohio Valley states, and Missouri Territory had a lucrative trade in lead and salt as well as sending pelts and furs up the Ohio. The lead mines that were scattered over a wide area some fifty miles from Ste. Genevieve and the large salt springs below that place, both engaged in a considerable trade to the Ohio Valley. In the first decade of the century the Pittsburgh area received much of its salt down the Allegheny from the Onondaga region, but after 1810 more and more began to be received from salt works on the Great Kanawha.[49]

This internal trade which had gone on through the early years of the century was greatly boosted by the War of 1812. Far more of the products of the lower Mississippi now found their way to Pittsburgh instead of being sent through New Orleans and then through the British blockades. At the same time the lack of imported British manufactured goods gave a fresh impetus to manufacturing at a time when the growth in internal trade was helping to enrich western cities and provide capital for investment.

Western Pennsylvania and Pittsburgh benefited most from all this, but

View of West Point with Fulton's steamship *Clermont*. Probably by Saint-Mémin. (Stokes Collection, The New York Public Library)

its effects were felt throughout the West; existing industries were expanded, and new ones put into operation. Steam engines now became a more common feature of the western scene. At Pittsburgh there was a wire-drawing mill, tilt hammers, and paper, textile, and flour mills propelled by steam, and there was "an incessant din of clattering hammers, and blowing of bellowses from morning till night." [50] At Cincinnati a new steam mill constructed during the war was the biggest building there, with twenty-four doors and ninety windows. It was designed to manufacture flour as well as to receive wool and cotton machinery, a flaxseed oil mill, and a fulling mill. Lexington's steam-driven flour mill could supply the whole town, and was a far cry from the 1780s when Kentuckians were crushing their corn in a mortar and pestle.[51]

The expansion of western industry since 1800 had created a small class of urban workmen, and these were far better off than their European counterparts. Before the War of 1812, which brought inflation, wages were high and living comparatively cheap. Carpenters, masons, shoemakers, or any skilled workmen could earn at least $1 a day in the more important western towns by 1812, and occasionally as much as $1.25 or even $1.50. Ordinary laborers could obtain 50 cents or more a day, but the price of food was cheap. In the towns pork could be obtained for three cents a pound, and beef for four to five cents; flour was about five dollars a barrel. In England during the same period the price of beef was four or five times as high, and flour three times, although wages were lower. In Kentucky even at this early date slaves were used extensively in the urban manufactures to solve the labor problem, particularly in the various hemp industries, although there was still a considerable demand for white skilled workmen.[52]

Before 1815 the West had taken great strides in its economic development in spite of extensive obstacles. In many areas subsistence farming had been succeeded by the growth of a surplus and cash crops. In the towns a prosperous merchant class had developed, and profits from trading were increasingly being invested not only in banks but also in manufacturing. The already extensive internal trade was greatly stimulated by the War of 1812. Yet there were still many difficulties. In England were stockpiles of manufactured goods waiting to flood into the United States when the war was over to compete with the products of the infant American industries. Transportation posed massive problems. Traffic up the Mississippi Valley was slow, precarious, and expensive, although the first one or two steamboats appeared on western waters from 1812. The main necessity was an efficient communication system to connect the West with the biggest market for farm produce in the East, but before this market could be fully utilized the Appalachians had to be breached to weld the West economically to the nation. Internal improvements to link the East with the Mississippi Valley were badly needed. Until better communications were established the West had difficulty making full use of its fertility, and the East was unable to take full advantage of the huge market that was developing in the Mississippi Valley.

◁ **9** ▷

The West and the War of 1812

W▸▸

hile the West was being settled in the years after the Revolution, the United States was going through an almost continual crisis in her foreign relations. In the 1780s the disunited Confederation government had failed to earn the respect of foreign nations, and after 1789 the United States had been embroiled in the turmoil created by the French Revolution and the ensuing European wars. The war betwen England and France, which began in 1793, proved particularly harassing for the infant United States, with the major difficulties being experienced at sea. Neither belligerent wished the neutral shipping of the United States to aid the other power, and between 1793 and the outbreak of war between the United States and Great Britain in 1812 they tried a variety of expedients to restrict American commerce. For the most part the British regulations were felt far more severely than the French, for England had the greater navy. The Americans objected to British blockades of the coast of Europe, the stopping and searching of American ships, the effort to stop trade between the French West Indies and France, and the practice of impressment, by which Great Britain claimed the right to stop American merchant vessels and take off British deserters.

Tension between England and the United States was increased by the entangling of British and American interests along the frontier of the Old Northwest. After the American Revolution England did not evacuate the

166

Northwest posts and continued to interfere in the area south of the Great Lakes ceded to the United States in 1783. The combination of British maritime restrictions in the Atlantic and Britain's aid to the Indians south of Detroit produced a crisis in British-American relations at the beginning of the wars between England and France in 1793–1794.

For the frontiersmen of the Mississippi Valley this crisis had little direct commercial importance. They might well respond to the insults to the American flag, but their participation in overseas commerce was as yet small, and certainly hardly enough to produce an extensive reaction to Brtish maritime practices. What was more important to the West in the early 1790s was the British activity on the borders of the Old Northwest—the aid and comfort given to hostile Indians by British Indian agents working out of Detroit. After the outbreak of war with France the British authorities in Canada acted rashly. They helped organize and arm the Indians who were assembling south of Detroit to resist the American forces in the Old Northwest. Through the summer of 1793 and into 1794 the United States faced a two-pronged crisis. American shipping was unsafe at sea, and the British were organizing the northwestern Indians. The crisis between the two countries was not eased until Jay's Treaty of November 1794. This agreement, combined with American military victory over the Indians, inaugurated almost a decade of improved relations between the United States and Great Britain.[1]

The years after 1803 brought a new and more dangerous crisis in Anglo-American relations; the problem originated in British actions at sea, but it soon directly involved the West. The post-1803 trans-Appalachian West was much different from that of 1793. Ten years earlier Kentucky had just become a state; Tennessee was under Indian attack; and there were few settlers north of the Ohio. In 1803 Kentucky and Tennessee were well established; Ohio became a state; and the United States by the Louisiana Purchase acquired control of the Mississippi River, possession of New Orleans, and a vast new extent of territory. No longer chiefly concerned with survival, the West was hoping for large profits from the export of an agricultural surplus. Indians still stirred the emotions, and at times dominated discussion on the edges of settlement, but for much of the trans-Appalachian West they were no longer a menace.

As Napoleon in these years won increasing control of the Continent, England tightened her domination of the sea, particularly after the victory at Trafalgar in 1805. After 1803 England feared invasion by France, and, desperate to man her navy, increased the practice of impressment. Also, even after the fear of invasion died away, England decided that blockade of the Continent was essential to victory. She tightened her commercial noose, first by the *Essex* decision of 1805, and then under the Orders in Council of 1807, which prohibited all trade with France or French possessions except by British license.[2]

Before the main Orders in Council had been put into effect in November 1807 the renewed crisis in foreign affairs had again brought specific problems to the northwest frontier. In June 1807, in an incident off the American coast, the American ship *Chesapeake* was fired on by the British *Leopard*. The resulting outcry in the United States made war seem likely and brought prompt action from British officials in Canada. Since 1794 the British in Canada had neglected the Indians, but now they decided that if the United States declared war an Indian alliance would be necessary for the defense of Canada. British leaders in Canada did not intend to encourage the Indians to make premature attacks on the American frontier, but they did allow their agents at Fort Malden near Detroit to tell the Indians of the American designs on their lands and of the possibility of a future war in which their support would be ardently desired by the British.[3]

In 1807 Indians from American territory visited Amherstburg, Canada, for supplies and encouragement, and this renewed activity on the part of the British Indian Department was well noted by the frontiersmen of the Old Northwest. The British could argue that they were attempting to enlist Indian support for a future war, not instigate immediate hostilities, but such a distinction carried little weight with Indian-hating settlers. Since the bloody days of the American Revolution, the West had looked with anger at the British-Indian alliance. This hatred of British frontier policy had been kept alive by the frontier wars of 1783 to 1794 and now was revived by the renewed British backing for the Indians. There is no doubt that this Anglo-Indian alliance made the British a natural enemy of the frontiersmen.

Yet in discussing the origins of the War of 1812 it is easy to make too much of frontier hatred of the British-Indian alliance. It had long been known that the Indians could be defeated by direct military action even if they had indirect British support, and they were certainly easier to defeat if the British armies were not openly committed to the conflict. Settlers on the very edge of the frontier might well have been all-absorbed by the Indian danger, but many in the West were, by 1812, more concerned with markets, the price of imports, and the difficulty of exports than with Indian attacks. Although westerners were delighted to take advantage of the War of 1812 to attack the British posts in upper Canada from which the Indans were supplied, it needed more than this old grievance to persuade most Americans, in the West as well as in the rest of the country, that war was the only solution to their difficulties.

Another regional factor, in the Southwest, complicates discussions of the War of 1812. In that area there was some expression of the feeling that war could be used as an excuse to invade and conquer the Floridas, the possession of Britain's ally Spain. Yet, as in the case of Indian hostility, the interest in Florida seems an insufficient reason to explain the declaration of war, even though Spain and England were allied from 1808. In September 1810 the revolution in West Florida gave Madison the opportunity to annex land up to the Perdido River, although only the area to the Pearl River was actually occupied. And since the Americans of the Southwest were gradually winning control of the Floridas, it was certainly questionable whether a declaration of war against England, with her powerful navy, would make the conquest of the Floridas any easier. The desire to conquer Florida was not a basic reason for the American declaration of war against England in 1812. It might well have made some in the Southwest more willing to accept the idea of war, but it does not appear even to have been as important a reason for swaying western sentiment as British support for the Indians.[4]

Before the War of 1812 Indians and southern expansion were less important than the pressures of British maritime policies. The westerners were angered by these policies in two important regards. First, the export of farm produce was becoming increasingly important to the western economy. The frontiersmen had difficulty in exporting farm produce and importing manufactured goods, and blamed the British, rather than the basic problems of inadequate communications and inefficient marketing, for the difficulties in making a profit. Moreover, the anger of the frontiersmen at the British lack of regard for American rights at sea cannot be viewed simply in terms of economic difficulties, for the frontiersmen were also most sensitive to any insults to American national honor. They showed the ardent nationalism common to empire builders. Removed from the centers of settlement, they spoke even more earnestly than the easterners of the glories of the Revolution and of America's contribution to liberty. They were carving a nation out of the wilderness, risking their lives, and could not stomach the United States accepting without resistance British infringements of American rights. Even before the autumn of 1807, when the British again began to cultivate the support of the Indians, westerners were calling for the defense of American rights against the British aggressions.

In the years following the *Chesapeake* incident in June 1807, the whole Mississippi Valley demonstrated a willingness to accept the policies decided upon by the American President. The new states were ardent supporters of the Democratic-Republican party, and they accepted Jefferson's argument that the United States would have to win respect for her rights at sea by temporary self-denial. In December 1807 the United States passed both a Non-Importation Act against certain British products and a general embargo, which forbade American ships from sailing for foreign ports. Jefferson had decided that the belligerents would be denied American trade until they respected American rights. Like the Democratic-Republican South, the farmers of the Ohio Valley gave general support to an embargo policy which ruined their chance of a profitable export trade. What is more surprising is that these agricultural areas supported Jefferson's and Madison's policies of economic coercion, even though from the time of the Embargo Act the Mississippi Valley as well as large areas of the south Atlantic states were suffering an agricultural depression. The prices that westerners could obtain at New Orleans for their products fell sharply in the years from 1807 to 1812. Moreover, this drop in prices did not affect the cost of imported goods to the Mississippi Valley farmers; these prices if anything increased.[5]

When Great Britain failed to make maritime concessions in response to the Jeffersonian Embargo and when that measure was followed by the watered-down Non-Intercourse Act of March 1809 and the even more diluted Macon's Bill No. 2 of May 1810, a general feeling of disgust settled over those who so ardently desired to change British policy, win back freedom for American commerce, and restore the tarnished national honor. The western regions felt the American failure particularly bitterly and after 1810 increasingly began to demand war.

In the elections of 1810 nearly half of the members of the House of Representatives were not returned to office. Although this represented no wholesale repudiation, enough new faces were added to those already pressing for a change in American policy to produce an entirely different atmosphere in the new Congress. Those who had asked for more forceful action now found themselves members of a cohesive group, and, what is more, a remarkable degree of leadership was exercised by the young politicians. The group of War Hawks that gathered around Henry Clay of Kentucky included a hard core of young men, men who had not fought in the Revolution but were disgusted at the manner in which the victories of their fathers had been dissipated by a vacillating policy. They called for a restoration of Revolutionary ideals, a restoration which they hoped would also bring about renewed economic prosperity.

The leader of the War Hawks came from the trans-Appalachian West. Henry Clay, who had previously only served in Congress to fill out two unexpired senatorial terms, quickly assumed the leadership when the Twelfth Congress assembled in November 1811. He was only thirty-four years old and was new to the House of Representatives, but was immediately elected Speaker. Clay, a Virginian, emigrated to Kentucky as a young man, practiced law, and worked his way up in Kentucky politics. The beleagured outposts of the Revolution now provided leaders to take the United States toward war, for with Clay from Kentucky came two other powerful War Hawks, Richard M. Johnson and Joseph Desha. From Tennessee came Felix M. Grundy—a notable advocate of the war effort—John Rhea, and John Sevier. The Northwest provided none of the important spokesmen—only Ohio sent representatives to Congress—but the one Ohio member of the House of Representatives was to vote for war. Allied with those from new states were War Hawks from other regions, notably the South: John C. Calhoun, Langdon Cheves, and David R. Williams of South Carolina, Peter B. Porter of New York, and John A. Harper of New Hampshire, all added their influence to the demand for war.

The struggle to declare war in the Twelfth Congress proved a long and difficult affair. As Congress met, the members received the news from Indiana that Governor Harrison had clashed with Tecumseh's Indian forces at

Tippecanoe on November 7, 1811, and that the British had added frontier blood to the long list of maritime insults. In general the Federalists in Congress, many of them from New England, opposed the conflict, while Democratic-Republicans for the most part favored it. The Democratic-Republicans, however, had trouble moving rapidly toward war. As they could not agree on the methods by which the war could be fought and what would be necessary to win it, they argued among themselves.[6]

In their speeches the westerners, and the War Hawks in general, had few doubts as to why the United States should go to war. They declaimed with passion that American national honor, maritime rights, and prosperity should be defended. To a lesser extent they discussed British activities among the Indians, and there were some allusions to the possibilities of expansion both in North and South should the war come. Henry Clay told Congress on December 31 that by maintaining the peace the country would lose its "commerce, character, a nation's best treasure, honor!" Richard M. Johnson of Kentucky asked Great Britain "to treat us as an independent people," and Felix M. Grundy of Tennessee stated that the point of contention between the United States and Great Britain "is the right of exporting the productions of our own soil and industry to foreign markets."[7]

In spite of the appeals of the War Hawks, the move for war proceeded slowly. The Federalists put up an energetic opposition, and the Democratic-Republicans could not agree on a united policy. There was considerable disagreement in regard to the inadequate army and navy. The army was under 10,000 men, and efforts to increase it ran into difficulties, particularly in regard to the problem of whether or not militia could be used outside the country. An effort to increase the navy failed completely; it was opposed by many of the westerners and other Democratic-Republicans who feared the power this would give to the commercial classes. They thought England could be brought to terms far more simply by the conquest of Canada than by naval action. Many Republicans also objected to increased taxes, even with a war in sight, and eventually taxes were increased on the understanding that they would go into effect only on the outbreak of war.[8]

Yet, in spite of all the difficulties, it became obvious that a majority of Congress thought that American honor and prosperity could be restored only by war against England, a war which they thought could be carried to a successful conclusion by the conquest of Canada. On June 4, 1812, the House of Representatives finally agreed to a declaration of war by a vote of 79 to 49. As the West had so few representatives in Congress, it played less part in the actual vote than in the debates leading up to it, although Kentucky, Ohio, and Tennessee cast all nine of their votes for war (Clay as speaker of course did not vote). Vermont also supported war by a vote of 3 to 1. In general, the bulk of the votes for war came from southern and middle state Republicans. The Federalists were generally opposed to war. The war measure met with some delay and considerable opposition in the Senate, but eventually on June 17 it was passed by a vote of 19 to 13 and signed by the President on the following day.

The debates leading to war with England marked the coming of age of western politicians on the national scene. In the years immediately after the Revolution there had been no opportunity for the frontier areas to have any direct impact on the national government; the government evolved a policy for the West, and the westerners were in most respects treated as colonials. The possiblity of the West exerting direct influence on the national scene had come in the 1790s; and after 1800, with the admission of new states to the Union and the debates on war with England, the western representatives took the opportunity to play a part of great importance in the formulation of national policy. The new areas of the country had few votes, but their representatives were particularly vocal in their support for war. And Henry Clay was the directing force behind the war movement. Although this was a war that involved support from all parts of the country, the representatives from the new areas across the Appalachians had played a role far out of proportion to their numbers; they had proved themselves to be ardent and vocal opponents of the British and earnest advocates of an independent, proud America.[9]

At the beginning of the War of 1812 the United States expected to invade and conquer Canada, thus forcing a change in British maritime policies. The United States hoped to invade Canada on three fronts—the Hudson Valley–Lake Champlain route to Montreal, the Niagara frontier, and across the Detroit River into upper Canada. Ideally, the main American effort should have been directed against Montreal, for this would have severed the St. Lawrence–Great Lakes navigation system far to the east and cut off all the settlements to the west. If this main onslaught had been timed to coincide with attacks at Niagara and Fort Malden and if the United States had used her advantage in population and resources to win naval control of the Great Lakes, then the invasion might indeed have been a success. As it was, naval control of the Lakes was contested during most of the war, and the United States never succeeded in invading Canada either along the Champlain Valley or across the Niagara frontier. Invasion plans bogged down in a morass of inadequate preparations, an incompetent supply system, and inept leadership. The United States hoped to conquer Canada with ease at the beginning of the war, but instead drifted into long-drawn-out campaigns. In spite of the necessity for a supreme effort in the East, much of the fighting took place in the West.

The reason for extensive western hostilities stemmed both from western enthusiasm at the beginning of the war and from western fears that the British-Indian alliance would threaten the frontier as it had in the Revolution. Although strategy called for the main effort to be northward along Lake Champlain, much of New England opposed the conflict, and many of the available recruits were in Kentucky or Ohio. The battle at Tippecanoe and the sporadic Indian hostilities in the Old Northwest had stirred the old fears of outright Indian onslaught. The American government in the years since 1783 had failed to convince the Indians that American expansion would be to their benefit. Since 1789 great hope had been placed in the assumption that the Indians would accept American civilization, voluntarily cede their lands, and become full-time farmers rather than hunters. The American government completely underestimated the desire of the Indians to retain their own culture, and in any case American pioneers had advanced far too swiftly to permit a civilizing policy to work. By 1812 Indian tribes throughout the eastern half of the Mississippi Valley were infuriated at the pressures on their lands. They regretted the cessions made since the Revolution and still dreamed of driving the Americans from their territory. Yet, in spite of this Indian dream, most of the American frontier was far safer than during the Revolution. The Indians of the Old Northwest were much weakened, and the settlers far more numerous. Only south of Tennessee, in Mississippi Territory, was a sparse pioneer settlement threatened by a major Indian force.[10]

The main western campaigns of the war were fought along the Detroit frontier and in the South against the Creeks, but the struggle extended even to the fur trading regions west of Lake Michigan. In 1812 British influence was still paramount in the area that is now Wisconsin and Minnesota. British fur trading interests working out of Canada kept the allegiance of the Indians and prevented the expansion of American interests into the region. Trader Robert Dickson had been recruiting Indians for the British cause on the upper Mississippi before the war even started, and by the time news of the declaration of war arrived at the British post of St. Joseph (east of Mackinac) on July 8, Dickson was already there with a force of warriors. The British commander at St. Joseph, Captain Charles Roberts, immediately organized an expedition against Mackinac. He had over one hundred warriors brought by Dickson, two or three hundred Ottawa and Chippewa, and two hundred French Canadians. This force took Mackinac on July 17 without resistance. The American commander had not even heard of the declaration of war when he was summoned to surrender.

The failure continued. In the middle of August 1812 the few American troops at Fort Dearborn (Chicago) attempted to retreat with their families to a less exposed position. They were fallen on by the Indians and overwhelmed after brief, fierce fighting. Some were killed, others captured, and Fort Dearborn was lost to the Americans for the remainder of the war. The American garrison at Fort Madison on the upper Mississippi managed to repel an Indian attack in September 1812, but the fort was abandoned by the Americans in the fall of 1813.

By the end of 1812 the region west of Lake Michigan was firmly in the hands of the British. Mackinac and Fort Dearborn had fallen, Fort Madison was isolated, and Green Bay and Prairie du Chien were pro-British. Warriors from west of Lake Michigan were able to travel to aid the British on battle-fronts farther to the east, and the Indians of the whole region were given the confidence to attack any isolated American settlements. Since the battle of Tippecanoe the governors of Illinois and Indiana territories had warned the secretary of war of isolated incidents and sporadic raids, and in both areas some settlers had taken their families to the safety of Kentucky or Ohio. Although the territories did not have to endure the all-out attack experienced by Kentucky in the Revolution, pioneers from Indiana to Missouri had to huddle around their forts and blockhouses, and from time to time news came that another family had been killed and scalped.[11]

The danger to outlying American settlements was considerably increased by the disasters on the more important Detroit frontier in this first summer of the war. When war started, General William Hull, the governor of Michigan Territory, was already on the march with an army from Ohio to Detroit. It was expected that he would invade upper Canada and capture Fort Malden. He reached Detroit at the beginning of July and on the 12th crossed the Detroit River. Then he vacillated, unwilling to risk an immediate attack on Fort Malden. The Americans did not have naval control of Lake Erie, and Hull's communications depended on a precarious trail by land from Detroit to Ohio that was particularly vulnerable to Indian attack. At the beginning

Post St. Joseph. Watercolor by Edward Walsh. (Clements Library, University of Michigan)

of August he heard of the fall of Mackinac, and now he feared that more Indians would swarm down from the region west of Lake Michigan. He still might have saved the day by a bold attack on Fort Malden, but instead he retreated back across the Detroit River to take refuge in Detroit. In the middle of August the British took the initiative under the leadership of Major General Isaac Brock. With their Indian allies they crossed the Detroit River, and Brock warned Hull that if he had to take Detroit by storm he could not guarantee the protection of the citizens and troops from the Indians. A nervous Hull yielded to this psychological warfare, and on August 16 surrendered his army of some two thousand men to a lesser British force. Hull's once enthusiastic troops now talked of treason, and the general was court-martialed, sentenced to be shot, and saved only by the intervention of the President.[12]

The complete failure of the western wing of the attack on Canada was only the beginning, for the other two drives against Canada, on the Niagara and Champlain fronts, also ended without success for the Americans. The attack across the Niagara River against Queenston in October 1812 resulted in the death of General Brock, who had hurried east to organize the British defense, but the American attack was repulsed. Even more disastrous to morale was the fiasco along the Hudson River—Lake Champlain route. Here General Henry Dearborn hoped to lead the main attack against Canada. He did not begin the main move northward until November; his officers argued among themselves; and he discovered that the militia would not cross the border to fight. Eventually, he turned back without engaging the enemy.[13]

These first months of the war had crushed American hopes of an easy

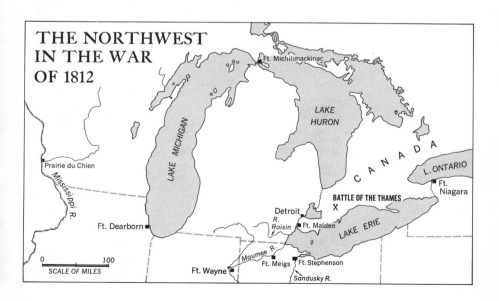

THE NORTHWEST
IN THE WAR
OF 1812

Ft. Michilimackinac

LAKE HURON

LAKE MICHIGAN

CANADA

L. ONTARIO

Prairie du Chien

Mississippi R.

Ft. Niagara

BATTLE OF THE THAMES
X

Detroit

Ft. Dearborn

R. Raisin

Ft. Malden

LAKE ERIE

0   100
SCALE OF MILES

Maumee R.

Ft. Meigs   Ft. Stephenson

Ft. Wayne

Sandusky R.

parade into Canada, and although there was later to be some measure of success in the West, American forces never succeeded in making important inroads into British territory on the Niagara and Lake Champlain fronts. The inadequate preparations, the incredibly difficult problems of communication, and the lack of a firm naval control on the Great Lakes ruined American hopes of the conquest of Canada. The only consolation for most of the settlers in the Old Northwest was that in this war they did not have to endure the repeated and bloody attacks of the Revolution. For the most part the large trans-Appalachian population was able to organize its own defense, and except in the sparsely populated territories families did not have to live in terror for their lives.

After the capitulation of Detroit new western armies were raised, and under the command of General William Henry Harrison preparations were made for regaining lost territory; first there were further disappointments. Harrison decided to take the initiative by a risky winter campaign against Fort Malden. This attempt was blocked even before it really began by the mistakes of General James Winchester, who commanded the American column on the Maumee. At the rapids he had a force of 1300 men, nearly all Kentuckians, who had enlisted with fervor early in the summer and who had suffered great hardships owing to the inadequacies of their supplies. Winchester had been informed by French inhabitants of Frenchtown on the River Raisin below Detroit that there was a considerable quantity of British stores there and decided to move his army to secure them. This he did with ease, but on January 22 the Americans were overwhelmed by a British force which had advanced rapidly from Fort Malden. Over five hundred Kentuckians were captured, a hundred or so killed, and the frontier was shocked by an Indian massacre after the battle. The Kentucky wounded were left at the Raisin with little protection when the British retreated to Malden; the next morning the Indians set fire to the houses in which they were sheltered, and thirty or forty were tomahawked or shot.

In the spring of 1813 the British, having successfully repulsed attempts at the invasion of Canada, tried to take the initiative on the Detroit frontier. Colonel Henry Procter, the victor of Frenchtown, in April led a force along the Maumee from Fort Malden in an effort to capture the American Fort Meigs which had been constructed at the rapids. The Americans successfully resisted the British attack, but again the Kentuckians suffered a disaster. When news reached General Harrison in the fort that Brigadier General Green Clay was advancing to his relief with another 1200 enthusiastic Kentuckians, he ordered Clay to attack the British batteries on the opposite side of the River. The initial attack succeeded, but the Kentuckians stayed too long on the field instead of spiking the guns and retreating, and were routed by a British and Indian counterattack. As at the Raisin some of the American prisoners were killed by the Indians, and only the personal intervention of Tecumseh stopped the slaughter. Yet the British had not captured the fort, and Procter failed again in July when once more he led a large British and Indian force up the Maumee.

The stalemate on the Detroit front was finally broken in the fall of 1813, when the Americans at last accomplished a small part of the objectives with which they had begun hostilities. In September 1813 Commander Oliver H. Perry won naval control of Lake Erie at the Battle of Put-in-Bay. This naval victory accomplished what the long campaigns in the Old Northwest had been unable to do. Procter at Fort Malden decided that with his supply line severed his position was untenable, and a retreat was essential. Tecumseh and his Indians wanted Procter to stand and fight at Fort Malden, but he retreated, with Indians leaving him daily. The British force and their remaining allies were overtaken by the Americans under Harrison at Moraviantown on the Thames River. Although the British established defensive positions in a wood, Harrison ignored orthodox military procedure and sent his mounted Kentuckians charging into the British lines, knowing that the westerners were well experienced at riding in wooded country. The British troops were demoralized by their retreat and fled from the battle; the remaining Indians put up a fierce resistance but gave way after the death of Tecumseh. What was left of the British force and their allies now retreated to the head of Lake Ontario, leaving the Detroit region in the hands of the Americans.[14]

The death of Tecumseh and the withdrawal of the British ended the last real Indian resistance in the Old Northwest. Only thirty years before the whole region had been Indian country, and until the mid-1790s the Indians had retained the hope that the American frontier advance would stop at the Ohio. Now the Indians were completely at the mercy of the frontiersmen. These northern battles had not won control of Canada for the frontiersmen, but they had extinguished the last Indian hopes of retaining, under British protection, a substantial portion of the Old Northwest.

It was as well for the Americans that the British had been defeated on the Detroit frontier and part of upper Canada occupied, for in the region west of Lake Michigan the United States had to depend on the peace negotiations rather than military victories for possession. In the spring of 1814 an American force from St. Louis temporarily gained possession of Prairie du Chien, but the British at Mackinac reacted quickly and recaptured it in July.

The Americans also failed in a major effort to regain control of Mackinac in the summer of 1814. In July a force of some eight hundred men sailed from Detroit under the command of Colonel George Croghan. The troops landed on Mackinac Island, only to be driven off by the British and Indians. Two American vessels were left to blockade Mackinac, but the British compounded the American embarrassment by capturing them. Prairie du Chien and Mackinac remained in British hands until the end of the war.[15] American efforts to conquer Canada had been an abysmal failure. On the Niagara and Champlain fronts there had not even been the partial success experienced farther west. Fighting on the Niagara frontier had been particularly bitter,

The battle of the Thames (Moraviantown), October 5, 1813. (Library of Congress)

with burning and looting on both sides of the river. American attempts to invade Canada via the Hudson Valley–Lake Champlain route and along the St. Lawrence had been an unmitigated disaster. The Canadian population center along the St. Lawrence remained untouched. The West had done far more than its share in providing troops for the invading armies, but this could not compensate for the lack of adequate preparations and the paucity of able leadership.

On the southern frontiers the war brought Indian dangers reminiscent of those of the Revolution. For much of the war the struggle with the Indians rather than the British absorbed the energies of the settlers, although the conflict began with deceptive calmness. In spite of later assertions that some supported the declaration of war with the intention of obtaining the Floridas, the American government did not even allow any attack on that area in the first months of the war. The first move in this direction was made in the fall of 1812, when it seemed for a time that the government had at last decided to attack West Florida. Governor Willie Blount of Tennessee was ordered to send 1500 men to the lower Mississippi, and such was the enthusiasm that there were more volunteers than were needed. Eventually 2500 assembled at Nashville in December 1812. Their commander was Andrew Jackson, as yet only a local figure, but anxious for action against British, Indians, or Spanish.

From Nashville the Tennessee army began a journey of great difficulty to Natchez in Mississippi Territory. Jackson, with two regiments of infantry went down the Cumberland, Ohio, and Mississippi rivers, while Colonel John Coffee led his cavalry along the Natchez Trace. It took Jackson over five weeks to reach Natchez, and he found Coffee's force waiting for him. The Tennesseans had responded with enthusiasm to government orders, but they were now given nothing to do but sit in camp near Natchez. The idea of invading Florida had bogged down in the Senate, and in February 1813 the new secretary of war John Armstrong ordered Jackson to disband his troops, hundreds of miles from their homes. Jackson refused to do this, and instead led them back over the Natchez Trace to Tennessee, where they were disbanded late in May. Jackson's first chance for national glory had ended in anticlimax, although in the spring of 1813 American forces did, without re-sistance, occupy the Mobile district, which had already been formally an-nexed before the war started. In spite of the opportunity presented by the war with England, the United States went no further in occupying the Spanish Floridas at this time.[16]

The first year of the war had brought little action on the southern front-iers, but in the summer of 1813 the Creeks began an all-out onslaught on the American settlements. Like all the Indians of the Mississippi Valley, the Creeks were hopeful that some day they might get the chance to regain the possessions they had lost. They had been visited by Tecumseh in 1811 and 1812, and he had told them of British support and of successes on the Canadi-

A view of the port of Buffalo. From *Port-Folio*, July–December 1815. (The New York Public Library)

an frontier. They were divided as to what action they should take, but many of them began to raid the frontiers of Mississippi Territory.

On August 30, 1813, the Creek hostiles fell on Fort Mims, some forty-five miles north of Mobile on the Alabama River. A thousand Creek warriors were led by Chief William Weatherford, whose father was Scotch and mother half-French, in the attack on the fort garrisoned by about a hundred Mississippi volunteers. Also sheltered within its walls were numerous frontiersmen and their families who had deserted their farms. The Creeks struck so suddenly that they found the front gate open, and a desperate struggle went on around it and for the buildings inside the fort. All afternoon the battle raged, but at last with the fort and its buildings on fire, those who tried to escape the flames were hacked down by the warriors. Several hundred settlers and troops were killed, and terror spread throughout the settlements in what is now Alabama. Settlers in the hundreds left their farms and fled downriver to Mobile.[17]

The news of the massacre at Fort Mims reached Tennessee early in September, and later that month a special session of the legislature empowered the governor to call out another 3500 men in addition to the 1500 already authorized. Andrew Jackson was given command, and the campaign began in the fall. Although Jackson experienced considerable difficulty in obtaining supplies for his troops and in coordinating with the army of eastern Tennesseans led by Major General John Cocke, he looked upon the campaign as an opportunity to destroy Creek power.

In early November Coffee's cavalry and mounted riflemen were detached by Jackson to attack the Creek town of Tallassahatche (near the site of Jacksonville, Alabama). They flung themselves into the town just after sunrise on November 3 when the drums were already beating the warriors to action. It was a massacre. No quarter was given to the Indian men, and even women and children were killed in the heat of the battle. The revenge for Fort Mims had begun. The Americans found 186 Indian dead after the battle, and took only 84 women and children prisoners. Of Coffee's force five were killed, and forty-one wounded.[18]

A few days later at Talladega Jackson continued the destruction of the Creeks. His plan of battle was as old as Hannibal. The cavalry on his two wings were to encircle the enemy, and his infantry in the center was preceded by an advance force which fell back when attacked to draw the enemy into the sack. Some Indians broke through when part of Jackson's troops gave way, but his force of 2000 made short shrift of the rest of the Creeks, who had less than half his numbers in the field. Nearly three hundred Creeks were found dead, while Jackson lost seventeen with over eighty wounded.[19]

Jackson's campaign now stalled, as many of his men insisted on returning home, having fulfilled the terms of their enlistments, but pressure was to some extent maintained by other troops. On November 18 a detachment of eastern Tennesseans under General James White attacked the Hillibee town which had already submitted to Jackson. The Americans killed 60 warriors and took 250 prisoners, while suffering no casualties. Georgians and Mississippians were also in the field. Near the end of November nearly a thousand Georgian militia with several hundred friendly Indians attacked Auttose on the Tallapoosa River, killing some two hundred for the loss of only eleven Americans.[20]

The Creek losses had been incredibly high in November 1813, but the American forces had still not penetrated to the heart of the Creek nation. In December and January, while Jackson tried to raise another army of Tennesseans, both Georgians and Mississippians fought inconclusive actions against strong Creek forces, but there was no doubt that a further heavy blow was needed before the Creeks could be ruined as an effective fighting force.

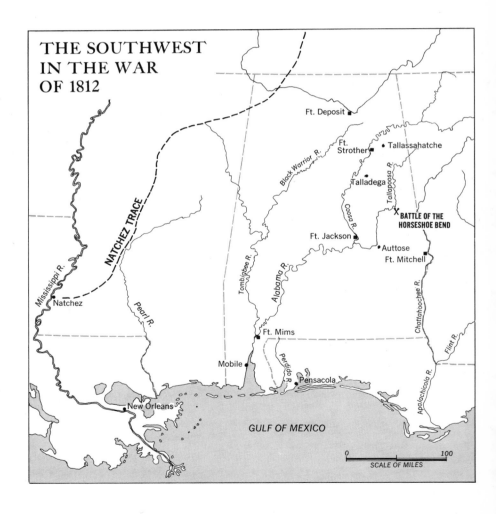

THE SOUTHWEST
IN THE WAR
OF 1812

By January 1814 Jackson was ready to move again with fresh Tennessee militia and friendly Cherokee and Creeks, who showed no compunction at completing the ruin of their own nation. His first expedition against the Creeks now entrenched on the Tallapoosa was unsuccessful, and Jackson had to retreat, but in March he moved again. The whole campaign reached a climax at Horseshoe Bend on the Tallapoosa River on March 27. Here, where the river curved into the shape of a horseshoe, the Creeks had built a strong breastwork across the resulting neck of land. Jackson's infantry stormed the defenses after a desperate battle, and the general told his wife "it was after dark before we finished killing them." Three Creek warriors were taken prisoner, over 550 dead were counted on the peninsula, and hundreds died trying to cross the river; Jackson's horsemen were on the other bank. The slaughter did not revolt Jackson. He told his wife "kiss my little andrew for me, tell him I have a warriors bow and quiver for him." These Tennesseans remembered Fort Mims and the burning cabins and scalped families along the Cumberland in the early 1790s. "The power of the Creeks," wrote Jackson, "is I think forever broken." [21]

When in August 1814 the Creeks signed a treaty with the United States at Fort Jackson, they were forced to cede more than half of their lands; part of Georgia and much of Alabama was now cleared of Indian title.[22] The victories in the North at the Thames, and in the south at Horseshoe Bend had broken Indian resistance east of the Mississippi River. The great wars that had been fought for this area since the Revolution were over. After the War of 1812 nothing was left but a pathetic mopping-up operation.

Although the Indians were crushed, the United States was still in danger in 1814. With Napoleon overthrown, the British were preparing to launch major attacks across the Atlantic. They intended to use their triumphant European veterans to invade the United States both in the North and South and thus secure a peace in which large areas of land in the Northeast and the Mississippi Valley would come under British control. In the North Sir George Prevost marched with a powerful British army along the Lake Champlain route. It seemed he would be able to take Plattsburg, sweep on to New York, and isolate disaffected New England from the Union. Again naval power proved decisive. In September 1814 at the battle of Plattsburg Bay the American naval force on Lake Champlain defeated the British, and Prevost retreated northward without engaging the American army.[23]

In the South the whole coastline was at the mercy of the now overwhelming British naval strength. While Prevost advanced south along Lake Champlain, a British force landed in Chesapeake Bay, routed the Americans at Bladensburg on August 24, 1814, and burned the public buildings at Washington. The British then turned against Baltimore but were repulsed. This setback combined with the far more decisive defeat inflicted on Prevost's force meant that the great British hopes of crushing American resistance with reinforcements from Europe had vanished.[24]

Macdonough's victory on Lake Champlain. (Stokes Collection, The New York Public Library)

At Ghent the British peace commissioners who had been engaged in long discussions with the Americans were instructed to reach agreement. England was ready to extricate herself from more than two decades of war, and on December 24, 1814, the Treaty of Ghent was signed. The treaty was a simple one. With the war in Europe over, maritime problems had disappeared, and they were omitted from the treaty. Neither side had been able to assert decisive control over the territory of the other, and it was decided that there would be a mutual restoration of territory. The area west of Lake Michigan was saved for the Americans, and England now abandoned her long-lived hopes of establishing a buffer state in the Old Northwest.[25]

Although the war was over, slow communications allowed its most dramatic battle to take place. This last battle was unnecessary but important; it demonstrated to the rest of the country the new strength of the West, boosted morale, and helped to make a President. In December 1814 and January 1815 a large British force, composed of European veterans and commanded by officers who had served under Wellington, landed in the Gulf of Mexico to attack New Orleans. In May 1814 Andrew Jackson had been made a United States Major General and was given control of the seventh military district, which included New Orleans. In December, as the British prepared to attack, he hurried there to organize its defenses.

After landing near New Orleans before Christmas, the British missed a chance of advancing rapidly into the city and waited to build up the strength of their forces. By the time the main assault was made on January 8, Jackson was well entrenched behind ditch and parapet, and the British moved forward across a narrow strip of ground, hemmed in by the Mississippi on their left and a swamp on their right. A force laboriously sent across the Mississippi to flank the Americans had some success but the main attack was swept by the grape from the American guns and a relentless fire from the western riflemen. As these British veterans of the peninsula turned in retreat, their dead and wounded were strewn over the battlefield. British casualties totaled some two-thousand compared to less than one hundred for the Americans. Andrew Jackson was firmly on the road to the Presidency, and an indecisive war had ended with a crushing western victory over the best soldiers England could muster.[26]

Only on the frontiers of Mississippi Territory did the War of 1812 produce the death and devastation of the Revolution. Other outlying areas were attacked, but they were not in a state of siege as the Kentuckians had been over thirty years before. Most trans-Appalachian areas were safe during the war. The British did not have the resources to penetrate deeply south of Detroit, and it was much too risky for the Indians to attempt to raid into the more settled areas of Ohio, Kentucky, or Tennessee.

Noticeable in the war was the general patriotism of the West. In the years following the Revolution there had been fears that the western settlements would break away from the United States, that the isolated pioneers would feel no sense of allegiance to a distant eastern government. By 1812 there had been a sharp reversal of attitude. Western senators and representatives gave enthusiastic support to national policies while many New Englanders flouted federal authority and some even threatened disunion. These westerners had thrown off their old allegiances to specific eastern states. Their allegiances to new states were less tenacious and tempered by a sense of nationalism.

The West supported the War of 1812 out of proportion to its numbers and won the two most decisive land battles for the United States—at the Thames in upper Canada and at New Orleans. At the battle of New Orleans the West won its own war of independence from England, sending a surge of pride through the rest of the country. The men of Kentucky, Tennessee, Louisiana, and Mississippi met a large, organized body of experienced British regulars and won a crushing victory. After forty years of frontier raids and pioneers threatened by a British-Indian alliance, the West had made plain its newly gained strength. Since 1783 pioneers had crossed the Appalachians in such numbers that they could now defend themselves effectively against both Indian and British attack.

The achievements since 1783 had been massive. At the end of the Revolution the Confederation government had been struggling to persuade its own states to cede their lands between the Appalachians and the Mississippi. In 1815 not only had all these cessions been accomplished, but a new public domain stretched westward across the Mississippi to the Rockies. In 1783 thirteen disunited states, on the eastern limits of the North American continent, seemed in danger of falling apart. England and Spain were ready to pick up the pieces, and looked eagerly at the isolated settlers across the Appalachians. By 1815 Vermont, Kentucky Tennessee, Ohio, and Louisiana had all been added to the Union; Spain was clinging precariously to her possessions in Florida; and England had been pushed firmly north of the Great Lakes.

Of vital importance had been the decision to expand as a nation rather than by adding colonial possessions. This avoided the danger of a nation of thirteen states deserted by dependencies west of the mountains. The pioneers who left the old states to seek new opportunities in the West were soon able to contribute their vitality directly to national strength, and their leaders were able to participate on the national scene, not disappear into a colonial obscurity. By 1815 it was becoming increasingly obvious that much of the North American continent was to be settled by pioneers from the United States. For all the hopes and diplomatic maneuverings of France, Spain, and England, these nations had to contend with the practically insuperable obstacle of a constantly expanding American population.

The victims of this advance were, of course, the Indians. Although some American leaders hoped to include the aboriginal population as equals with in the expanding American state, they never conceived that this could be accomplished through cultural pluralism. Even those who hoped to save the Indian believed that this could be done only if the Indians became American farmers. Assimilation, extinction, or expulsion were the choices. For the most part the frontiersmen would not concede even this much, for if the Indians became American farmers they would need land. The frontiersmen did not want to relinquish even a small portion of land they had struggled so hard to settle. The Indians, like the animals, would have to go. The government when forced to choose between its own pioneers and the Indians inevitably chose the former. In spite of all the hopes of assimilation the normal method of advance had been by military victory followed by supposedly willing Indian land cessions.

Throughout these years it is more realistic to think of a patchwork of frontier regions rather than any continuous line far to the west. Although in 1815 American pioneers were pushing across the Mississippi, settlers were still developing new lands in western New York, western Pennsylvania, western North Carolina and Georgia. Frequently the most noticed advances created only the bare bones of settlement; the well-rounded and solid development often took years of encroachment on the more undesirable lands. Kentucky pioneers struggling over the Cumberland Gap in the Revolution or the first Ohio Company settlers landing at the mouth of the Muskingum attract immediate attention; less noticeable are the thousands who moved into Kentucky or Ohio year after year, long after statehood, until most of the land was sold.

This patchwork development also confuses discussions on the development of frontier society. Even after a state was admitted to the Union, there were frequently both large undeveloped areas and regions where the settlers existed on the most primitive level. Pittsburgh, Cincinnati, Lexington, and the other main urban settlements performed a vital function in the transition to economic prosperity and in the perpetuation of a cultural tradition, but they were atypical of western society in the years before 1815. Promoters and a variety of land speculators were deeply involved in the frontier advance, but for the United States the acquisition and retention of much of the North American continent depended upon the efforts of millions of farmers anxious to create a better life for themselves and their families.

During the war emigrants continued to cross the Appalachians into the more settled areas. The publicity and campaigns prepared the ground for a massive emigration after the war ended. Indian resistance was shattered both in North and South, and as settlers crowded the roads west in the fall of 1815 it was hard to believe that only thirty years before a few squatters had huddled on the north bank of the Ohio while powerful tribes roamed through the land to the north. In the South, thirty years before, Spain had controlled the Mississippi and the southern tribes majestically ruled their vast territories. Now the Cherokee had been squeezed between eastern and western Tennessee and were left as uneasy pensioners of the American government. Most of the Creek warriors were dead, slaughtered with Old Testament exactness by the Tennesseans and their allies. The Georgians were pushing westward across their state; Mississippi and Alabama were open for settlement; and frontiersmen in the thousands were crossing the Mississippi River to new frontiers.

NOTES

Chapter 1: Expansion and Diplomacy in the Southwest, 1783–1796

[1] *Historical Statistics of the United States. Colonial Times to 1957* (Washington, 1960), p. 13.

[2] See Avery O. Craven, *Soil Exhaustion as a Factor in the Agricultural History of Virginia and Maryland, 1606–1860* (Urbana, Ill., 1925), pp. 72–84, 118–120; Cornelius O. Cathey, *Agricultural Developments in North Carolina, 1783–1860* (Chapel Hill, N.C., 1956), pp. 45–47.

[3] "Journal of Richard Butler," in Neville B. Craig, ed., *The Olden Time*, 2 vols. (Pittsburgh, 1848; reprinted, Cincinnati, 1876), vol. II, p. 447; Francis Baily, *Journal of a Tour in Unsettled Parts of North America in 1796 & 1797* (London, 1856), p. 191; *The Journal of Andrew Ellicott* (Philadelphia, 1803), p. 12; Victor Collot, *A Journey in North America*, 2 vols. (Paris, 1826), vol. I, pp. 61–62. The population of what is now West Virginia increased from some 55,000 in 1790 to over 78,000 in 1800. See Charles H. Ambler and Festus P. Summers, *West Virginia: The Mountain State* (2d ed.; Englewood Cliffs, N.J., 1958). pp. 103–119; Charles H. Ambler, *Sectionalism in Virginia from 1776–1861* (Chicago, 1910), pp. 42–47, 82–88.

[4] *The Backwoods Preacher: An Autobiography of Peter Cartwright*, ed. by W. P. Strickland (London, 1858), p. 4.

[5] See Hugh Hammond Bennet, *The Soils and Agriculture of the Southern States* (New York, 1921), pp. 193–212; Everett Dick, *The Dixie Frontier* (New York, 1948), pp. 3–5; Lewis C. Gray, *History of Agriculture in the Southern United States to 1860*, 2 vols. (Washington, 1933), vol. II, p. 861.

[6] "A Memorandum of M. Austin's Journey from the Lead Mines in the County of Wythe in the State of Virginia to the Lead Mines in the Province of Louisiana West of the Mississippi, 1796–1797," *American Historical Review*, V (April 1900), 525; William A. Pusey, *The Wilderness Road to Kentucky* (New York, 1921); Balthasar H. Meyer. ed., *History of Transportation in the United States before 1860* (Washington, 1917), pp. 8–9; Robert L. Kincaid, *The Wilderness Road* (Indianapolis, 1947).

[7] Leland D. Baldwin, *The Keelboat Age on the Western Waters* (Pittsburgh, 1941), pp. 134–158; John D. Barnhart, *Valley of Democracy: The Frontier Versus the Plantation in the Ohio Valley, 1775–1818* (Bloomington, Ind., 1953), p. 31; John Pope, *A Tour Through the Southern and Western Territories of the United States of North America* (Richmond, 1792; reprinted, New York, 1888), p. 18; "The Diary of Major William Stanley, 1790–1810," *Quarterly Publication of the Historical and Philosophical Society of Ohio*, XIV (1919), 20.

[8] "Journal of Richard Butler," in Craig, ed., *Olden Time*, vol. II, p. 499; "Journal of Arthur Lee," in *ibid.*, vol. II, pp. 339–340; "Journal of Joseph Buell," in S. P. Hildreth, *Pioneer History* (Cincinnati, 1848), pp. 151, 161. Between October 1786 and December 1788 some 857 boats passed Fort Harmar on their way down the Ohio, and they carried 16,203 passengers. Between August 1. 1786, and December 7, 1789, the total passengers amounted to 23,618. See Barnhart, *Valley of Democracy*, pp. 38–41.

[9] "Journal of Richard Butler," in Craig, ed., *Olden Time*, vol. II, p. 448; see also "Journal of Peter Muhlenberg," in Henry A. Muhlenberg, *The Life of Major-General Peter Muhlenberg of the Revolutionary Army* (Philadelphia, 1849), p. 4; John Filson, *The Discovery, Settlement, and Present State of Kentucke* (Wilmington, Del., 1784), pp. 27–28.

[10] Daniel Drake, *Pioneer Life in Kentucky. A Series of Reminiscential Letters from Daniel Drake, M.D. of Cincinnati to his Children,* ed. by Charles D. Drake (Cincinnati, 1870), p. 181.

[11] *Ibid.,* p. 25; "Journal of Richard Butler," in Craig, ed., *Olden Time,* vol. II, p. 451; James P. Finley, *Autobiography of Rev. James B. Finley, or, Pioneer Life in the West,* ed. by W. P. Strickland (Cincinnati, 1857), pp. 38–39, 44.

[12] John Filson, "Two Westward Journeys of John Filson, 1785," ed. by Beverley W. Bond, Jr., *Mississippi Valley Historical Review,* IX (March 1923), 324; Baily, *Journal of a Tour,* p. 194; "Journal of Peter Muhlenberg," in *Life of Muhlenberg,* pp. 435–436; *Journal of Andrew Ellicott,* p. 19; "Memorandum of M. Austin," *American Historical Review,* V, 527.

[13] Richard C. Wade, *The Urban Frontier: The Rise of Western Cities, 1790–1830* (Cambridge, Mass., 1959), pp. 18–21, 49–52; Bernard Mayo, "Lexington: Frontier Metropolis," in Eric F. Goldman, ed., *Historiography and Urbanization: Essays in American History in Honor of W. Stull Holt* (Baltimore, 1941), pp. 21–42; *Return of the Whole Number of Persons within the Several Districts of the United States: According to "An Act for the second census or enumeration of the inhabitants of the United States," Passed February the 28th, One Thousand Eight Hundred* (Washington, 1802), pp. 83–84, and inset facing p. 88. Hereafter cited as *Second Census.*

[14] Baily, *Journal of a Tour,* p. 242.

[15] Gray, *History of Agriculture,* vol. II, pp. 622–626; Filson, *Kentucke,* pp. 36–37; "Journal of Richard Butler," in Craig, ed., *Olden Time,* vol. II, p. 507.

[16] Baily, *Journal of a Tour,* pp. 194–195.

[17] *Autobiography of Peter Cartwright,* ed. by Strickland, pp. 4–7; Gray, *History of Agriculture,* vol. II, p. 863.

[18] Thomas P. Abernethy, *From Frontier to Plantation in Tennessee: A Study in Frontier Democracy* (Chapel Hill, N.C., 1932), pp. 154–156; Gray, *History of Agriculture,* vol. II, pp. 863–864. Samuel C. Williams, *Dawn of Tennessee Valley and Tennessee History* (Johnson City, Tenn. 1937), considers the history of the Tennessee region in the years before the Revolution. For North Carolina see Archibald Henderson, ed., *North Carolina: The Old North State and the New,* 5 vols. (Chicago, 1941), vol. II, pp. 7–11; Hugh Talmage Lefler and Albert Ray Newsome, *North Carolina* (Chapel Hill, N.C., 1963), pp. 253–255.

[19] Abernethy, *Frontier to Plantation,* pp. 155–156.

[20] Gray, *History of Agriculture,* vol. II, pp. 626–628. The N. Carolina land law of 1783 set a price of £10 specie for 100 acres. Individual land warrants were not to exceed 5000 acres, but speculators obtained numerous warrants. Also Abernethy, *Frontier to Plantation,* pp. 49–54; Robert S. Cotterill, *The Southern Indians: The Story of the Civilized Tribes before Removal* (Norman, Okla., 1954), pp. 57–67.

[21] Samuel C. Williams, *History of the Lost State of Franklin* (New York, 1933), pp. 1–12, 77–79; Thomas P. Abernethy, *Western Lands and the American Revolution* (New York, 1937), pp. 290–293; Abernethy, *Frontier to Plantation,* pp. 68–90; Barnhart, *Valley of Democracy,* pp. 61–65; Carl S. Driver, *John Sevier: Pioneer of the Old Southwest* (Chapel Hill, N.C., 1932), pp. 79–98.

[22] For the formation of a southern Indian policy see *Journals of the Continental Congress,* 34 vols. (Washington, 1904–1937), vol. XXV, p. 692 note 1, vol. XXVII, pp. 453–465, 550–553, vol. XXVIII, pp. 118–120, 134 note 2, 136–139, 159–162, 195.

[23] Minutes of the Hopewell treaty are in *American State Papers, Indian Affairs,* (Washington, 1832), vol. I, pp. 40–43, and the treaty in 7 U.S. *Statutes at Large,* pp. 18–21. Also William H. Masterson, *William Blount* (Baton Rouge, La., 1954), pp. 102–106; *Journals of the Continental Congress,* vol. XXVIII, p. 297; Williams, *Lost State of Franklin,* pp. 102–103.

24 Clarence E. Carter, ed., *The Territorial Papers of the United States* (Washington, 1934–   ), vol. IV, pp. 3–19; Masterson, *Blount*, pp. 174–179.

25 Carter, ed., *Territorial Papers,* vol. IV, pp. 60–67, 346–370 *passim;* Francis P. Prucha, *American Indian Policy in the Formative Years: The Indian Trade and Intercourse Acts, 1790–1834* (Cambridge, Mass., 1962), pp. 149–154; *American State Papers, Indian Affairs,* vol. I, pp. 639–640; 7 U.S. *Statutes at Large,* pp. 62–65; Baily, *Journal of a Tour,* pp. 436–437.

26 Carter, ed., *Territorial Papers,* vol. IV, pp. 81, 378 note 96, 404–405.

27 Baily, *Journal of a Tour,* pp. 409–418; Samuel C. Williams, *Early Travels in the Tennessee Country, 1540–1800* (Johnson City, Tenn., 1928), p. 508.

28 E. Merton Coulter, *Georgia: A Short History* (Chapel Hill, N.C., 1960), pp. 196–197; *Historical Statistics of the United States,* p. 13. Also Ulrich B. Phillips, "Georgia and State Rights," American Historical Association, *Annual Report,* 1901, II (Washington, 1902), 39–41; *American State Papers, Indian Affairs,* vol. I, pp. 17, 19–20, 23–24.

29 J. Sumner to Henry Knox, December 14, 1788, Henry Knox Papers, Massachusetts Historical Society. The activities of McGillivray can be followed from the introduction and correspondence in John Caughey, *McGillivray of the Creeks* (Norman, Okla., 1938).

30 Thomas Perkins Abernethy, *The South in the New Nation, 1789–1819* (Wendell H. Stephenson and E. Merton Coulter, eds., "History of the South," vol. IV; Louisiana State University Press, 1961), pp. 43–44; Caughey, *McGillivray of the Creeks,* pp. 24–27, 64–67.

31 Arthur P. Whitaker, *The Spanish-American Frontier, 1783–1795* (1927; reprinted, Gloucester, Mass., 1962), pp. 63–77.

32 Abernethy, *South in the New Nation,* p. 46; Abernethy, *Frontier to Plantation,* pp. 92–94.

33 The activities of Wilkinson and the Spanish conspiracy of this time can be followed in Abernethy, *South in the New Nation,* pp. 47–68. Spanish policy is treated in Whitaker, *Spanish-American Frontier,* pp. 78–122.

34 *American State Papers, Indian Affairs,* vol. I, pp. 54–55.

35 *Ibid.,* vol. I, pp. 65–68; Caughey, *McGillivray of the Creeks,* 40–45, 259–262, 273–279. Treaty is in 7 U.S. *Statutes at Large,* pp. 35–38.

36 Whitaker, *Spanish-American Frontier,* pp. 163–170.

37 Abernethy, *South in the New Nation,* pp. 74–93; Abernethy, *Western Lands and the American Revolution,* pp. 260–261, 288–289, 312–315.

38 Abernethy, *South in the New Nation,* pp. 136–168. An older, but still useful account, is that of Charles H. Haskins, "The Yazoo Land Companies," American Historical Association, *Papers,* V, no. 4 (1891), 395–437.

39 Abernethy, *South in the New Nation,* pp. 104–125.

40 See Whitaker, *Spanish-American Frontier,* pp. 201–212, and Samuel F. Bemis, *Pinckney's Treaty: A Study of America's Advantage from Europe's Distress, 1783–1800* (Baltimore, 1926); Abernethy, *South in the New Nation,* pp. 206–216.

41 This subject is discussed in Reginald Horsman, *Expansion and American Indian Policy, 1783–1812* (Lansing, Mich., 1967).

Chapter 2: Northern Expansion, 1783–1795

1 See Lois K. Mathews, *The Expansion of New England: The Spread of New England Settlement and Institutions to the Mississippi River* (1909; reprinted, New York, 1962); Richard J. Purcell, *Connecticut in Transition, 1775–1818* (Washington, 1918), pp. 139–155.

2 Lewis D. Stilwell, *Migration from Vermont, 1776–1860* (Montpelier, Vt., 1937), pp. 67–90.

[3] David M. Ludlum, *Social Ferment in Vermont, 1791–1850* (New York, 1939), pp. 10–15; Mathews, *Expansion of New England,* pp. 142–145; Stilwell, *Migration from Vermont,* pp. 95–97, 124–130.

[4] Mathews, *Expansion of New England,* pp. 140–142; *Historical Statistics of the United States,* p. 13; Clarence A. Day, *A History of Maine Agriculture, 1604–1860* (University of Maine Studies, 2d Series, No. 68; Orono, Maine, 1954) pp. 62–70.

[5] Ruth L. Higgins, *Expansion in New York with Especial Reference to the Eighteenth Century* (Columbus, 1931), pp. 100–162; Ralph H. Brown, *Mirror for Americans. Likeness of the Eastern Seaboard: 1810* (New York, 1943), pp. 160–161; Dixon R. Fox, *Yankees and Yorkers* (New York, 1940), pp. 184–185.

[6] There has been much writing on the history of western New York in these years. There is considerable material in Orsamus Turner, *History of the Pioneer Settlement of Phelp's and Gorham's Purchase, and Morris' Reserve* (Rochester, N.Y., 1851). See also George G. Humphrey, *Nathaniel Gorham* (Rochester, N.Y., 1927), and Eleanor Young, *Forgotten Patriot: Robert Morris* (New York, 1950). Activities of the Pulteney associates are covered in Paul D. Evans, "The Pulteney Purchase," *Quarterly Journal of the New York State Historical Association,* III (April 1922), 83–104. Also Neil A. McNall, *An Agricultural History of the Genesee Valley, 1790–1860* (Philadelphia, 1952), pp. 11–16. Settlement in the Susquehanna Valley is dealt with in James A. Frost, *Life on the Upper Susquehanna, 1783–1860* (New York, 1951), pp. 7–74.

[7] McNall, *Agricultural History of the Genesee Valley,* pp. 1–5, 18–35, 66–70, 75–77; Mathews, *Expansion of New England,* pp. 153–167; Helen I. Cowan, *Charles Williamson, Genesee Promoter—Friend of Anglo-American Rapprochement* (Rochester, N.Y., 1941), *passim;* Brown, *Mirror for Americans,* pp. 164–165, 169–170.

[8] Jeannette B. Sherwood, "The Military Tract," *Quarterly Journal of the New York State Historical Association,* VII (July 1926), 169–179; Brown, *Mirror for Americans,* pp. 168–169.

[9] John Lincklaen, *Travels in the Years 1791 and 1792 in Pennsylvania, New York, and Vermont* (New York, 1897), p. 103.

[10] Charles H. Leete, "The St. Lawrence Ten Towns," *Quarterly Journal of the New York State Historical Association,* X (October 1929), 318–327; Higgins, *Expansion in New York,* pp. 138–149.

[11] Solon J. Buck, *The Planting of Civilization in Western Pennsylvania* (Pittsburgh, 1939), pp. 204–228; Elizabeth K. Henderson, "The Northwestern Lands of Pennsylvania, 1790–1812," *Pennsylvania Magazine of History and Biography,* LX (April 1936), 131–160; Stevenson W. Fletcher, *Pennsylvania Agriculture and Country Life, 1640–1840* (Harrisburg, Pa., 1950), pp. 24–32.

[12] This argument is discussed in two articles by Merrill Jensen, "The Cession of the Old Northwest," *Mississippi Valley Historical Review,* XXIII (June 1936), 27–48, and "The Creation of the National Domain, 1781–1784," *ibid.,* XXVI (December 1939), 323–342.

[13] For the Virginia cession see Carter, ed., *Territorial Papers,* vol. II, pp. 6–9. The importance of the military bounty lands in this struggle over the public domain is discussed in Rudolf Freund, "Military Bounty Lands and the Origin of the Public Domain," *Agricultural History,* XX (January 1946) 8–18.

[14] Carter, ed., *Territorial Papers,* vol. II, pp. 10–12, 22–24, vol. IV, pp. 3–13, vol. V, pp. 142–146; Robert S. Cotterill, "The South Carolina Cession," *Mississippi Valley Historical Review,* XII (December 1925), 376–384; Abernethy, *Frontier to Plantation,* pp. 55–57, 112–113.

[15] *Journals of the Continental Congress,* vol. XVIII, pp. 915–916.

[16] *Ibid.,* vol. XXVI, pp. 118–120, 246–252, 255–260, 274–279.

[17] The different methods and policies of western settlement are discussed in Amelia C. Ford, *Colonial Precedents of Our National Land System as it Existed in 1800*

(Madison, Wis., 1910), and Marshall Harris, *Origin of the Land Tenure System in the United States* (Ames, Iowa, 1953).

18 The best discussion of the Ordinance of 1785, its background, and early operation is in William D. Pattison, *Beginnings of the American Rectangular Land Survey System, 1784–1800* (Chicago, 1957). The actual sale of land is discussed in Malcolm J. Rohrbough, *The Land Office Business: The Settlement and Administration of American Public Lands, 1789–1837* (New York, 1968). The Ordinance is printed in Carter, ed., *Territorial Papers*, vol. II, pp. 12–18.

19 "Journal of Richard Butler," in Craig, ed., *Olden Time*, vol. II, pp. 437–443; Barnhart, *Valley of Democracy*, pp. 40, 129–131.

20 A. L. Burt, *The United States, Great Britain, and British North America, from the Revolution to the Establishment of Peace after the War of 1812* (New Haven, Conn., 1940), pp. 82–105, presents the standard modern account of the reasons for the British retention of the posts. His arguments perhaps place too great an emphasis on the desire to prevent Indian war.

21 British backing of the Indians is discussed in Reginald Horsman, *Matthew Elliott: British Indian Agent* (Detroit, 1964).

22 Horsman, *Expansion and American Indian Policy*, pp. 10–12, 17–23.

23 Shaw Livermore, *Early American Land Companies* (New York, 1939), pp. 134–138.

24 *Ibid.*, pp. 138–140, 145; Carter, ed., *Territorial Papers*, vol. II, pp. 29, 52–54, 61–63, 80–88; Archer B. Hulbert, *The Records of the Original Proceedings of the Ohio Company*, 2 vols. (Marietta, Ohio, 1917), vol. I, pp. xlviii–lxxvii; Beverley W. Bond, Jr., *The Civilization of the Old Northwest* (New York, 1934), pp. 279–280. In 1792 the company was unable to pay the money it owed, and obtained a settlement from the government by which it was allowed to keep over 1,000,000 acres. The original $500,000 paid for 750,000 acres, while over 200,000 acres was paid for in military warrants. By 1796 the company had practically wound up its affairs.

25 Carter, ed., *Territorial Papers*, vol. II, pp. 39–50. Jack E. Eblen, "Origins of the United States Colonial System: The Ordinance of 1787," *Wisconsin Magazine of History*, 51 (Summer 1968), 294–314 shows that the Northwest Ordinance was being planned before pressure from the Ohio Company.

26 Hulbert, ed., *Records of the Original Proceedings of the Ohio Company*, vol. I, pp. xcviii–cii; Barnhart, *Valley of Democracy*, pp. 138–139; Carter, ed., *Territorial Papers*, vol. II, p. 294.

27 *Journals of the Continental Congress*, vol. XXXI, pp. 916–918. See also Leonard C. Helderman, "The Northwest Expedition of Clark," *Mississippi Valley Historical Review*, XXV (December 1938), 317–334; Charles G. Talbert, *Benjamin Logan: Kentucky Frontiersman* (Lexington, Ky., 1952), pp. 203–221.

28 The minutes of the Fort Harmar treaties are in Draper Manuscripts, State Historical Society of Wisconsin, 23U75–142. The treaties are in 7 U.S. *Statutes at Large*, 28–29, 33–34.

29 Hildreth, *Pioneer History*, pp. 389–390.

30 *American State Papers, Indian Affairs*, vol. I, pp. 92–93, 100, 104; Gayle Thornbrough, ed., *Outpost on the Wabash, 1787–1791* (Indiana Historical Society "Publications," vol. 19; Indianapolis, 1957), pp. 259–264; "Military Journal of Major Ebeneezer Denny," *Memoirs of the Historical Society of Pennsylvania*, VII (Philadelphia, 1860), 343–353.

31 *American State Papers, Indian Affairs*, vol. I, pp. 112–113, 129–135; William H. Smith, ed., *The St. Clair Papers: The Life and Public Services of Arthur St. Clair*, 2 vols. (Cincinnati, 1882), vol. II, pp. 200–201, 212–216, 222–223, 227–229; James R. Jacobs, *The Beginning of the U.S. Army, 1783–1812* (Princeton, N.J., 1947), pp. 66–123.

32 Julia Perkins Cutler, *Life and Times of Ephraim Cutler Prepared from his Journals*

and Correspondence (Cincinnati, 1890), pp. 22–24; Dwight L. Smith, ed., *The Western Journals of John May* (Cincinnati, 1961), pp. 48–69, 122–124.

³³ Cutler, *Life and Times*, pp. 24–27, 29.

³⁴ See Archer B. Hulbert, "The Methods and Operations of the Scioto Group of Speculators," *Mississippi Valley Historical Review*, I (March 1915), 502–515, and II (June 1915), 56–73.

³⁵ Collot, *Journey*, vol. I, p. 80; *Journal of Andrew Ellicott*, p. 13. See also Carter, ed., *Territorial Papers*, vol. II, pp. 311–312, 337, 422–428,, 462–469; H. M. Brackenridge, *Recollections of Persons and Places in the West* (Philadelphia, 1834), pp. 41–47.

³⁶ Beverley W. Bond, ed., *The Correspondence of John Cleves Symmes: Founder of the Miami Purchase* (New York, 1926), pp. 1–24.

³⁷ *Ibid.*, pp. 13–21, 125–128; Carter, ed., *Territorial Papers*, vol. II, p. 470.

³⁸ Pattison, *Beginnings of the American Rectangular Survey System*, pp. 104–168.

³⁹ The peace missions of these years are discussed in Horsman, *Expansion and American Indian Policy*, pp. 90–98.

⁴⁰ British aims are discussed in Samuel F. Bemis, *Jay's Treaty: A Study in Commerce and Diplomacy* (1924; revised edition, New Haven, 1962), pp. 147–182. See also *American State Papers, Indian Affairs*, vol. I, pp. 227, 229–230, 235; Rowena Buell, ed., *Memoirs of Rufus Putnam and Certain Official Papers and Correspondence* (Boston, 1903), pp. 273–278, 301–304, 311–312, 313–316.

⁴¹ *American State Papers, Indian Affairs*, vol. I, pp. 356–357.

⁴² See correspondence in Richard C. Knopf, ed., *Anthony Wayne: A Name in Arms: Soldier, Diplomat, Defender of Expansion Westward of a Nation: The Wayne-Knox-Pickering-McHenry Correspondence* (Pittsburgh, 1960), pp. 275–277, 281–284. At the time the name of fort was frequently written as "Fort Greene Ville." I have used the customary modern spelling of the name.

⁴³ Horsman, *Matthew Elliott*, pp. 92–105.

⁴⁴ Bemis, *Jay's Treaty, passim;* Louis P. Kellogg, *The British Régime in Wisconsin and the Northwest* (Madison, Wis., 1935), pp. 233–235.

⁴⁵ *American State Papers, Indian Affairs*, vol. I, pp. 564–582; 7 U.S. *Statutes at Large*, pp. 49–54.

Chapter 3: Southern Settlement, 1796–1815

¹ *Historical Statistics of the United States*, p. 13.

² François André Michaux, "Travels West of the Alleghany Mountains, 1802," in Reuben G. Thwaites ed., *Early Western Travels, 1748–1846*, 32 vols. (Cleveland, 1904–1907), vol. III, p. 174; John Melish, *Travels in the United States of America in the Years 1806 & 1807, and 1809, 1810 & 1811*, 2 vols. (Philadelphia, 1812), vol. II, pp. 96–97. Salt was one of the few other items that brought profit to the region.

³ "Fortescue Cuming's Tour to the Western Country, 1807–1809," in Thwaites, ed., *Early Western Travels*, vol. IV, pp. 112–113; Samuel J. Mills and Daniel Smith, *Report of a Missionary Tour through that Part of the United States which lies West of the Allegany Mountains* (Andover, Mass., 1815), p. 8.

⁴ F. A. Michaux, "Travels," in Thwaites, ed., *Early Western Travels*, vol. III, pp. 171–172; *The Navigator* (8th ed.; Pittsburgh, 1814), p. 85; Christian Schultz, Jr., *Travels on an Inland Voyage . . . in the Years 1807 and 1808*, 2 vols. (New York, 1810), vol. I, pp. 135–136.

⁵ Thaddeus Mason Harris, "Journal of a Tour Northwest of the Alleghany Mountains, 1803," in Thwaites, ed., *Early Western Travels*, vol. III, pp. 357–358.

⁶ Melish, *Travels*, vol. II, p. 94, also pp. 111–112.

⁷ *Census for 1820*, Book 1 (Washington, 1821), p. 1; Drake, *Pioneer Life*, p. 206;

Melish, *Travels,* vol. II, p. 207; also Lorenzo Dow, *History of Cosmopolite* (Wheeling, Va., 1848), p. 343.

8 "Cuming's Tour," Thwaites, ed., *Early Western Travels,* vol. IV, p. 171.

9 F. A. Michaux, "Travels," *ibid.,* vol. III, pp. 195–196; Schultz, *Travels,* vol. I, pp. 179–180; Melish, *Travels,* vol. II, p. 200.

10 Melish, *Travels,* vol. II, pp. 183–184; "Cuming's Tour," Thwaites, ed., *Early Western Travels,* vol. IV, pp. 182–185.

11 Francis Asbury, *Journal of Rev. Francis Asbury,* 3 vols. (New York, 1852), vol. III, p. 349.

12 Josiah Espy, "Memorandums of a Tour made by Josiah Espy in the States of Ohio and Kentucky and Indiana Territory in 1805," *Ohio Valley Historical Series, Miscellanies,* no. 1 (Cincinnati, 1870), 15; "Cuming's Tour," Thwaites, ed., *Early Western Travels,* vol. IV, pp. 258–259; Melish, *Travels,* vol. II, p. 154; Wade, *Urban Frontier,* pp. 13–17, 64–66.

13 John F. Schermerhorn and Samuel J. Mills, *A Correct View of that Part of the United States which Lies West of the Allegany Mountains with Regard to Religion and Morals* (Hartford, Conn. 1814), p. 22, also pp. 19–23.

14 *Journal of Asbury,* vol. III, p. 132; see also F. A. Michaux, "Travels," in Thwaites, ed., *Early Western Travels,* vol. III, pp. 269–270.

15 Horsman, *Expansion and American Indian Policy,* pp. 82, 105, 127–128.

16 Schermerhorn and Mills, *Correct View,* p. 24; Henry Ker, *Travels through the Western Interior of the United States from the Year 1808 up to the Year 1816* (Elizabethtown, N.J., 1816), pp. 307, 309–310.

17 Schermerhorn and Mills, *Correct View,* p. 26; Ker, *Travels,* pp. 304–307; Abernethy, *Frontier to Plantation,* pp. 194–207, 277.

18 *Second Census,* p. 88.

19 See *American State Papers, Indian Affairs,* vol. I, pp. 668–681; War Department, Secretary's Office, Letters Sent, Indian Affairs, National Archives, A: pp. 199–202, 225, 238–239, B: pp. 41–42, 88, 154–160; 7 U.S. *Statutes at Large,* pp. 68–70, 96–98.

20 James C. Bonner, *A History of Georgia Agriculture, 1732–1860* (Athens, Ga., 1964), pp. 38–39; Coulter, *Georgia,* pp. 219–220; *Historical Statistics of the United States,* p. 13; Ker, *Travels,* pp. 341–344.

21 There is considerable information on the Louisiana problem in Arthur P. Whitaker, *The Mississippi Question, 1795–1803* (New York, 1934), and in E. Wilson Lyon, *Louisiana in French Diplomacy, 1759–1804* (Norman, Okla., 1934).

22 The modern standard account of the Burr conspiracy is Thomas P. Abernethy, *The Burr Conspiracy* (New York, 1954). More favorable to Burr is Walter F. McCaleb, *The Aaron Burr Conspiracy* (New York, 1936).

23 For the history of the Natchez region prior to the American period see John H. Moore, *Agriculture in Ante-Bellum Mississippi* (New York, 1958), pp. 13–18; Abernethy, *South in the New Nation,* pp. 444–445; Gray, *History of Agriculture,* vol. II, p. 897; Dunbar Rowland, *History of Mississippi: The Heart of the South,* 2 vols. (Chicago, 1925), vol. I, pp. 165–336; Jack D. L. Holmes, *Gayoso: The Life of a Spanish Governor in the Mississippi Valley, 1789–1799* (Baton Rouge, La., 1965).

24 *Historical Statistics of the United States,* p. 13; Baily, *Journal,* pp. 279–284, 345, 350–351; Carter, ed., *Territorial Papers,* vol. V, p. 65.

25 Abernethy, *South in the New Nation,* pp. 447–451; Carter, ed., *Territorial Papers,* vol. V, pp. 192–205; *Third Census,* p. 83.

26 Mills and Smith, *Report of a Missionary Tour,* pp. 26–27; *Navigator* (1814), pp. 214–215.

27 *Second Census,* pp. 85–86; Abernethy, *South in the New Nation,* p. 246; Carter, ed., *Territorial Papers,* vol. V, pp. 292–295.

²⁸ Ephraim Kirby to Jefferson, May 1804, Carter, ed., *Territorial Papers,* vol. V, pp. 322–324.

²⁹ *Ibid.,* vol. V, pp. 317–319, 443–444.

³⁰ *Ibid.,* vol. V, pp. 684–692; *Third Census,* p. 83; Abernethy, *South in the New Nation,* p. 456; *Navigator* (1814), pp. 352–357.

³¹ Clement Eaton, *The Growth of Southern Civilization* (Henry S. Commager and Richard B. Morris, ed., "New American Nation" series; New York, 1961), pp. 128–129.

³² Carter, ed., *Territorial Papers,* vol. IX, pp. 16, 28–33, 147–149; Abernethy, *South in the New Nation,* pp. 252–253; Baily, *Journal,* pp. 295–296.

³³ Baily, *Journal,* pp. 300–306; John F. Watson, "Notitia of Incidents at New Orleans in 1804 and 1805," in John S. Williams, ed., *American Pioneer,* 2 vols. (Cincinnati, 1842–1843), vol. II, pp. 228–233; Ker, *Travels,* pp. 46–48; Schultz, *Travels,* vol. II, pp. 190–198.

³⁴ Major Amos Stoddard, *Sketches, Historical and Descriptive of Louisiana* (Philadelphia, 1812), p. 328; Watson, "Notitia," Williams, ed., *American Pioneer,* II, 234–236; Schultz, *Travels,* vol. II, pp. 193–195.

³⁵ Carter, ed., *Territorial Papers,* vol. IX, pp. 161–162; 299; Watson, "Notitia," Williams, ed., *American Pioneer,* vol. II, p. 235.

³⁶ Stoddard, *Sketches,* pp. 180–183; Carter, ed., *Territorial Papers,* vol. IX, pp. 677–678; Henry M. Brackenridge, *Views of Louisiana: Together With a Journal of a Voyage up the Missouri in 1811* (Pittsburgh, 1814; reprinted Chicago, 1962), pp. 169–171.

³⁷ Stoddard, *Sketches,* pp. 185–189; Ker, *Travels,* pp. 82–83; Brackenridge, *Views of Louisiana,* pp. 161–167.

³⁸ *Third Census,* p. 82. For the annexation of West Florida see Isaac J. Cox, *The West Florida Controversy, 1798–1813: A Study in American Diplomacy* (Baltimore, 1918), pp. 312–436, 487–529. There is also information in Rembert W. Patrick, *Florida Fiasco: Rampant Rebels on the Georgia-Florida Border, 1810–1815* (Athens, Ga., 1954). Only the area up to the Pearl River was actually occupied before the War of 1812.

³⁹ Stoddard, *Sketches,* pp. 206–212; "Cuming's Tour," Thwaites, ed., *Early Western Travels,* vol. IV, pp. 281–282, 299; Schultz, *Travels,* vol. II, pp. 103, 105–106; Dow. *History of Cosmopolite,* pp. 344–346.

⁴⁰ Schultz, *Travels,* vol. II, p. 62.

⁴¹ *Ibid.,* vol. II, pp. 48–67, 78; Stoddard, *Sketches,* pp. 214–218; Collot, *Journey,* vol. I, p. 252; Brackenridge, *Recollections,* pp. 25–31; "Memorandum of M. Austin," *American Historical Review,* V, 540–541.

⁴² Collot, *Journey,* vol. I, p. 277.

⁴³ Stoddard, *Sketches,* pp. 218–224; Schultz, *Travels,* vol. II, pp. 39–41, 47; Edwin C. McReynolds, *Missouri: A History of the Crossroads State* (Norman, Okla., 1962), pp. 51–71. Hattie M. Anderson, "Missouri, 1804–1828: Peopling a Frontier State," *Missouri Historical Review,* XXXI (January 1937), 150–180.

Chapter 4: Northern Settlement, 1795–1815

¹ Melish, *Travels,* vol. II, p. 383.

² Brown, *Mirror for Americans,* pp. 168–169; McNall, *Agricultural History of the Genesee Valley,* pp. 68–69.

³ Higgins, *Expansion in New York,* pp. 132–137; also Paul D. Evans, *The Holland Land Company* (Buffalo, N.Y., 1924), and Orsamus Turner, *Pioneer History of the Holland Land Purchase of Western New York* (Buffalo, N.Y., 1849).

⁴ Melish, *Travels,* vol. II, pp. 308, 312–319, 351–356; Schultz, *Travels,* vol. I, p. 95.

⁵ Buck, *Planting of Civilization in Western Pennsylvania,* pp. 204–228; Schultz, *Travels,* vol. I, pp. 106–112; Melish, *Travels,* vol. II, pp. 304–306.

⁶ *Navigator* (1814), pp. 66–68; Schultz, *Travels*, vol. I, p. 124; "Cuming's Tour," Thwaites, ed., *Early Western Travels*, vol. IV, pp. 76–87.

⁷ Alfred B. Sears, *Thomas Worthington: Father of Ohio Statehood* (Columbus, 1958), pp. 13–24; David M. Massie, *Nathaniel Massie: A Pioneer of Ohio* (Cincinnati, 1896), pp. 23–64.

⁸ For Connecticut cession see Carter, ed., *Territorial Papers*, vol. II, pp. 22–24. The Connecticut Land Company is treated in Claude L. Shepard, "The Connecticut Land Company and Accompanying Papers," Western Reserve Historical Society, *Annual Report*, 1915–1916, Part II, Tract No. 96, 59–221; see also Harland Hatcher, *The Western Reserve: The Story of New Connecticut in Ohio* (Indianapolis, 1949), pp. 13–88.

⁹ Carter, ed., *Territorial Papers*, vol. II, pp. 552–557; Payson J. Treat, *The National Land System, 1785–1820* (New York, 1910), pp. 66–94, 100.

¹⁰ Carter, ed., *Territorial Papers*, vol. II, pp. 638–640, vol. III, pp. 88–97.

¹¹ *Ibid.*, vol. VII, pp. 173–184; Treat, *National Land System*, pp. 94–142.

¹² *Journal of Asbury*, vol. III, p. 165; *Second Census*, p. 85.

¹³ Clement L. Martzolff, "Zane's Trace," *Ohio Archaeological and Historical Quarterly*, XIII (1904), 297–331; Archer B. Hulbert, *Pioneer Roads and Experiences of Travellers*, 2 vols. (*Historic Highways of America*, vols. 11 and 12; Cleveland, 1904), vol. I, pp. 151–166; Max Farrand, ed., *A Journey to Ohio in 1810 as Recorded in the Journal of Margaret Van Horn Dwight* (New Haven, Conn. 1912), pp. 36–37.

¹⁴ Archer B. Hulbert, *The Cumberland Road* (*Historic Highways of America*, vol. 10; Cleveland, 1904), pp. 15–54; Philip D. Jordan, *The National Road* (New York, 1948), pp. 69–89.

¹⁵ Espy, "Memorandums of a Tour," pp. 22–23 (1805); Farrand, ed., *Journey to Ohio*, p. 47.

¹⁶ *Historical Statistics of the United States*, p. 13; Brackenridge, *Recollections*, p. 219.

¹⁷ Melish, *Travels*, vol. II, p. 147.

¹⁸ Schermerhorn and Mills, *Correct View*, pp. 11–12; "Cuming's Tour," Thwaites, ed., *Early Western Travels*, vol. IV, p. 107; Schultz, *Travels*, vol. I. pp. 134–135; Melish, *Travels*, vol. II, pp. 89–91; *Navigator* (1814), p. 81.

¹⁹ Schultz, *Travels*, vol. II, p. 143; also F. A. Michaux, "Travels," Thwaites, ed., *Early Western Travels*, vol. III, p. 177; "Cuming's Tour," *ibid.*, vol. IV, pp. 123–124.

²⁰ Melish, *Travels*, vol. II, pp. 102–103, 295.

²¹ Schermerhorn and Mills, *Correct View*, p. 17; also Espy, "Memorandums of a Tour," pp. 24–25.

²² "Cuming's Tour," Thwaites, ed., *Early Western Travels*, vol. IV, pp. 215–217; Espy, "Memorandums of a Tour," pp. 17–18; Melish, *Travels*, vol. II, pp. 219–221.

²³ Daniel Drake, *Natural and Statistical View or Picture of Cincinnati and the Miami Country* (Cincinnati, 1815), pp. 167, 37, 134–135, 170.

²⁴ Melish, *Travels*, vol. II, pp. 262–264, 273–274.

²⁵ "Two Westward Journeys of John Filson, 1785," *Mississippi Valley Historical Review*, IX, 330; see also "Journal of Buell," Hildreth, *Pioneer History*, p. 155.

²⁶ Symmes to Robert Morris, June 22, 1790, Bond, ed., *Correspondence of Symmes*, pp. 287–290 (quotations); Barnhart, *Valley of Democracy*, p. 163; "Memorandum of M. Austin," *American Historical Review*, V, 528–529.

²⁷ "Memorandum of M. Austin," *American Historical Review*, V, 527.

²⁸ André Michaux, "Travels in Kentucky. 1793–1796." Thwaites, ed., *Early Western Travels*, vol. III, pp. 66–67.

²⁹ Baily, *Journal*, pp. 245–246.

³⁰ *Second Census*, p. 87; Barnhart, *Valley of Democracy*, pp. 163–164.

³¹ See John Badollet to Albert Gallatin, December 21, 1807, Gayle Thornbrough,

ed., *The Correspondence of John Badollet and Albert Gallatin, 1804–1836* (Indiana Historical Society *Publications,* vol. 22; Indianapolis, 1963), pp. 91–94.

32 Espy, "Memorandums of a Tour," pp. 11–14; Schultz, *Travels,* vol. I, p. 192.

33 See Chelsea L. Lawlis, "Whitewater Settlement, 1790–1810," *Indiana Magazine of History,* XLIII (March 1947), 23–40. Settlement in general is discussed in Barnhart, *Valley of Democracy,* pp. 164–166; L. C. Rudolph, *Hoosier Zion: The Presbyterians in Early Indiana* (New Haven, Conn. 1963), pp. 3–13; *Third Census,* pp. 85–86.

34 For Harrison's treaties see Dorothy Burne Goebel, *William Henry Harrison: A Political Biography* (Indiana Historical *Collections,* vol. XIV; Indianapolis, 1926), pp. 98–127; Logan Esarey, ed., *Messages and Letters of William Henry Harrison,* 2 vols. (Indiana Historical *Collections,* vols. VII and IX; Indianapolis, 1922), vol. I, *passim.* The most recent biography of Tecumseh is Glenn Tucker, *Tecumseh: Vision of Glory* (Indianapolis, 1956).

35 Jared Mansfield to Gallatin, Carter, ed *Territorial Papers,* vol. VII, pp. 425–426; Mills and Smith, *Report of a Missionary Tour,* p. 11. For estimates of population see *ibid.,* p. 15, and Carter, ed., *Territorial Papers* vol. VIII, p. 364.

36 Report of St. Clair to Jefferson, February 10, 1791, Carter, ed., *Territorial Papers,* vol. II, pp. 323–327; also petition of American inhabitants of Illinois to St. Clair, May 23, 1790, *ibid.,* vol. II, pp. 252–253.

37 André Michaux, "Travels," Thwaites, ed., *Early Western Travels,* vol. III, p. 70.

38 Collot, *Journey,* vol. I, pp. 232–233: see also "Memorandum of M. Austin," *American Historical Review,* V, 534–538.

39 Schultz, *Travels,* vol. II, p. 37.

40 *Third Census,* p. 87; Arthur C. Boggess, *The Settlement of Illinois, 1778–1830* (Chicago, 1908), pp. 9–133; Clarence W. Alvord, *The Illinois Country, 1763–1818* ("Centennial History of Illinois"; Springfield, 1920), pp. 398–464; Carter, ed., *Territorial Papers,* vol. III, pp. 76–77, vol. XVI, p. 93; Mills and Smith, *Report of a Missionary Tour,* pp. 16–17.

41 Clarence M. Burton, *The City of Detroit, Michigan 1701–1922,* 5 vols. (Detroit, 1922), vol. II, p. 1503; Nelson Vance Russell, *The British Regime in Michigan and the Old Northwest, 1760–1796* (Northfield, Minn., 1939), pp. 102–106; Carter, ed., *Territorial Papers,* vol. III, pp. 121–122.

Chapter 5: The Organization of Government

1 Chilton Williamson, *American Suffrage from Property to Democracy, 1760–1860* (Princeton, N.J., 1960), pp. 82, 92–97, 115–116, 132–136, 138–157, 181.

2 Earle Newton, *The Vermont Story: A History of the People of the Green Mountain State, 1749–1949* (Montpelier, Vt., 1949), pp. 76–77; Ludlum, *Social Ferment in Vermont,* pp. 6–7.

3 Abernethy, *Western Lands and the American Revolution,* pp. 303–304; Barnhart, *Valley of Democracy,* pp. 68–70; Talbert, *Benjamin Logan,* pp. 192–196.

4 Williamson. *American Suffrage,* p. 211; Talbert, *Benjamin Logan,* pp. 196–197.

5 Abernethy, *Western Lands and the American Revolution,* pp. 305–309, 319–326, 346–352; Barnhart, *Valley of Democracy,* pp. 70–80; Talbert, *Benjamin Logan,* pp. 197–202, 222–247.

6 Barnhart, *Valley of Democracy,* pp. 80–105; Abernethy, *South in the New Nation,* pp. 69–72; 220–221; Talbert, *Benjamin Logan,* pp. 258–260; Arthur K. Moore, *The Frontier Mind: A Cultural Analysis of the Kentucky Frontiersman* (Lexington, Ky., 1957), pp. 149–150.

7 Carter, ed., *Territorial Papers,* vol. II, pp. 39–50; Williamson, *American Suffrage,* p. 117.

8 Charles Thomson, Minutes of the Proceedings in Congress, August 18, 1786, Edmund C. Burnett, ed., *Letters of Members of the Continental Congress*, 8 vols. (Washington, 1921–1936), VIII, p. 440.

9 Barnhart, *Valley of Democracy*, p. 143; St. Clair to Washington, August 1789, Carter, ed., *Territorial Papers*, vol. II, p. 206.

10 Carter, ed., *Territorial Papers*, vol. II, pp. 472–473.

11 *Ibid.*, vol. II, pp. 479, 499–500; Bond, *Civilization of the Old Northwest*, pp. 56–61, 71–88.

12 Carter, ed., *Territorial Papers*, vol. III, pp. 514–515; Williamson, *American Suffrage*, p. 212.

13 Bond, *Civilization of the Old Northwest*, pp. 89–102; Barnhart, *Valley of Democracy*, pp. 147–149; Sears, *Thomas Worthington*, pp. 47–56.

14 St. Clair to Paul Fearing, December 25, 1801, Carter, ed., *Territorial Papers*, vol. III, p. 187; also Sears, *Thomas Worthington*, pp. 56–66.

15 William Goforth to Jefferson, January 5, 1802, Carter, ed., *Territorial Papers*, vol. III, p. 198; see also Symmes to Jefferson, January 23, 1802, *ibid.* vol. III, pp. 205–207.

16 Sears, *Thomas Worthington*, pp. 73–93; Ohio population is in Carter, ed., *Territorial Papers*, vol. III, pp. 199–200; Worthington to Jefferson, November 8, 1802; *ibid.*, vol. III, p. 254; Madison to St. Clair, November 22, 1802, *ibid.*, vol. III, p. 260.

17 Barnhart, *Valley of Democracy*, pp. 150–159; Sears, *Thomas Worthington*, pp. 94–107.

18 Bond, *Civilization of the Old Northwest*, pp. 60–66, 80–81; Petition by Inhabitants of Knox County, January 1, 1800, Carter, ed., *Territorial Papers*, vol. VII, pp 3–4. For bill to separate territory see *ibid.*, vol. VII, pp. 7–10, vol. III, pp. 6–8.

19 For first stage of territorial government in Indiana see Barnhart, *Valley of Democracy*, pp. 167–170; Bond, *Civilization of the Old Northwest*, pp. 152–159.

20 Carter, ed., *Territorial Papers*, vol. VII, p. 502; also Badollet to Gallatin, January 23, 1808, Thornbrough, ed., *Correspondence of Badollet and Gallatin*, p. 97.

21 Carter, ed., *Territorial Papers*, vol. VII, p. 526; Williamson, *American Suffrage*, p. 213.

22 Carter, ed., *Territorial Papers*, vol. VII, pp. 600–601, 604–605, 608; *Annals of Congress*, 10th Cong., 2d Sess., pp. 1821–1822.

23 See Carter, ed., *Territorial Papers*, vol. VII, pp. 687–694, vol. VIII, pp. 111–113; Williamson, *American Suffrage*, pp. 216, 219.

24 Carter, ed., *Territorial Papers*, vol. VIII, p. 151.

25 *Ibid.*, vol. VIII, pp. 147–148; Barnhart, *Valley of Democracy*, pp. 178–180.

26 Solon J. Buck, *Illinois in 1818* (Springfield, Ill., 1917), pp. 181–193. There is considerable information on the complaints of the Illinois region in Carter, ed., *Territorial Papers*, vol. VII, pp. 129–145, 157–158, 326, 545–550, 601–602.

27 Carter, ed., *Territorial Papers*, vol. XVI, pp. 6–8; Barnhart, *Valley of Democracy*, pp. 197–199; Bond, *Civilization of the Old Northwest*, pp. 202–203.

28 Edwards to Johnson, March 14, 1812, Carter, ed., *Territorial Papers*, vol. XVI, pp. 199–202; petition of March 24, 1812, *ibid.*, vol. XVI, pp. 203–204.

29 Bond, *Civilization of the Old Northwest*, pp. 204–205; Barnhart, *Valley of Democracy*, pp. 200–201.

30 Reginald Horsman, *Frontier Detroit, 1760–1812* ("Michigan in Perspective" Conference, Occasional Publication No. 1; Detroit, 1964), pp. 1–17; F. Clever Bald, *Detroit's First American Decade: 1796–1805* (Ann Arbor, Mich. 1948), pp. 42, 55–57, 137–145, 207–208, 221, 235–236, 272; Burton, *City of Detroit*, vol. I, pp. 156, 309–310, 312–320.

31 Carter, ed., *Territorial Papers*, vol. IV, pp. 18–19.

32 Blount to John Sevier, May 31, 1793, Carter, ed., *Territorial Papers*, vol. IV, p. 266; Masterson, *William Blount*, pp. 174–179.

33 Carter, ed., *Territorial Papers,* vol. IV, pp. 309–310, 319, 328, 350–351; Abernethy, *Frontier to Plantation,* p. 133.

34 Carter, ed., *Territorial Papers,* vol. IV., pp. 404–408; Barnhart, *Valley of Democracy,* pp. 110–111.

35 Abernethy, *Frontier to Plantation,* pp. 135–140; Barnhart, *Valley of Democracy,* pp. 111–119.

36 Carter, ed., *Territorial Papers,* vol. IV, pp. 420, 422–425; Abernethy, *South in the New Nation,* pp. 170–171.

37 Carter, ed., *Territorial Papers,* vol. V, pp. 18–22.

38 *Ibid.,* vol. V, pp. 27–29, 63–68.

39 *Ibid.,* vol. V, pp. 78–82.

40 For arguments, see Sargent and Judges McGuire and Bruin to Committee of Inhabitants, October 5, 1799, *ibid.,* vol. V, pp. 86–87, also 87–89, 92–98, 105–123, 126. See also Sargent to Timothy Pickering, November 1, 1799, Dunbar Rowland, ed., *The Mississippi Territorial Archives, 1798–1803* (Nashville, Tenn., 1905), pp. 182–187, and Robert V. Haynes, "The Revolution of 1800 in Mississippi," *Journal of Mississippi History,* XIX (October 1957), 234–251.

41 Carter, ed., *Territorial Papers,* vol. V, pp. 159–174, 361–362, 505, 588, vol. VI, pp. 411–413.

42 *Ibid.,* vol. V, pp. 733–737 (May 1809), vol. VI, pp. 36–39 (Dec. 1809).

43 The memorial of December 27, 1814 is in *ibid.,* vol. VI, pp. 484–487. For earlier efforts to enter the Union see *ibid.,* vol. VI, pp. 242–243, 253–257, 339–341.

44 Carter, ed., *Territorial Papers,* vol. IX, pp. 89–90, 202–213.

45 *Ibid.,* vol. IX, pp. 242–243, 245–248, 261, 304–305; Abernethy, *South in the New Nation,* p. 266.

46 Carter, ed., *Territorial Papers,* vol. IX, pp. 405–407, 478–481, 657, 660–661, 873–877.

47 Abernethy, *South in the New Nation,* pp. 364–366; Garnie William McGinty, *A History of Louisiana* (New York, 1949), p. 113.

48 Carter, ed., *Territorial Papers,* vol. VII, pp. 188–189 n.; McReynolds, *Missouri,* pp. 33–38.

49 Carter, ed., *Territorial Papers,* vol. XIV, pp. 252–256, 357–358, 362–364, 484–486, 552–559.

Chapter 6: The Life of the Settlers

1 See F. A. Michaux, "Travels," Thwaites, ed., *Early Western Travels,* vol. III, pp. 189–194; "Bradbury's Travels in the Interior of America, 1809–1811," *ibid.,* vol. V, pp. 281–282; Collot, *Journey,* vol. I, pp. 109–113; Baily, *Journal,* pp. 217–218; Melish, *Travels,* vol. II, pp. 97–98; Isaac Weld, Jr., *Travels Through the States of North America and the Provinces of Upper and Lower Canada during the Years 1795, 1796, and 1797* (London, 1799), p. 434.

2 Weld, *Travels,* p. 434 ("morose and savage"); Baily, *Journal,* p. 217 ("a race").

3 F. A. Michaux, "Travels," Thwaites, ed., *Early Western Travels,* vol. III, p. 193.

4 John S. Williams, "Our Cabin; Or, Life in the Woods," Williams, ed., *American Pioneer,* vol. II, p. 442.

5 For this discussion of a log cabin and its contents see *ibid.,* II, 444–445; F. A. Michaux, "Travels," Thwaites, ed., *Early Western Travels,* vol. III, pp. 136–137; Strickland, ed., *Autobiography of Finley,* pp. 70–73; Baily, *Journal,* pp. 197–200, 218–219, 289, 305–309, 409, 421; Ker, *Travels,* p. 43; Stoddard, *Sketches,* pp. 328–329; Drake, *Pioneer Life,* pp. 14–21, 42, 259–261.

6 Schultz, *Travels,* vol. II, p. 21.

7 Williams, "Our Cabin," Williams, ed., *American Pioneer,* vol. II, pp. 459–461.

[8] Drake, *Pioneer Life,* p. 107.

[9] For the clearing of land, and first crops and stock, see *ibid.,* pp. 35–36, 45–47, 69, 72–75; "Bradbury's Travels," Thwaites, ed., *Early Western Travels,* vol. V, pp. 310–311; Melish, *Travels,* vol. II, pp. 211–212; Williams, "Our Cabin," Williams, ed., *American Pioneer,* vol. II, p. 451; Drake, *Natural and Statistical View,* pp. 56, 83.

[10] Schultz, *Travels,* vol. II, p. 23; see also J. Cutler, *A Topographical Description of the State of Ohio, Indiana Territory, and Louisiana* (Boston, 1812), p. 23.

[11] Isaac J. Finley and Rufus Putnam, *Pioneer Record and Reminiscences of the Early Settlers and Settlement of Ross County, Ohio* (Cincinnati, 1871), p. 6.

[12] Drake, *Pioneer Life,* pp. 57–58; Strickland, ed., *Autobiography of Finley,* p. 73.

[13] Hildreth, *Pioneer History,* pp. 364, 375–377; *Journal of Ellicott,* pp. 11–12; Schultz, *Travels,* vol. I, p. 189, vol. II, p. 188; *Journal of Asbury,* vol. II, p. 477.

[14] Drake, *Pioneer Life,* pp. 58–60.

[15] Strickland, ed., *Autobiography of Finley,* pp. 73–96, 151–152; Muhlenberg, *Life of Muhlenberg,* p. 438; Drake, *Pioneer Life,* pp. 21–22.

[16] Cutler, *Life of Ephraim Cutler,* p. 31; Drake, *Pioneer Life,* pp. 60–61; Strickland, ed., *Autobiography of Finley,* p. 152.

[17] Samuel Wilkeson, "Early Recollections of the West," Williams, ed., *American Pioneer,* vol. II, pp. 158–159.

[18] Hildreth, *Pioneer History,* pp. 355–356.

[19] Filson, *Kentucke,* pp. 23–24; Baily, *Journal,* pp. 177–182, 223; Drake, *Pioneer Life,* pp. 85–86.

[20] Williams, "Our Cabin," Williams, ed., *American Pioneer,* vol. II, p. 447; also Drake, *Pioneer Life,* pp. 46–47.

[21] Hildreth, *Pioneer History,* pp. 351–358; Drake, *Pioneer Life,* pp. 21, 129–132; Williams, "Our Cabin," Williams, ed., *American Pioneer,* vol. II, pp. 447, 455; Strickland, ed., *Autobiography of Cartwright,* p. 6.

[22] Drake, *Pioneer Life,* pp. 11–13, 47–52, 62–63, 212; Baily, *Journal,* pp. 417–418; Williams, "Our Cabin," Williams, ed., *American Pioneer,* vol. II, p. 451; Strickland, ed., *Autobiography of Finley,* pp. 69, 111–112; Muhlenberg, *Life of Muhlenberg,* p. 447; William Priest, *Travels in the United States of America* (London, 1802), pp. 36–37; John Lambert, *Travels through Lower Canada and the United States of North America in the Years 1806, 1807, and 1808,* 3 vols. (London, 1810), vol. III, pp. 496–497.

[23] Strickland, ed., *Autobiography of Cartwright,* p. 49; see also Williams, "Our Cabin," Williams, ed., *American Pioneer,* vol. II, p. 452; Melish, *Travels,* vol. II, p. 258; Drake, *Pioneer Life,* p. 44.

[24] "Cuming's Tour," Thwaites, ed., *Early Western Travels,* vol. IV, p. 353.

[25] Baily, *Journal,* p. 417.

[26] Drake, *Pioneer Life,* pp. 96–97; Thomas Ashe, *Travels in America Performed in 1806,* 3 vols. (London, 1808), vol. II, pp. 280–281; "John Lipscomb's Diary, 1784," in Samuel Cole Williams, ed., *Early Travels in the Tennessee Country, 1540–1800* (Johnson City, Tenn. 1928), p. 275; Baily, *Journal,* pp. 199–200, 409–410, 423, 438; F. A. Michaux, "Travels," Thwaites, ed., *Early Western Travels,* vol. III, pp. 138–139; Morris Birkbeck, *Notes on a Journey in America, from the Coast of Virginia to the Territory of Illinois* (Philadelphia, 1817), pp. 98–100.

[27] Baily, *Journal,* p. 201; "Cuming's Tour," Thwaites, ed., *Early Western Travels,* vol. IV, p. 221.

[28] Drake, *Pioneer Life,* pp. 107–108, 155, 223.

[29] Brackenridge, *Recollections,* p. 25.

[30] "Cuming's Tour," Thwaites, ed., *Early Western Travels,* vol. IV, pp. 330, 339–341, 352–353; Ashe, *Travels,* vol. III, pp. 261–262; Watson, "Notitia," Williams, ed., *American Pioneer,* vol. II, p. 233; Stoddard, *Sketches,* pp. 325–326. It was mentioned that the Indians and the Negroes were exceedingly fond of the tail of the alligator, John Pope,

A Tour through the Southern and Western Territories of North-America (Richmond, 1792; reprinted New York, 1888), p. 42; Schultz, *Travels*, vol. II, p. 177.

31 "Lipscomb's Diary," Williams, ed., *Early Travels*, p. 272.

32 Drake, *Natural and Statistical View*, pp. 140–142.

33 Strickland, ed., *Autobiography of Finley*, p. 248. See also *Journal of Asbury*, vol. II, p. 37; Drake, *Pioneer Life*, pp. 82–84; F. A. Michaux, "Travels," Thwaites, ed., *Early Western Travels*, vol. III, p. 144; Melish, *Travels*, vol. II, pp. 51–52.

34 Pope, *Tour*, p. 25; also Ashe, *Travels*, vol. II, p. 280; "Letter of George Sempl," Williams, ed., *American Pioneer*, I, 157; *Journal of Asbury*, vol. II, p. 148; Wilkeson, "Early Recollections," Williams, ed., *American Pioneer*, vol. II, p. 215.

35 Mills and Smith, *Report of a Missionary Tour*, p. 43; Baily, *Journal*, p. 310.

36 Schultz, *Travels*, vol. I, pp. 140–141. For Kentucky see F. A. Michaux, "Travels," Thwaites, ed., *Early Western Travels*, vol. III, pp. 223–224; Drake, *Pioneer Life*, pp. 79–80.

37 Schultz, *Travels*, vol. II, pp. 199–200; Watson, "Notitia," Williams, ed., *American Pioneer*, vol. II, p. 233.

38 See Drake, *Pioneer Life*, pp. 70, 76–79, 85, 92–96; "Cuming's Tour," Thwaites, ed., *Early Western Travels*, vol. IV, p. 101; Farrand, ed., *Journey to Ohio*, p. 49.

39 For frontier dress in this period see Strickland, ed., *Autobiography of Finley*, pp. 70, 84–98; Hildreth, *Pioneer History*, pp. 392–393; Williams, "Our Cabin," Williams, ed., *American Pioneer*, vol. II, pp. 453–454; "Letter of Felix Renick," *ibid.*, I, 274; Wilkeson, "Early Recollections," *ibid.*, II, 159–160; Drake, *Pioneer Life*, pp. 68–69, 74, 99–103, 192, 231; "Bradbury's Travels," Thwaites, ed., *Early Western Travels*, vol. V, pp. 284–285; Strickland, ed., *Autobiography of Cartwright*, p. 6.

40 A classic work, by a pioneer doctor, is Daniel Drake, *A Systematic Treatise, Historical, Etiological, and Practical on the Principal Diseases of the Interior Valley of North America*, 2 vols. (Philadelphia, 1850, 1854). See also C. F. Volney, *A View of the Soil and Climate of the United States of America* (Philadelphia, 1804), p. 229; Strickland, ed., *Autobiography of Finley*, p. 107; "Cuming's Tour," Thwaites, ed., *Early Western Travels*, vol. IV, p. 349; "Bradbury's Travels," *ibid.*, vol. V, p. 310; Schultz, *Travels*, vol. II, pp. 22–23; *Journal of Ellicott*, p. 288; Alfred Tischendorf and E. Taylor Parks, eds., *The Diary and Journal of Richard Clough Anderson, Jr., 1814–1826* (Durham, N.C., 1964), pp. 13, 17; Carter, ed., *Territorial Papers*, vol. IX, p. 299.

41 *Navigator* (1814), p. 22.

42 Drake, *Systematic Treatise*, vol. II, p. 594; also Hildreth, *Pioneer History*, pp. 378–379.

43 Muhlenberg, *Life of Muhlenberg*, p. 444; "The Diary of Major William Stanley, 1790–1810," *Quarterly Publication of the Historical and Philosophical Society of Ohio*, XIV (1919), 22; Hildreth, *Pioneer History*, pp. 391–392; Drake, *Natural and Statistical View*, p. 184; Drake, *Systematic Treatise*, vol. II, p. 572, 577.

44 André Michaux, "Travels," Thwaites, ed., *Early Western Travels*, vol. III, p. 92.

45 Drake, *Pioneer Life*, p. 54.

46 *Ibid.*, p. 185.

47 For amusements in these years see *ibid.*, pp. 54–56, 63–66, 132–133, 183–187; Williams, "Our Cabin," Williams, ed., *American Pioneer*, vol. II, pp. 457–458; Strickland, ed., *Autobiography of Finley*, pp. 71–72; Strickland, ed., *Autobiography of Cartwright*, p. 11.

Chapter 7: The Development of Frontier Society

1 Strickland, ed., *Autobiography of Cartwright*, pp. 4–6 for "the barrens." The comment on Knoxville is in "Report of Steiner and Schweinitz," Williams, ed., *Early Travels*, p. 455. For Alabama and for Natchez, see Dow, *History of Cosmopolite*, pp. 164, 218.

2 Mills and Smith, *Report of a Missionary Tour*, p. 8.

3 Ker, *Travels*, p. 41.

4 "Bradbury's Travels," Thwaites, ed., *Early Western Travels*, vol. V, p. 211.

5 "Butler's Journal," Craig, ed., *Olden Time*, vol. II, pp. 493–495.

6 Ashe, *Travels*, vol. II, p. 269; Schultz, *Travels*, vol. I, pp. 202–203.

7 Drake, *Pioneer Life*, p. 189; also *"Cuming's Tour,"* Thwaites, ed., *Early Western Travels*, vol. IV, p. 352.

8 *Ibid.*, vol. IV, pp. 137–138.

9 Melish, *Travels*, vol. II, p. 206; see also *Journal of Ellicott*, p. 25.

10 *Journal of Asbury*, vol. III, p. 134.

11 William W. Sweet, *Religion in the Development of American Culture, 1765–1840* (New York, 1952), p. 91; Clifton E. Olmstead, *History of Religion in the United States* (Englewood Cliffs, N.J., 1960), pp. 218–221; Bernard A. Weisberger, *They Gathered at the River: The Story of the Great Revivalists and their Impact upon Religion in America* (Boston, 1958), pp. 3–19 modifies this view.

12 "Report of Steiner and Schweinitz," Williams, ed., *Early Travels*, p. 513.

13 Sweet, *Religion in the Development of American Culture*, p. 109; William W. Manross, *A History of the American Episcopal Church* (2d ed.; New York, 1950), pp. 172–201, 247–254; Bond, *Civilization of the Old Northwest*, p. 473.

14 John T. Ellis, ed., *Documents of American Catholic History* (2nd ed.; Milwaukee, 1962), pp. 177–179.

15 Olmstead, *History of Religion*, pp. 254–256; Ellis, ed., *Documents of American Catholic History*, pp. 179–184; Mary R. Mattingley, *The Catholic Church on the Kentucky Frontier, 1785–1812* (Washington, D.C., 1936).

16 Olmstead, *History of Religion*, pp. 242–243; Gaius G. Atkins and Frederick L. Fagley, *History of American Congregationalism* (Boston, 1942), pp. 122–148.

17 Ludlum, *Social Ferment in Vermont*, pp. 19–20, 26–30, 40–49; Stilwell, *Migration from Vermont*, pp. 109–112; [Rev. Nathan Perkins], *A Narrative of a Tour Through the State of Vermont from April 27 to June 12, 1789. By the Revd Nathan Perkins of Hartford* (Rutland, Vt., 1964), p. 32.

18 Whitney R. Cross, *The Burned-over District: The Social and Intellectual History of Enthusiastic Religion in Western New York, 1800–1850* (Ithaca, N.Y., 1950), pp. 3–51. Mathews, *Expansion of New England*, pp. 161–164.

19 Cross, *Burned-over District*, pp. 18–21; Olmstead, *History of Religion*, pp. 245–247; Bond, *Civilization of the Old Northwest*, pp. 467–468.

20 There is a general discussion of revivalism in Peter G. Mode, "Revivalism as a Phase of Frontier Life," *Journal of Religion*, I, (July 1921), 337–354. For early signs of revival see Ernest T. Thompson, *Presbyterians in the South*, vol. 1: 1607–1861 (Richmond, Va., 1963), pp. 126–130.

21 Catharine C. Cleveland, *The Great Revival in the West, 1797–1805* (Chicago, 1916), pp. 37–42. The eastern phase of the revival is treated in Charles R. Keller, *The Second Great Awakening in Connecticut* (New Haven, Conn. 1942).

22 Strickland, ed., *Autobiography of Finley*, p. 166.

23 See Cleveland, *Great Revival*, pp. 62–85; Charles A. Johnson, *The Frontier Camp Meeting: Religion's Harvest Time* (Dallas, 1955), pp. 41–68; Dow, *History of Cosmopolite*, p. 235; F. A. Michaux, "Travels," Thwaites, ed., *Early Western Travels*, vol. III, pp. 248–249.

24 Strickland, ed., *Autobiography of Finley*, p. 165.

25 Cleveland, *Great Revival*, pp. 87–127; Johnson, *Frontier Camp Meeting*, pp. 208–228; Dow, *History of Cosmopolite*, pp. 181–183, 214–215; Strickland, ed., *Autobiography of Cartwright*, pp. 19–22.

26 Cleveland, *Great Revival*, p. 164.

27 Strickland, ed., *Autobiography of Cartwright*, p. ix.

[28] *Ibid.*, pp. x, 14–15; also Elizabeth K. Nottingham, *Methodism on the Frontier: Indiana Proving Ground* (New York, 1941). p. 44; Olmstead, *History of Religion*, pp. 251–252; Schermerhorn and Mills, *Correct View*, pp. 40–41; *Journal of Asbury*, vol. II, pp. 84–85, 479, vol. III, p. 125.

[29] *Ibid.*, vol. II, p. 476; Olmstead, *History of Religion*, p. 253; James M. Miller, *The Genesis of Western Culture: The Upper Ohio Valley, 1800–1825* (Columbus, 1938), p. 125.

[30] Bond, *Civilization of the Old Northwest*, pp. 475–477; Edwin S. Gaustad, *Historical Atlas of Religion in America* (New York, 1962), pp. 74–78; Emory S. Bucke, ed., *History of American Methodism, 3 vols.* (New York, 1964), vol. I, pp. 488–545.

[31] William W. Sweet, *Religion on the American Frontier: The Baptists, 1783–1830: A Collection of Source Material* (New York, 1931), pp. 36–57; Walter B. Posey, *The Baptist Church in the Lower Mississippi Valley, 1776–1845* (Lexington, Ky., 1957), pp. 18–37; Nottingham, *Methodism on the Frontier*, pp. 43–44; Schermerhorn and Mills, *Correct View*, pp. 38–40.

[32] Sweet, *Religion on the American Frontier: The Baptists*, pp. 18–35; Posey, *Baptist Church in the Lower Mississippi Valley*, pp. 5, 140; Williams, *History of the Lost State of Franklin*, pp. 270–274; Ludlum, *Social Ferment in Vermont*, p. 35; Bond, *Civilization of the Old Northwest*, pp. 470–473; Rudolph, *Hoosier Zion*, pp. 20–36; Filson, *Kentucke*, p. 29; Schermerhorn and Mills, *Correct View*, p. 32.

[33] Mills and Smith, *Report of a Missionary Tour*, p. 16.

[34] William W. McKinney, *Early Pittsburgh Presbyterianism* (Pittsburgh, 1938), pp. 67–152; Gaustad, *Historical Atlas of Religion*, p. 21; Bond, *Civilization of the Old Northwest*, pp. 468–470; Rudolph, *Hoosier Zion*, p. 42; Schermerhorn and Mills, *Correct View*, pp. 35–37.

[35] Ernest T. Thompson, *Presbyterians in the South*, vol. 1: 1607–1861 (Richmond, Va., 1963), pp. 112–118, 144–155; Sweet, *Religion in the Development of American Culture*, pp. 216–219; Schermerhorn and Mills, *Correct View*, pp. 37–38.

[36] Sweet, *Religion in the Development of American Culture*, pp. 219–224; Schermerhorn and Mills, *Correct View*, pp. 30–31, 41–42; Thompson, *Presbyterians in the South*, vol. I, pp. 155–165.

[37] Miller, *Genesis of Western Culture*, pp. 131–134; Bond, *Civilization of the Old Northwest*, pp. 487–489; Edward D. Andrews, *The People Called Shakers: A Search for the Perfect Society* (New York, 1953), pp. 70–93.

[38] Bond, *Civilization of the Old Northwest*, pp. 491–492.

[39] *Ibid.*, p. 127.

[40] See petition from Mississippi Territory, November 26, 1798, Carter, ed., *Territorial Papers*, vol. V, pp. 50–51. The inhabitants of Wayne County asked for a land grant to support religion in their petition of September 2, 1800, "religion & Morality being essentially necessary to the well being & support of a free Government," *ibid.*, vol. III, p. 105.

[41] For the Ohio efforts see Bond, *Civilization of the Old Northwest*, pp. 133–134; quotation is from Schermerhorn and Mills, *Correct View*, p. 12.

[42] Strickland, ed., *Autobiography of Finley*, pp. 229–230; *Journal of Asbury*, vol. III, p. 127.

[43] Schermerhorn and Mills, *Correct View*, p. 17 (1812); Melish, *Travels*, vol. II, p. 226.

[44] Hildreth, *Pioneer History*, p. 379; Melish, *Travels*, vol. II, p. 354.

[45] See Cutler, *Life of Ephraim Cutler*, p. 88; Williams, "Our Cabin," Williams, ed., *American Pioneer*, II, 456; Wilkeson, "Early Recollections," *ibid.*, II, 204; Drake, *Pioneer Life*, pp. 142–155; Thomas Dilworth, *A New Guide to the English Tongue* (new ed.; Boston, 1789), p. 6; Strickland, ed., *Autobiography of Finley*, pp. 154–155; "Report of Steiner

and Schweinitz," Williams, ed., *Early Travels*, p. 517; F. A. Michaux, "Travels," Thwaites, ed., *Early Western Travels*, vol. III, p. 250.

[46] Petition of December 31, 1801, Carter, ed., *Territorial Papers*, vol. III, pp. 43–44; John Badollet to Gallatin, June 30, 1812, Thornbrough, ed., *Correspondence of Badollet and Gallatin*, p. 245.

[47] For education in Ohio in these years see Miller, *Genesis of Western Culture*, pp. 71, 100–103; Bond, *Civilization of the Old Northwest*, pp. 424–430; W. H. Venable, *Beginnings of Literary Culture in the Ohio Valley* (Cincinnati, 1891), pp. 172–196. For land grants see George W. Knight, "History and Management of Land Grants for Education in the Northwest Territory," American Historical Association, *Papers*, vol. I, no. 3, pp. 79–247. For Mississippi's problems see Carter, ed., *Territorial Papers*, vol. V, pp. 181–182, 588–589, vol. VI, pp. 344–345, 465–466, 480–481.

[48] Ludlum, *Social Ferment in Vermont*, pp. 222–224.

[49] Thomas D. Clark, *History of Kentucky* (New York, 1937). pp. 303–310; Schermerhorn and Mills, *Correct View*, pp. 24, 26.

[50] Miller, *Genesis of Western Culture*, pp. 106–107; Clark, *History of Kentucky*, pp. 320–327. See also Niels H. Sonne, *Liberal Kentucky, 1780–1828* (New York, 1939), pp. 46–77.

[51] For Ohio see Bond, *Civilization of the Old Northwest*, pp. 428–429; Miller, *Genesis of Western Culture*, pp. 101–102. There is mention of the Tennessee colleges in Schermerhorn and Mills, *Correct View*, p. 26, and of those in western Pennsylvania in Mills and Smith, *Report of a Missionary Tour*, pp. 7–8.

[52] "Cuming's Tour," Thwaites, ed., *Early Western Travels*, vol. IV, p. 352; Stoddard, *Sketches*, pp. 309–310.

[53] Carter, ed., *Territorial Papers*, vol. VII. pp. 492–493, vol. VIII, pp. 357–360; Bond, *Civilization of the Old Northwest*, pp. 426, 430–431. Similar efforts were made in Louisiana, where there was only slow educational development in this period, see Carter, ed., *Territorial Papers*, vol. IX, pp. 21–22, 38, 231–232, 424–425, 543–544, 1016.

[54] Melish, *Travels*, vol. II, p. 238.

[55] Ralph L. Rusk, *The Literature of the Middle Western Frontier*, 2 vols. (New York, 1925), vol. I, pp. 143–145. 156; Walter Sutton, *The Western Book Trade: Cincinnati as a Nineteenth Century Publishing and Book Trade Center* (Columbus, 1961). pp. 10–12.

[56] Miller, *Genesis of Western Culture*, pp. 77, 80–90; Rusk, *Literature of the Middle Western Frontier*, vol. I, pp. 132–141; Venable, *Beginnings of Literary Culture*, pp. 37–40; Abernethy, *Frontier to Plantation*, pp. 130, 199, 206; Bond, *Civilization of the Old Northwest*, pp. 437–450.

[57] Wade, *Urban Frontier*, p. 130.

[58] Bond, *Civilization of the Old Northwest*, pp. 432–436; Miller, *Genesis of Western Culture*, p. 160; Sutton, *Western Book Trade*, pp. 19, 26.

[59] Howard H. Peckham, "Books and Reading on the Ohio Valley Frontier." *Mississippi Valley Historical Review*, XLIV (March 1958), pp. 650–653, 657–663; Miller, *Genesis of Western Culture*, pp. 78–80.

[60] David Kaser, *Joseph Charless: Printer in the Western Country* (Philadelphia, 1963). pp. 36–41, 49–50.

[61] Louis B. Wright, *Culture on the Moving Frontier* (Bloomington, Ind., 1955), pp. 72, 118; Miller, *Genesis of Western Culture*, pp. 147–151; Venable, *Beginnings of Literary Culture*, pp. 129–147; 263–264; Ray A. Billington, *America's Frontier Heritage* (Billington, ed., "Histories of the American Frontier" series; New York, 1966), pp. 82–84. Peckham, "Books and Reading," *Mississippi Valley Historical Review*, XLIV, 653–657; Drake, *Natural and Statistical View*, p. 160.

[62] Rusk, *Literature of the Middle Western Frontier*, vol. I, pp. 352–364, 435–436;

Miller, *Genesis of Western Culture,* pp. 153–155; Bond, *Civilization of the Old Northwest,* pp. 453–455.

63 Melish, *Travels,* vol. II, pp. 186–189; "Cuming's Tour," Thwaites, ed., *Early Western Travels,* vol. IV, pp. 187–188; *Navigator* (1814), pp. 263–264.

64 *Navigator* (1814), p. 356.

Chapter 8: The Growth of Frontier Prosperity

1 Stilwell, *Migration from Vermont,* pp. 9–10, 98–101. There is a discussion of agricultural development in Maine in these years in Day, *History of Maine Agriculture,* pp. 66–107.

2 Percy W. Bidwell and John I. Falconer, *History of Agriculture in the Northern United States, 1620–1860* (1925; reprinted New York, 1941), pp. 171, 177–178; McNall, *Agricultural History of the Genesee Valley,* pp. 88–92; Bond, *Civilization of the Old Northwest,* pp. 319–324; William T. Utter, *The Frontier State, 1803–1825* (Carl Wittke, ed., *The History of the State of Ohio,* vol. II; Columbus, 1942), pp. 120–172.

3 Bond, *Civilization of the Old Northwest,* pp. 344–349; Carter, ed., *Territorial Papers,* vol. VIII, pp. 224–226, 311–312.

4 Gray, *History of Agriculture in the Southern United States,* vol. II, pp. 754–755, 875–877; Ambler, *Sectionalism in Virginia,* pp. 45–47; James F. Hopkins, *A History of the Hemp Industry in Kentucky* (Lexington, 1951).

5 Gray, *History of Agriculture in the Southern United States,* vol. II, pp. 687, 754–755, 766, 878; Abernethy, *Frontier to Plantation,* pp. 150–151; F. A. Michaux, "Travels," Thwaites, ed., *Early Western Travels,* vol. III, pp. 276–277.

6 John H. Moore, *Agriculture in Ante-Bellum Mississippi* (New York, 1958), pp. 19–32; Gray, *History of Agriculture in the Southern United States,* vol. II, p. 688; Baily, *Journal,* pp. 285–286.

7 Eaton, *Growth of Southern Civilization,* p. 133; Gray, *History of Agriculture in the Southern United States,* vol. II, pp. 687–689, 739–740, 896–897; Abernethy, *South in the New Nation,* p. 257; J. Carlyle Sitterson, *Sugar Country: The Cane Sugar Industry in the South, 1753–1950* (Lexington, Ky., 1953), pp. 3–28.

8 Melish, *Travels,* vol. II, p. 234.

9 Wade, *Urban Frontier,* pp. 43–45.

10 Hildreth, *Pioneer History,* p. 473; Randolph C. Downes, "Trade in Frontier Ohio," *Mississippi Valley Historical Review,* vol. XVI (March 1930), pp. 472–494.

11 Melish, *Travels,* vol. II, p. 395.

12 Stilwell, *Migration from Vermont,* pp. 10, 104–105; Curtis P. Nettels, *The Emergence of a National Economy, 1775–1815* (Henry David *et. al.,* eds., *The Economic History of the United States,* vol. II, New York, 1962), p. 174; Lincklaen, *Journals,* p. 86; Lambert, *Travels,* vol. III, p. 476; McNall, *Agricultural History of the Genesee Valley,* pp. 88–89, 176; Bidwell and Falconer, *History of Agriculture,* p. 171.

13 Charles H. Ambler, *A History of Transportation in the Ohio Valley* (Glendale, Calif., 1932), pp. 35–37; Baldwin, *Keelboat Age,* p. 184.

14 Abernethy, *Frontier to Plantation,* p. 155; Gray, *History of Agriculture in the Southern United States,* vol. II, pp. 868–869; F. A. Michaux, "Travels," Thwaites, ed., *Early Western Travels,* vol. III, pp. 265–266, 280–282.

15 Downes, "Trade in Frontier Ohio," *Mississippi Valley Historical Review,* XVI, 493–494; Paul C. Henlein, *Cattle Kingdom in the Ohio Valley, 1783–1860* (Lexington, Ky., 1959), pp. 8–11.

16 Cutler, *Life of Ephraim Cutler,* pp. 89–103; also Strickland, ed., *Autobiography of Finley,* p. 115; Melish, *Travels,* vol. II, p. 249.

17 F. A. Michaux, "Travels," Thwaites, ed., *Early Western Travels,* vol. III, pp. 243–247.

[18] Baldwin, *Keelboat Age*, pp. 68–70, 81–83; George Rogers Taylor, "Prices in the Mississippi Valley Preceding the War of 1812," *Journal of Economic and Business History*, III (November 1930), 148.

[19] Whitaker, *Mississippi Question*, pp. 79–85; Baldwin, *Keelboat Age*, pp. 20–29.

[20] Wilkeson, "Early Recollections," Williams, ed., *American Pioneer*, vol. II, p. 163.

[21] F. A. Michaux, "Travels," Thwaites, ed., *Early Western Travels*, vol. III, pp. 156–160; Thaddeus Mason Harris, "Journal of a Tour Northwest of the Alleghany Mountains, 1803," *ibid.*, vol. III, p. 343; Baily, *Journal*, p. 148; Schultz, *Travels*, vol. II, p. 11.

[22] Harris, "Journal," Thwaites, ed., *Early Western Travels*, vol. III, pp. 343–344; F. A. Michaux, "Travels," *ibid.*, vol. III, pp. 191–192; Schultz, *Travels*, vol. II, pp. 21–22; Drake, *Pioneer Life*, p. 235.

[23] "Cuming's Tour," Thwaites, ed., *Early Western Travels*, vol. IV, p. 116; *Navigator* (1814), p. 33.

[24] "Diary of Stanley," *Quarterly Publication of the Historical and Philosophical Society of Ohio*, XIV, 22–23; Baily, *Journal*, p. 201; cf. Birkbeck, *Notes on a Journey*, pp. 116–117.

[25] Bond, *Civilization of the Old Northwest*, pp. 401–405; Bray Hammond, *Banks and Politics in America, from the Revolution to the Civil War* (Princeton, N.J., 1957), pp. 170–171; John Jay Knox, *A History of Banking in the United States* (New York, 1900), pp. 668–669, 692; Wade, *Urban Frontier*, p. 69; Utter, *The Frontier State*, pp. 264–272; Drake, *Natural and Statistical View*, pp. 150–151.

[26] Ashe, *Travels*, vol. II, p. 176; Drake, *Natural and Statistical View*, pp. 148–149.

[27] Espy, "Memorandums of a Tour," *Ohio Valley Historical Series, Miscellanies*, no. 1, p. 8.

[28] Ashe, *Travels*, vol. II, pp. 151–152; Wade, *Urban Frontier*, pp. 49–53, 64–66.

[29] "Report of Steiner and Schweinitz," Williams, ed., *Early Travels*, pp. 516–517; F. A. Michaux, "Travels," Thwaites, ed., *Early Western Travels*, vol. III, pp. 250–252.

[30] Whitaker, *Mississippi Question*, pp. 51–52, 85–97, 130–154, 189–236; Bemis, *Pinckney's Treaty*, pp. 335–358; Wade, *Urban Frontier*, pp. 39–42.

[31] Baldwin, *Keelboat Age*, pp. 42–49, 66, 124–127, 182–186; W. Wallace Carson, "Transportation and Traffic on the Ohio and Mississippi before the Steamboat," *Mississippi Valley Historical Review*, VII (June 1920), 26–38; Wilkeson, "Early Recollections," Williams, ed., *American Pioneer*, vol. II, p. 163; F. A. Michaux, "Travels," Thwaites, ed., *Early Western Travels*, vol. III, pp. 159–160, 239.

[32] Dawson A. Phelps, "Travel on the Natchez Trace: A Study of its Economic Aspects," *The Journal of Mississippi History*, XV (July 1953), 155–164; Robert S. Cotterill, "The Natchez Trace," *Tennessee Historical Magazine*, VII (April 1921), 27–35.

[33] Schultz, *Travels*, vol. II, p. 200; Melish, *Travels*, vol. II, p. 259; Ashe, *Travels*, vol. III, pp. 253–254, 259; *Navigator* (1814), pp. 14–15.

[34] Taylor, "Prices in the Mississippi Valley," *Journal of Economic and Business History*, vol. III, pp. 154–163.

[35] Victor S. Clark, *History of Manufactures in the United States*, 3 vols. (rev. ed.; New York, 1929), vol. I, pp. 438–440; Buck, *Planting of Civilization in Western Pennsylvania*, pp. 273–287; Isaac Lippincott, *A History of Manufactures in the Ohio Valley to the year 1860* (New York, 1914), p. 40; Bidwell and Falconer, *History of Agriculture in the Northern United States*, pp. 126–131.

[36] Journal of Arthur Lee" (1784), Craig, ed., *Olden Time*, vol. II, p. 339; Collot, *Journey*, vol. I, pp. 37–39; Abernethy, *Frontier to Plantation*, p. 152.

[37] Baldwin, *Keelboat Age*, pp. 52–53, 161–174; Ambler, *History of Transportation in the Ohio Valley*, pp. 81–106; Archer B. Hulbert, "Western Ship-Building," *American Historical Review*, XXI (July, 1916), 720–733; Schultz, *Travels*, vol. I, pp. 142–143. The first steamboats were introduced on western rivers only at the end of this period. The *New Orleans* sailed from Pittsburgh to New Orleans in 1812, see Louis C. Hunter, *Steam-*

boats on the Western Rivers: An Economic and Technological History (Cambridge, Mass., 1949), pp. 6–19.

38 F. A. Michaux, "Travels," Thwaites, ed., *Early Western Travels,* vol. III, p. 200; "Cuming's Tour," Thwaites, ed., *Early Western Travels,* vol. IV, p. 186.

39 "Cuming's Tour," *ibid.,* vol. IV, pp. 185–187; Hammond, *Banks and Politics,* pp. 168–170; Wade, *Urban Frontier,* pp. 51–52, 69.

40 "Cuming's Tour," Thwaites, ed., *Early Western Travels,* vol. IV, p. 255.

41 *Ibid.,* vol. IV, pp. 245–255; Schultz, *Travels,* vol. I, pp. 124–126.

42 Melish, *Travels,* vol. II, p. 60.

43 *Ibid.,* vol. II, pp. 54–58; Dow, *History of Cosmopolite,* p. 339.

44 Melish, *Travels,* vol. II, pp. 373, 378, 381–383, 384–391.

45 *Ibid.,* vol. II, pp. 126–128, 220; Sears, *Thomas Worthington,* pp. 26–27.

46 Melish, *Travels,* vol. II, pp. 149, 179, 181, 185–189.

47 *Ibid.,* vol. II, p. 105; Pope, *Tour,* p. 27; Baldwin, *Keelboat Age,* p. 66.

48 *Navigator* (1814), pp. 28–29, 110; Drake, *Natural and Statistical View,* pp. 148–150; "Cuming's Tour," Thwaites, ed., *Early Western Travels,* vol. IV, p. 91.

49 F. A. Michaux, "Travels," Thwaites, ed., *Early Western Travels,* vol. III, p. 280; Melish, *Travels,* vol. II, pp. 59–60; Schultz, *Travels,* vol. II, pp. 54–56, 73–74; *Navigator* (1814), pp. 18–22.

50 *Navigator* (1814), p. 58, also pp. 55–67.

51 Drake, *Natural and Statistical View,* pp. 137–138; Ker, *Travels,* p. 319.

52 F. A. Michaux, "Travels," Thwaites, ed., *Early Western Travels,* vol. III, p. 201; Melish, *Travels,* vol. II, pp. 56–58, 127–128, 186–189, 253, 372; *Navigator* (1814), p. 264.

Chapter 9:   The West and the War of 1812

1 The Anglo-American problems of these years are treated in detail in Burt, *United States, Great Britain,* pp. 1–165, and in Bemis, *Jay's Treaty, passim.* The standard work on British-American relations in the years of rapprochement is Bradford Perkins. *The First Rapprochement: England and the United States, 1795–1805* (Philadelphia, 1955). The decline of Franco-American relations is considered in Alexander De Conde, *Entangling Alliance: Politics and Diplomacy under George Washington* (Durham, N.C., 1958), and *The Quasi-War: The Politics and Diplomacy of the Undeclared War with France, 1797–1801* (New York, 1966).

2 Commercial relations between England and the United States in the 1803–1807 period are discussed in Reginald Horsman, *The Causes of the War of 1812* (Philadelphia, 1962), pp. 24–122, and in Bradford Perkins, *Prologue to War: England and the United States, 1805–1812* (Berkeley and Los Angeles, Calif., 1961), pp. 1–222.

3 For the renewal of British interest in the Indians in 1807–1808 see Horsman, *Matthew Elliott,* pp. 157–176.

4 The best presentation of the case of the importance of the demand for the Floridas is in Julius W. Pratt, *Expansionists of 1812* (New York, 1925), pp. 60–125.

5 Taylor, "Prices in the Mississippi Valley," *Journal of Economic and Business History,* III, 148; George R. Taylor, "Agrarian Discontent in the Mississippi Valley Preceding the War of 1812," *Journal of Political Economy,* XXXIX (1931), 471–505; Horsman, *Causes of the War of 1812,* pp. 174–175.

6 There are recent treatments of the War Hawks in Reginald Horsman, "Who Were the War Hawks?" and Roger H. Brown, "The War Hawks of 1812: An Historical Myth," *Indiana Magazine of History,* LX (June 1964), 121–151. Roger H. Brown, *The Republic in Peril: 1812* (New York, 1964) presents a detailed treatment of the Twelfth Congress, and Norman K. Risjord, "1812: Conservatives, War Hawks, and the Nation's Honor," *William and Mary Quarterly,* 3d Series, XVIII (April 1961), 196–210 stresses the importance of national honor in the coming of the war.

[7] *Annals of Congress,* 12th Cong., 1st Sess., pp. 599, 457, 424; Horsman, *Causes of the War of 1812,* pp. 229–232.

[8] Horsman, *Causes of the War of 1812,* pp. 237–242.

[9] Perkins, *Prologue to War,* pp. 403–415; Brown, *Republic in Peril,* pp. 44–45 and *passim;* Horsman, *Causes of the War of 1812;* pp. 260–262, 293.

[10] See Thomas D. Clark, "Kentucky in the Northwest Campaign," Horsman, "The Role of the Indian in the War," and C. P. Stacey, "Naval Power on the Lakes, 1812–1814," in Philip P. Mason, ed., *After Tippecanoe: Some Aspects of the War of 1812* (East Lansing, Mich., 1963), pp. 78–87, 63–64, 49–52; also Horsman, *Expansion and American Indian Policy.*

[11] These events west of Lake Michigan are treated in more detail in Reginald Horsman, "Wisconsin and the War of 1812," *Wisconsin Magazine of History,* XLVI (Autumn 1962), 3–15, and in Louise P. Kellogg, *The British Régime in Wisconsin and the Northwest* (Madison, Wis., 1935), pp. 283–329. See also Ninian W. Edwards, *History of Illinois from 1778 to 1833; and Life and Times of Ninian Edwards* (Springfield, Ill., 1870), pp. 294–348.

[12] Alec R. Gilpin, *The War of 1812 in the Old Northwest* (East Lansing, Mich., 1958), pp. 23–125.

[13] See Henry Adams, *History of the United States,* 9 vols. (New York, 1889–1891), vol. VI, pp. 336–361.

[14] Gilpin, *War of 1812 in the Old Northwest,* pp. 126–234; Horsman, "The Role of the Indian in the War," Mason, ed., *After Tippecanoe,* pp. 69–74.

[15] Kellogg, *British Régime,* pp. 313–316.

[16] John Spencer Bassett, ed., *The Correspondence of Andrew Jackson,* 7 vols. (Washington, 1926–1935), vol. I, pp. 242–243, 252–253, 256–268, 275–276, 291–292; James Parton, *Life of Andrew Jackson,* 3 vols. (Boston, 1887), vol. I, pp. 360–386; Pratt, *Expansionists of 1812,* pp. 218–231.

[17] Ferdinand L. Claiborne to General Flournoy, September 3, 1813, John Brannan, ed., *Official Letters of the Military and Naval Officers of the United States during the War with Great Britain in the Years 1812, 13, 14 & 15* (Washington, 1823), pp. 202–205.

[18] Bassett, ed., *Jackson Correspondence,* vol. I, pp. 319–320, 326–328, 331, 336–337, 341; Brannan, ed., *Official Letters,* pp. 255–256.

[19] Bassett, ed., *Jackson Correspondence,* vol. I, 348–350; Brannan. ed., *Official Letters,* pp. 264–266.

[20] Brannan, ed., *Official Letters,* pp. 281–285; Bassett, ed., *Jackson Correspondence,* vol. I, pp. 345–346, 354–355, 361.

[21] Jackson to his wife, April 1, 1814, Bassett, ed., *Jackson Correspondence,* vol. I, pp. 492–494, also pp. 444–454, 488–492; Jackson to Thomas Pinckney, March 28, 1814, Brannan, ed., *Official Letters,* pp. 319–320, also 294–305. The Creek campaigns are treated in Parton, *Life of Jackson,* vol. I, pp. 411–457; Adams, *History of the United States,* vol. VII, pp. 206–244; Eron Rowland, *Andrew Jackson's Campaign Against the British, or the Mississippi Territory in the War of 1812* (New York, 1926), pp. 26–218.

[22] 7 U.S. *Statutes at Large,* pp. 120–122; Bassett, ed., *Jackson Correspondence,* vol. II, p. 24.

[23] Adams, *History of the United States,* vol. VIII, pp. 91–119.

[24] *Ibid.,* vol. VIII, pp. 120–173; Francis F. Beirne, *The War of 1812* (New York, 1949), pp. 264–288, 308–321.

[25] For the peace negotiations see Bradford Perkins, *Castlereagh and Adams: England and the United States, 1812–1823* (Berkeley and Los Angeles, Calif., 1964), pp. 20–155.

[26] Adams, *History of the United States,* vol. VIII, pp. 311–385; Parton, *Life of Jackson,* vol. II, pp. 11–232; see also Charles B. Brooks, *The Siege of New Orleans* (Seattle, 1961).

BIBLIOGRAPHICAL NOTES

There is an abundance of both primary and secondary materials on the West in the years between 1783 and 1815. Each chapter could well use the space that can be allowed for the whole bibliography. Manuscript collections devoted to these years are abundant in the research libraries east of the Mississippi River. The National Archives in Washington, D.C., are particularly important for records relating to the Confederation period, to the government in the territories, and to military and Indian policy, and the program of microfilming is now making these records generally available. The Library of Congress is, of course, rich in collections of personal correspondence; most useful for the West in this period are the collections of William Henry Harrison, Andrew Jackson, and Thomas Worthington. Among the other eastern libraries the most valuable holdings are probably in the Massachusetts Historical Society, with the Timothy Pickering and the Henry Knox Papers, and in the Historical Society of Pennsylvania in Philadelphia; there is also extensive material in the libraries of the state historical societies and in regional societies. In the Mississippi Valley there is an abundance of resources, much of it in the state historical societies, of which the State Historical Society of Wisconsin is probably richest in its holdings for this period.

Western history during these years has also benefited from the extensive publication of primary sources. Indispensable is Clarence E. Carter, ed., *The Territorial Papers of the United States* (Washington, 1934–   ) and there is considerable information of value in many of the publications devoted to national history, particularly *American State Papers*, 38 vols. (Washington, 1832–1861). There is also an abundance of material in the state publications among which are the *Michigan Pioneer and Historical Collections,* 40 vols. (Lansing, Mich., 1877–1929); *Collections of the State Historical Society of Wisconsin,* 31 vols. (Madison, Wis., 1854–1931); *Collections of the Illinois State Historical Library* (Springfield, Ill., 1903–   ); and the *Indiana Historical Collections* (Indianapolis, 1916–   ).

The census reports for these first decades of the new country are sketchy in the extreme, but they at least show the population trends, and at times it is possible to secure a little more. Particularly useful in this regard is Tench Coxe, *A Statement of the Arts and Manufactures of the United States for the Year 1810* (Philadelphia, 1814), which was derived from the third census. There are a number of publications which help with the problem of population. Among the more useful are Stella H. Sutherland, *Population Distribution in Colonial America* (New York, 1936), Evarts B. Greene and Virginia D. Harrington, *American Population before the Federal Census of 1790* (New York, 1932), and several publications by the Bureau of the Census, particularly *Historical Statistics of the United States. Colonial Times to 1957* (Washington, 1960).

There are a number of general histories dealing with the West at this time. John Anthony Caruso's, *The Appalachian Frontier: America's First Surge Westward* (Indianapolis, 1959) and *The Great Lakes Frontier: An Epic of the Old Northwest*

(Indianapolis, 1961) both present readable accounts. Dale Van Every in *The Ark of Empire: The American Frontier, 1784–1803* (New York, 1963) and *The Final Challenge: The American Frontier, 1804–1845* (New York, 1964) stresses dramatic aspects of the frontier. Francis S. Philbrick, *The Rise of the West, 1754–1830* (Henry S. Commager and Richard B. Morris, eds., "New American Nation" series; New York, 1965) emphasizes political, legal, and diplomatic aspects.

Travel Accounts, Contemporary Narratives

Contemporary narratives of these years are quite abundant. They have been listed and described in several excellent publications. Of great value are Thomas D. Clark, ed., *Travels in the Old South: A Bibliography*, 3 vols. (Norman, Okla., 1956–1959), and Robert R. Hubach, *Early Midwestern Travel Narratives: An Annotated Bibliography, 1634–1850* (Detroit, 1961). These can be supplemented by William Matthews, comp., *An Annotated Bibliography of American Diaries Written Prior to the Year 1861* (Boston, 1959), and Robert W. G. Vail, *The Voice of the Old Frontier* (Philadelphia, 1949).

There are a number of publications which provide a group of travel accounts. The most comprehensive is Reuben G. Thwaites, ed., *Early Western Travels, 1748–1846*, 32 vols. (Cleveland, 1904–1907). Two older publications which contain useful material are Neville B. Craig, ed., *The Olden Time*, 2 vols. (Pittsburgh, 1846; reprinted Cincinnati, 1876) and John S. Williams, ed., the *American Pioneer*, 2 vols. (Cincinnati, 1842–1843). Samuel C. Williams, ed., *Early Travels in the Tennessee Country, 1540–1800* (Johnson City, Tenn., 1928) provides narratives for a particular region, and there are selections in John W. Harpster, ed., *Pen Pictures of Early Western Pennsylvania* (Pittsburgh, 1938).

Westerners provide accounts of their region in a number of works. A classic book of promotion by an early Kentucky resident is John Filson, *The Discovery, Settlement, and Present State of Kentucke* (Wilmington, Del., 1784). There is more Filson material in "Two Westward Journeys of John Filson, 1785," ed. by Beverley W. Bond, Jr., *Mississippi Valley Historical Review*, IX (March 1923), 320–330. Of great interest is Daniel Drake, *Pioneer Life in Kentucky. A Series of Reminiscential Letters from Daniel Drake, M.D. of Cincinnati to his Children*, ed. by Charles D. Drake (Cincinnati, 1870). There are a few details on the Louisville region at the end of this period in Alfred Tischendorf and E. Taylor Parks, ed., *The Diary and Journal of Richard Clough Anderson, Jr., 1814–1826* (Durham, N.C., 1964). An interesting contrast is provided by Henry A. Muhlenberg's journal of a trip to the falls of the Ohio in 1784, which is in the appendix to Henry A. Muhlenberg, *The Life of Major-General Peter Muhlenberg of the Revolutionary Army* (Philadelphia, 1849).

Valuable source materials on early Ohio are contained in S. P. Hildreth, *Pioneer History* (Cincinnati, 1848) and in Julia P. Cutler, *Life and Times of Ephraim Cutler Prepared from his Journals and Correspondence* (Cincinnati, 1890). An early description of the same region is in Dwight L. Smith, ed., *The Western Journals of John May* (Cincinnati, 1961). Daniel Drake, who moved from Kentucky to Ohio, demonstrated his considerable ability in his *Natural and Statistical View or Picture of Cincinnati and the Miami Country* (Cincinnati, 1815). There is a lively account of the route to Ohio in Max Farrand, ed., *A Journey to Ohio in 1810 As Recorded in the Journal of Margaret Van Horn Dwight* (New Haven, Conn., 1912).

There is a well-written description of settlements on the Mississippi in Henry M. Brackenridge, *Views of Louisiana: Together With a Journal of a Voyage up the Missouri in 1811* (Pittsburgh 1814; reprinted Chicago, 1962). The same author has an interesting volume of reminiscences in his *Recollections of Persons and Places in the West* (Philadelphia, 1834). A useful account by a soldier stationed on the lower Mississippi is that of Major Amos Stoddard, *Sketches, Historical and Descriptive of Louisiana* (Philadelphia, 1812).

In the 1790s and after 1800 the number of accounts, by foreigners as well as Americans, greatly increased. There is some information in books by two Frenchmen: C. F. Volney, *A View of the Soil and Climate of the United States of America* (Philadelphia, 1804; trs. by C. B. Brown) was in America from 1795 to 1798; and Victor Collot, *A Journey in North America*, 2 vols. (Paris, 1826) traveled west in 1796. The British came in greater numbers than the French. Of the early journals perhaps the best is Francis Baily, *Journal of a Tour in Unsettled Parts of North America in 1796 & 1797* (London, 1856), but the classic English account is John Melish, *Travels in the United States of America in the Years 1806 & 1807, and 1809, 1810 & 1811*, 2 vols. (Philadelphia, 1812). A very unfriendly English account is provided by Thomas Ashe, *Travels in America, Performed in 1806* (London, 1808), who plagiarizes more than most.

Among the other accounts which proved of use for this book are John Lincklaen, *Travels in the Years 1791 and 1792 in Pennsylvania, New York, and Vermont* (New York, 1897); John Pope, *A Tour through the Southern and Western Territories of the United States of North-America* (Richmond, 1792; reprinted New York, 1888); Isaac Weld, Jr., *Travels Through the States of North America and the Provinces of Upper and Lower Canada during the Years 1795, 1796, and 1797* (London, 1799); *The Journal of Andrew Ellicott . . . 1796, 1797, 1798, 1799, 1800* (Philadelphia, 1803); Christian Schultz, Jr., *Travels on an Inland Voyage . . . in the Years 1807 and 1808*, 2 vols. (New York, 1810); Henry Ker, *Travels through the Western Interior of the United States from the Year 1808 up to the Year 1816* (Elizabethtown, N.J., 1816).

Shorter, but of interest are "A Memorandum of M. Austin's Journey from the Lead Mines in the County of Wythe in the State of Virginia to the Lead Mines in the Province of Louisiana West of the Mississippi, 1796–1797," *American Historical Review*, V (April 1900), 518–542; Josiah Espy, "Memorandums of a Tour made by Josiah Espy in the States of Ohio and Kentucky and Indiana Territory in 1805," *Ohio Valley Historical Series, Miscellanies*, no. 1 (Cincinnati, 1870); "Personal Narrative of William Lytle," *The Quarterly Publication of the Historical and Philosophical Society of Ohio*, I (1906), 3–30; "The Diary of Major William Stanley, 1790–1810," *ibid.*, XIV (1919), 19–32.

The journals, diaries, and reminiscences of clergymen are often useful for more than the religious history of these years. Among the best for the West in this period are Francis Asbury, *Journal of Rev. Francis Asbury*, 3 vols. (New York, 1852); E. G. Holland, *Memoir of Rev. Joseph Badger* (3d ed.; New York, 1854); W. P. Strickland, ed., *The Backwoods Preacher: An Autobiography of Peter Cartwright* (London, 1858); Lorenzo Dow, *History of Cosmopolite* (Wheeling, Va., 1848); W. F. Strickland, *Autobiography of Rev. James B. Finley, or, Pioneer Life in the West* (Cincinnati, 1857). Two comprehensive reports of great interest are Samuel J. Mills and Daniel Smith, *Report of a Missionary Tour through that Part of the United States which Lies West of the Allegany Mountains performed under the Direction of the Massachusetts Missionary Society* (Andover, Mass., 1815), and John F. Schermerhorn and Samuel J. Mills, *A Correct View of that Part of the United States which Lies West of the Allegany Mountains with Regard to Religion and Morals* (Hartford, Conn., 1814).

For settlement along the Ohio a most useful source is provided by the various editions of *The Navigator*, first published at Pittsburgh in 1801, which served as a traveler's guide for the journey down the river.

Land Policy

Malcolm R. Rohrbough, *The Land Office Business: The Settlement and Administration of American Public Lands, 1789–1837* (New York, 1968) deals with the problem of the sale of lands. Standard for the general history of the public domain are Roy M. Robbins, *The Public Domain, 1776–1836* (Princeton, N.J., 1942), Benjamin H. Hibbard, *A History of the Public Land Policies* (New York, 1924), and the more detailed Payson J. Treat, *The National Land System, 1785-1820* (New York, 1910). There are also a number of useful essays in Vernon Carstensen, ed., *The Public Lands: Studies in the History of the Public Domain* (Madison, Wis., 1962). Some of the main documents are conveniently collected in Thomas C. Donaldson, ed., *The Public Domain: Its History* (Washington, 1884), and in *American State Papers, Class VIII, Public Lands*, 8 vols. (Washington, 1832–1861).

The problem of land cessions has been somewhat neglected in recent years. For a number of years the standard account was Herbert B. Adams, *Maryland's Influence upon Land Cessions to the United States* (Baltimore, 1885) but the part played by the land speculators was stressed in Merrill Jensen, "The Cession of the Old Northwest," *Mississippi Valley Historical Review*, XXIII (June 1936), 27–48, and "The Creation of the National Domain, 1781–1784," *ibid.*, XXVI (December 1939), 323–342. The strange South Carolina cession is discussed in Robert A. Cotterill, "The South Carolina Cession," *Mississippi Valley Historical Review*, XII (December 1925), 376–384, and the role of the military bounty lands is discussed in Rudolf Freund, "Military Bounty Lands and the Origin of the Public Domain," *Agricultural History*, XX (January 1946), 8–18.

On the colonial background of the Ordinance of 1785 a useful work is Marshall D. Harris, *Origin of the Land Tenure System in the United States* (Ames, Iowa, 1953). An older pioneering study is Amelia C. Ford, *Colonial Precedents of Our National Land System as it Existed in 1800* (Madison, Wis., 1910), and the early history of the Ordinance itself is treated in William D. Pattison, *Beginnings of the American Rectangular Land Survey System, 1784-1800* (Chicago, 1957). Norman J. W. Thrower, *Original Survey and Land Subdivision: A Comparative Study of the Form and Effect of Cadastral Surveys* (Chicago, 1966) compares two areas in Ohio.

Of the general works on land speculation in these years the most useful is Shaw Livermore, *Early American Land Companies* (New York, 1939). A less scholarly account is presented in Aaron M. Sakolski, *The Great American Land Bubble* (New York, 1932), and there is some information in Joseph S. Davis, *Essays in the Earlier History of American Corporations* (Cambridge, Mass., 1917).

Henry Tatter, "State and Federal Land Policy during the Confederation," *Agricultural History*, IX (October 1935), 176–186 has some general information, and a valuable article on some of the problems of the Kentucky land policies is Paul W. Gates, "Tenants of the Log Cabin," *Mississippi Valley Historical Review*, XLIX (June 1962), 3–31.

Two useful articles on specific applications of the public land system are Robert S. Cotterill, "The National Land System in the South, 1803–1812," *Mississippi Valley Historical Review*, XVI (March 1930), 495–506 and Harry L. Coles, Jr., "Applicability of the Public Land System to Louisiana," *Mississippi Valley Historical Review*, XLIII (June 1956), 39–58.

Indian Relations

Standard for American relations with the Indians in these years are Charles C. Royce, comp., *Indian Land Cessions in the United States* (American Bureau of Ethnology, Eighteenth Annual Report, 1896-1897; Washington, 1899); 7 U.S. *Statutes at Large* (Boston, 1853); Charles J. Kappler, *Indian Affairs, Laws and Treaties*, 3 vols. (Washington, 1913); and *American State Papers, Class II, Indian Affairs*, vol. I (Washington, 1832). Accounts of the formation of general national policy in these years are given in George D. Harmon, *Sixty Years of Indian Affairs: Political, Economic, and Diplomatic, 1789–1850* (Chapel Hill, N.C., 1941); Walter H. Mohr, *Federal Indian Relations, 1774–1788* (Philadelphia, 1933); and Reginald Horsman, *Expansion and American Indian Policy, 1783–1812* (East Lansing, Mich., 1967). American efforts to pursue more peaceful measures toward the Indians are considered in Francis P. Prucha, *American Indian Policy in the Formative Years: The Indian Trade and Intercourse Acts, 1790–1834* (Cambridge, Mass., 1962). There is an account of the factory system in Ora B. Peake, *A History of the United States Indian Factory System, 1795–1822* (Denver, Colo., 1954). This should be supplemented with Edgar B. Wesley, "The Government Factory System Among the Indians, 1795–1822," *Journal of Economic and Business History*, IV (May 1932), 487–511. An old but still useful work is Annie H. Abel, "The History of Events Resulting in Indian Consolidation West of the Mississippi," American Historical Association, *Annual Report, 1906* (Washington, 1908), 233–450. Robert K. Berkhofer, *Salvation and the Savage: An Analysis of Protestant Missions and American Indian Response, 1787–1862* (Lexington, Ky., 1965) attempts to analyze missionary attitudes and Indian response.

Important national figures in American Indian policy have been given inadequate treatment, although North Callahan, *Henry Knox* (New York, 1958) devotes some space to the problem of Indian relations. For an understanding of the general problems of waging war against the Indians, James R. Jacobs. *The Beginning of the U.S. Army, 1783–1812* (Princeton, N.J., 1947) and Harry M. Ward, *The Department of War, 1781–1795* (Pittsburgh, 1962) are useful. Documentary materials are readily available in *American State Papers, Class V, Military Affairs*, vol. I (Washington, 1832).

A sound general introduction to Indian relations in the South is provided by Robert S. Cotterill, *The Southern Indians: The Story of the Civilized Tribes before Removal* (Norman, Okla., 1954). Two other books of value are John W. Caughey, *McGillivray of the Creeks* (Norman, Okla., 1938), which consists of a useful introduction and documentary materials, and Merritt B. Pound, *Benjamin Hawkins: Indian Agent* (Athens, Ga., 1951). The career of Benjamin Hawkins can also be followed in *Letters of Benjamin Hawkins, 1796–1806* (Georgia Historical Society "Collections," IX; Savannah, Ga., 1916). There is also a variety of articles which deal with particular aspects of Indian policy in the South. Among the best are Robert S. Cotterill, "Federal Indian Management in the South, 1789–1825," *Mississippi Valley Historical Review*, XX (December 1933), 333–352, and three articles by Randolph C. Downes: "Creek-American Relations, 1782–1790," *Georgia Historical Quarterly*, XXI (1937), 142–184; "Creek-American Relations, 1790–1795," *Journal of Southern History*, VIII (August 1942), 350–373, and "Cherokee-American Relations in the Upper Tennessee Valley, 1776–1791," *Eastern Tennessee Historical Society, Publications*, VIII (1936), 35–53. Also of value are D. L. McMurray, "The Indian Policy of the Federal Government and the Economic Development of the Southwest, 1789–1795," *Tennessee Historical Magazine*, I (March and June 1915), 21–39, 106–119, and Martin Abbott, "Indian Policy and Management in the Mississippi Territory, 1798–1817," *Journal of Mississippi History*, XIV (July 1952), 153–169. An older work which is still of value is Charles C. Royce, "The Cherokee Nation of Indians: A Narrative of their Official Relations with the Colonial and Federal Governments," (American Bureau of Ethnology, *Fifth Annual Report, 1883–1884;* Washington, 1887), pp. 121–178.

An excellent general account of northwestern Indian policy is provided by Randolph C. Downes, *Council Fires on the Upper Ohio: A Narrative of Indian Affairs in the Upper Ohio Valley until 1795* (Pittsburgh, 1940). The first of the postwar treaties is given detailed treatment in Henry S. Manley, *The Treaty of Fort Stanwix, 1784* (Rome, N.Y., 1932), and there is useful information on negotiation with the Indians in the 1780s and 1790s in Octavius Pickering and Charles W. Upham, *The Life of Timothy Pickering*, 4 vols. (Boston, 1867–1873). There is a recent interpretation of Pickering in Edward H. Phillips, "Timothy Pickering At His Best: Indian Commissioner, 1790–1794," *Essex Institute Historical Collections*, CII (July 1966), 163–202. The efforts of Rufus Putnam can be followed in Rowena Buell, ed., *Memoir of Rufus Putnam and Certain Official Papers and Correspondence* (Boston, 1903), and there is a detailed account of the negotiations of 1793 in Benjamin Lincoln, "Journal of a Treaty Held in 1793, with the Indian Tribes Northwest of the Ohio, by Commissioners of the United States," Massachusetts Historical Society, *Collections*, 3d Series, V (Boston, 1836), 109–176. The Treaty of Greenville is discussed soundly in Dwight L. Smith, "Wayne's Peace with the Indians of the Old Northwest, 1795," *Ohio State Historical and Archaeological Quarterly*, LIX (July 1950), 239–255, and "Wayne and the Treaty of Greene Ville," *ibid.*, LXXIII (January 1954), 1–7. William Henry Harrison's negotiations with the Indians are dealt with in Dorothy B. Goebel, *William Henry Harrison: A Political Biography* (Indiana Historical "Collections," XIV; Indianapolis, 1926), and Logan Esarey, ed., *Messages and Letters of William Henry Harrison* (Indiana Historical "Collections," VII, IX, Indianapolis, 1922). Land cessions in Ohio and Michigan are discussed in Dwight L. Smith, "Indian Land Cessions in Northern Ohio and Southeastern Michigan, 1805–1808," *Northwest Ohio Quarterly*, XXIX (Winter, 1956–1957), 27–45.

There is considerable information on the warfare of these years in the Old Northwest. Two of the Kentucky military leaders have been treated in sound biographies; James A. James, *The Life of George Rogers Clark* (Chicago, 1928), and Charles G. Talbert, *Benjamin Logan: Kentucky Frontiersman* (Lexington, Ky., 1962). Also valuable is Leonard C. Helderman, "The Northwest Expedition of George Rogers Clark, 1786–1787," *Mississippi Valley Historical Review*, XXV (December 1938), 317–334. Hostilities in the Indiana region are considered in Gayle Thornbrough, ed., *Outpost on the Wabash, 1787-1791: Letters of Brigadier General Josiah Harmar and Major John Francis Hamtramck . . .* (Indianapolis, 1957), and there is considerable information on the whole northwestern region in William H. Smith, ed., *The St. Clair Papers: The Life and Public Services of Arthur St. Clair*, 2 vols. (Cincinnati, 1882). An intimate account of the campaigning is provided in Ebeneezer Denny, "Military Journal of Major Ebeneezer Denny," *Memoirs of the Historical Society of Pennsylvania*, VII (Philadelphia, 1860), 237–409.

Wayne's victory over the Indians can be followed in Thomas A. Boyd, *Mad Anthony Wayne* (New York, 1929) and in Harry E. Wildes, *Anthony Wayne: Trouble Shooter of the American Revolution* (New York, 1941). There is a full documentary account in Richard C. Knopf, *Anthony Wayne: a Name in Arms: Soldier, Diplomat, Defender of Expansion Westward of a Nation: The Wayne-Knox-Pickering-McHenry Correspondence* (Pittsburgh, 1960).

Among the main Indian leaders, Joseph Brant still lacks a comprehensive modern biography, although William L. Stone, *Life of Joseph Brant*, 2 vols. (New York, 1838) has valuable source material; and Harvey Chalmers and Ethel Brant Monture, *Joseph Brant, Mohawk* (East Lansing, Mich., 1955) is readable. Glenn Tucker, *Tecumseh: Vision of Glory* (Indianapolis, 1956) is colorful; but Benjamin Drake, *The Life of Tecumseh, and his Brother the Prophet* (Cincinnati, 1841) is still worth looking at.

Diplomatic Entanglements and the Frontier

There has been considerable writing on British involvement in the Old Northwest in these years. The pioneering work on the British decision to retain the Northwest posts was Andrew C. McLaughlin, "The Western Posts and British Debts," American Historical Association, *Annual Report, 1894* (Washington, 1895), pp. 413–444. This early interpretation has been revised in the work of A. L. Burt, notably in *The United States, Great Britain and British North America, from the Revolution to the Establishment of Peace after the War of 1812* (New Haven, Conn., 1940), which also deals with the whole question of the British-American-Indian involvement along the Canadian border in these years. Burt's view was supported in G. S. Graham, "The Indian Menace and the Retention of the Western Posts," *Canadian Historical Review*, XV (March 1934), 46–48. British relations with the Indians are dealt with more specifically in Orpha E. Leavitt, "British Policy on the Canadian Frontier 1782–1792: Mediation and an Indian Barrier State," Wisconsin Historical Society, *Proceedings*, 1915 (Madison, Wis., 1916),

151–185; Philip M. Hamer, "The British in Canada and the Southern Indians, 1790–94," East Tennessee Historical Society, *Publications*, II (1930), 107–134, and Reginald Horsman, *Matthew Elliott, British Indian Agent* (Detroit, 1964). The role of the fur trade is considered in Donald G. Creighton, *The Commercial Empire of the St. Lawrence, 1760–1850* (Toronto, 1937), and in Wayne E. Stevens, *The Northwest Fur Trade, 1763–1800* (Urbana, Ill., 1928). Extensive documentary material on British involvement in the years from 1783 to 1795 is contained in the *Michigan Pioneer and Historical Collections*, 40 vols. (Lansing, Mich., 1877–1929), and in Ernest A. Cruikshank, ed., *The Correspondence of Lieut. Governor John Graves Simcoe*, 5 vols. (Toronto, 1923–1931). The standard work on Jay's Treaty is Samuel F. Bemis, *Jay's Treaty: A Study in Commerce and Diplomacy* (1923; rev. ed., New Haven, Conn., 1962).

There are three sound general works on Spanish diplomacy in the Southwest in these years. Two by Arthur P. Whitaker, *The Spanish-American Frontier, 1783–1795: The Westward Movement and the Spanish Retreat in the Mississippi Valley* (Boston, 1927) and *The Mississippi Question, 1795–1803: A Study in Trade, Politics, and Diplomacy* (New York, 1934), effectively cover the whole period to the Louisiana Purchase; and Samuel F. Bemis, *Pinckney's Treaty: A Study of America's Advantage from Europe's Distress, 1783–1800* (Baltimore, 1926) is a careful diplomatic study. A useful collection of documents is Lawrence Kinnaird, ed., *Spain in the Mississippi Valley, 1765–1794*, 3 vols., American Historical Association, *Annual Report*, 1945, II–IV (Washington, 1946–1949). Spain's relations with the Indians are considered in Arthur P. Whitaker, "Spain and the Cherokee Indians, 1783–1798," *North Carolina Historical Review*, IV (July 1927), 252–267, and Jane M. Berry, "The Indian Policy of Spain in the Southwest, 1783–1795," *Mississippi Valley Historical Review*, III (March 1917), 462–477. A recent study of value is Jack D. L. Holmes, *Gayoso: The Life of a Spanish Governor in the Mississippi Valley, 1789–1799* (Baton Rouge, La., 1965). There is information on Spanish conspiracies in the Southwest in two biographies of James Wilkinson: James R. Jacobs, *Tarnished Warrior: Major-General James Wilkinson* (New York, 1938) and Thomas R. Ray and M. R. Werner, *The Admirable Trumpeter: A Biography of General James Wilkinson* (New York, 1941). A special aspect is dealt with in Archibald Henderson, "The Spanish Conspiracy in Tennessee," *Tennessee Historical Magazine*, III (December 1917), 229–243.

The impact of Genêt on the West is treated in Richard Lowitt, "Activities of Citizen Genêt in Kentucky, 1793–1794," *Filson Club Historical Quarterly*, XXII (October 1948), 252–267. This subject was dealt with effectively by Frederick Jackson Turner in "The Origin of Genêt's Projected Attack on Louisiana and the Florida s," *American Historical Review*, III (July 1898), 650–671, and in "The Policy of France Toward the Mississippi Valley in the Period of Washington and Adams," *American Historical Review*, X (January 1905), 249–279. There is also information in Archibald Henderson, "Isaac Shelby and the Genêt Mission," *Mississippi Valley Historical Review*, VI (March 1920), 451–469.

There has been a good deal of work on the Louisiana Purchase. E. Wilson Lyon has presented sound accounts of Louisiana in *French Diplomacy, 1759–1804* (Norman, Okla., 1934) and *The Man Who Sold Louisiana: The Career of François Barbé-Marbois* (Norman, Okla., 1942). Also useful are Mildred S. Fletcher, "Louisiana as a Factor in French Diplomacy from 1763 to 1800," *Mississippi Valley*

Historical Review, XVII (December 1930), 367–376; W. Edwin Hemphill, "The Jeffersonian Background of the Louisiana Purchase," *ibid.,* XXII (September 1935), 176–190; and André Lafargue, "The Louisiana Purchase: The French Viewpoint," *Louisiana Historical Quarterly,* XXIII (January 1940), 107–117.

The Burr conspiracy is carefully treated in Thomas P. Abernethy, *The Burr Conspiracy* (New York, 1954).

Settlement in the South

There is a lack of books on the reason for the emigration of settlers from the eastern states, although there is information in Avery O. Craven, *Soil Exhaustion as a Factor in the Agricultural History of Virginia and Maryland, 1616–1860* (Urbana, Ill., 1926), and Cornelius O. Cathey, *Agricultural Developments in North Carolina, 1783–1860* (Chapel Hill, N.C., 1956).

The role of the speculator in the years following the Revolution is considered in Thomas P. Abernethy, *Western Lands and the American Revolution* (New York, 1937). Abernethy also devotes considerable space to this subject in his volume *The South in the New Nation, 1789–1819* (Wendell H. Stephenson and E. Merton Coulter, eds., "History of the South," vol. IV; Louisiana State University Press, 1961) and presents a general analysis of one aspect in his *Three Virginia Frontiers* (Louisiana State University Press, 1940). The Tennessee experience is treated in his *From Frontier to Plantation in Tennessee: A Study in Frontier Democracy* (Chapel Hill, N.C., 1932), Also useful is Arthur P. Whitaker, "The Muscle Shoals Speculation, 1783–1789," *Mississippi Valley Historical Review,* XIII (December 1926), 365–386. The most recent work on the Yazoo speculations is C. Peter Magrath, *Yazoo: Law and Politics in the New Republic: The Case of Fletcher v Peck* (Providence, R.I., 1966). Still of value is Charles H. Haskins, "The Yazoo Land Companies," American Historical Association, *Papers,* V, no. 4 (1891), 61–103. There is information in Samuel B. Adams, "The Yazoo Fraud," *Georgia Historical Quarterly,* VII (June 1923), 155–165, and in John C. Parish, "The Intrigues of Doctor James O'Fallon," *Mississippi Valley Historical Review,* XVII (September 1930), 230–263. William H. Masterson, *William Blount* (Baton Rouge, La., 1954) is a competent biography of a key figure.

Settlement in West Virginia is discussed in Ruth W. Dayton, *Pioneers and their Homes on Upper Kanawha* (Charleston, W.Va., 1947); Lewis P. Summers, *History of Southwest Virginia, 1746–1786* (Richmond, Va., 1903); Lucullus McWhorter, *The Border Settlers of Northwestern Virginia from 1768 to 1795* (Hamilton, Ohio, 1915); and Charles D. Ambler, *Sectionalism in Virginia from 1776 to 1861* (Chicago, 1910). A useful one volume history of the state is Charles H. Ambler and Festus P. Summers, *West Virginia: The Mountain State* (Englewood Cliffs, N.J., 1958).

The Wilderness Road is dealt with in Robert L. Kincaid, *The Wilderness Road* (Indianapolis, 1947) and William A. Pusey, *The Wilderness Road to Kentucky* (New York, 1921). The Ohio route is considered in interesting fashion in Leland D. Baldwin, *The Keelboat Age on Western Waters* (Pittsburgh, 1941). A concise history of Kentucky is provided by Thomas D. Clark, *History of Kentucky* (New York, 1937). There is a more detailed account in Robert S. Cotterill, *History of Pioneer Kentucky* (Cincinnati, 1917). Much can also be learned from

Bernard Mayo, *Henry Clay: Spokesman of the New West* (Boston, 1937), which is rich in description and there is information on Kentucky's main town in Bernard Mayo, "Lexington: Frontier Metropolis," in Eric F. Goldman, ed., *Historiography and Urbanization: Essays in American History in Honor of W. Stull Holt* (Baltimore, 1941).

Expansion into western North Carolina is considered in Archibald Henderson, *North Carolina: The Old North State and the New*, 5 vols. (Chicago, 1941), and in Hugh T. Lefler and Albert R. Newsome, *North Carolina: The History of a Southern State* (Chapel Hill, N.C., 1954).

Early Tennessee has been treated in a number of books by Samuel C. Williams. Useful are his *Dawn of Tennessee Valley and Tennessee History* (Johnson City, Tenn., 1937), and *History of the Lost State of Franklin* (New York, 1933). General histories are James Phelan, *History of Tennessee* (Boston, 1888) and Philip M. Hamer, ed., *Tennessee, a History, 1673–1932*, 4 vols. (New York, 1933). There is information in James G. M. Ramsey, *The Annals of Tennessee to the End of the Eighteenth Century* (1853; reprinted Kingsport, Tenn., 1926). Harriette Simpson Arnouw delves into a variety of aspects of early Tennessee life in two volumes, *Seedtime on the Cumberland* (New York, 1960), and *Flowering of the Cumberland* (New York, 1963).

There is information on expansion in Georgia in Ulrich B. Phillips, "Georgia and States Rights," American Historical Association, *Annual Report*, 1901, vol. II (Washington, 1902), 3–224; James C. Bonner, *A History of Georgia Agriculture, 1732–1860* (Athens, Ga., 1964); and Samuel G. McLendon, *History of the Public Domain of Georgia* (Atlanta, 1924). A useful short history is E. Merton Coulter, *Georgia: A Short History* (Chapel Hill, N.C., 1960), and a detailed work on the Upper Savannah is his *Old Petersburg and the Broad River Valley of Georgia: Their Rise and Decline* (Athens, Ga., 1965). The beginnings of settlement in Mississippi Territory before 1815 are considered in Dunbar Rowland, *History of Mississippi: The Heart of the South*, 2 vols. (Chicago, 1925); John F. H. Clairborne, *Mississippi, as a Province, Territory, and State* (Jackson, Miss., 1880); John H. Moore, *Agriculture in Ante-Bellum Mississippi* (New York, 1958); and Albert B. Moore, *History of Alabama* (University, Ala., 1934).

There are accounts of the early history of Louisiana settlement in Garnie W. McGinty, *A History of Louisiana* (New York, 1949) and Charles E. Gayarré, *History of Louisiana*, 4 vols. (4th ed.; New Orleans, 1903). Also useful is Lawrence Kinnaird, "American Penetration into Spanish Louisiana," in *New Spain and the Anglo-American West: Historical Contributions Presented to H. E. Bolton*, 2 vols. (Los Angeles, Calif., 1932). The events in West Florida are considered in Isaac J. Cox, *The West Florida Controversy, 1798–1813: A Study in American Diplomacy* (Baltimore, 1918) and Rembert W. Patrick, *Florida Fiasco: Rampant Rebels on the Georgia-Florida Border, 1810–1815* (Athens, Ga., 1954). A useful one volume history of Missouri is Edwin C. McReynolds, *Missouri: A History of the Crossroads State* (Norman, Okla., 1962), and there is information in the older Louis Houck, *A History of Missouri*, 3 vols. (Chicago, 1908). Settlement in this period is dealt with in Hattie M. Anderson, "Missouri, 1804–1828: Peopling a Frontier State," *Missouri Historical Review*, XXXI (January 1937), 150–180, and in Jonas Vilas, "Population and Extent of Settlement in Missouri before 1804," *ibid.*, V (July 1911), 189–213.

Settlement in the North

There is some material on the reasons for emigration from New England in Lois Kimball Mathews, *The Expansion of New England: the Spread of New England Settlement and Institutions to the Mississippi River, 1620–1865* (Boston, 1909) and in Richard J. Purcell, *Connecticut in Transition, 1775–1818* (Washington, 1918). For northern New England the most useful work is Lewis D. Stilwell, *Migration from Vermont, 1776–1860* (Montpelier, Vt., 1937), which also deals with immigration into the state in the years after the Revolution. There is also information in the introduction to Frederick S. Allis, Jr., ed., *William Bingham's Maine Lands, 1790–1820* (Colonial Society of Massachusetts, "Publications," XXXVI, XXXVII; Boston, 1954) and Harold F. Wilson, *The Hill Country of Northern New England: Its Social and Economic History* (New York, 1936)

The New York frontier has attracted considerable attention. Among the most useful of these works are Ruth L. Higgins, *Expansion in New York: With Especial Reference to the Eighteenth Century* (Columbus, 1931); David M. Ellis, *Landlords and Farmers in the Hudson-Mohawk Region, 1790–1850* (Ithaca, N.Y., 1946); Alexander C. Flick, ed., *History of the State of New York*, 10 vols. (New York, 1932–1937); and the general Dixon R. Fox, *Yankees and Yorkers* (New York, 1940). Central New York is considered in Francis W. Halsey, *The Old New York Frontier* (New York, 1901) and in James A. Frost, *Life on the Upper Susquehanna, 1783–1860* (New York, 1951).

The history of Phelp's and Gorham's purchase can be followed in the compendious Orsamus Turner, *History of the Pioneer Settlement of Phelps and Gorham's Purchase, and Morris' Reserve* (Rochester, N.Y., 1851) and the Pulteney interests in the careful Paul D. Evans, "The Pulteney Purchase," *Quarterly Journal of the New York State Historical Association, III* (April 1922), 83–104. Indispensable is Neil A. McNall, *An Agricultural History of the Genesee Valley, 1790–1860* (Philadelphia, 1952), and there is considerable information in Helen I. Cowan, *Charles Williamson: Genesee Promoter* (Rochester, N.Y., 1941). The fate of the Holland Land Company is discussed in Paul D. Evans, *The Holland Land Company* (Buffalo, N.Y., 1924) and its settlers in Orsamus Turner, *Pioneer History of the Holland Purchase of Western New York* (Buffalo, N.Y., 1849).

Western Pennsylvania in these years is considered at length in Solon J. and Elizabeth H. Buck, *The Planting of Civilization in Western Pennsylvania* (Pittsburgh, 1939). Also useful are Elizabeth K. Henderson, "The Northwestern Lands of Pennsylvania, 1790–1812," *Pennsylvania Magazine of History and Biography*, LX (April 1936), 131–160, and R. Nelson Hale, "The Pennsylvania Population Company," *Pennsylvania History*, XVI (April 1949), 122–130.

On the Ohio Company there is a sound history in the introduction to Archer B. Hulbert, ed., *The Records of the Original Proceedings of the Ohio Company*, 2 vols. (Marietta, Ohio, 1917). The leading members of the company have been strangely neglected by historians in this century. Key figures in the company are looked at in William P. and Julia P. Cutler, *Life, Journals and Correspondence of Rev. Manasseh Cutler*, 2 vols. (Cincinnati, 1888) and Charles S. Hall and Mary Cone, *Life of Rufus Putnam* (Cleveland, 1886). A figure who was deeply involved in the speculations of the late 1780s is discussed in James Woodress, *A Yankee's Odyssey: The Life of Joel Barlow* (Philadelphia, 1958), which supplements the earlier Charles B. Todd, *Life and Letters of Joel Barlow* (New York, 1886). The Scioto speculation is discussed in Archer B. Hulbert, "The Methods and Operations of the Scioto Group of Speculators," *Mississippi Valley Historical Review*, I (March 1915), 502–515, II (June 1915), 56–73, and the Symmes purchase in Beverley W. Bond, Jr., ed., *The Correspondence of John Cleves Symmes: Founder of the Miami Purchase* (New York, 1926).

A careful general work is Beverley W. Bond, Jr., *The Civilization of the Old Northwest: A Study of Political, Social, and Economic Development, 1788–1812* (New York, 1934). Of great value are two volumes in *The History of the State of Ohio*, ed. by Carl Wittke: Beverley W. Bond, Jr., *The Foundations of Ohio* (Columbus, 1941), and William T. Utter, *The Frontier State, 1803–1825* (Columbus, 1942). Also useful is Randolph C. Downes, *Frontier Ohio, 1788–1803* (Columbus, 1935). A general account of the Western Reserve is provided in Harlan Hatcher, *The Western Reserve: The Story of New Connecticut in Ohio* (Indianapolis, 1949).

There is information on Indiana settlement in Logan Esarey, *A History of Indiana from Its Exploration to 1850* (Indianapolis, 1915) and in Chelsea L. Lawlis, "Whitewater Settlement, 1790–1810," *Indiana Magazine of History*, XLIII (March 1947), 23–40. Illinois in these years receives careful treatment in Arthur C. Boggess, *The Settlement of Illinois, 1778–1830* (Chicago, 1908) and more general treatment and interpretation in Clarence W. Alvord, *The Illinois Country, 1673–1818* ("Centennial History of Illinois," Springfield, Ill., 1920). There is also useful information in Solon J. Buck, *Illinois in 1818* ("Centennial History of Illinois," Springfield, Ill., 1917).

The tentative beginnings in Michigan can be followed in Nelson Vance Russell, *The British Régime in Michigan and the Old Northwest, 1760–1796* (Northfield, Minn. 1939) and in the introduction to Ernest J. Lajeunesse, C.S.B., ed., *The Windsor Border Region: Canada's Southernmost Frontier* (Toronto, 1960). Detroit itself in these years is best considered in F. Clever Bald, *Detroit's First American Decade, 1796–1805* (Ann Arbor, Mich., 1948) and in the older Clarence M. Burton, *The City of Detroit, Michigan*, 5 vols. (Detroit, 1922).

The Organization of Government

Writing on frontier governmental development in these years has been dominated by the argument concerning the role of the frontier in promoting American democracy. Basic to an understanding of the argument are the essays in Frederick Jackson Turner, *The Frontier in American History* (New York, 1920); also relevant are the essays in his *The Significance of Sections in American History* (New York, 1932). There have been a great variety of essays dealing with particular aspects of Turner's theories. Among the most important attacks on Turner's thesis of the frontier as a promoter of American democracy are Benjamin F. Wright, "American Democracy and the Frontier," *Yale Review*, XX (December 1930), 349–365, and "Political Institutions and the Frontier," in Dixon R. Fox, ed., *Sources of Culture in the Middle West* (New York, 1934). Some of the more important defenders of Turner in this regard are Roy F. Nichols, "The Territories: Seedbeds of Democracy," *Nebraska History*, XXXV (September 1954), 159–172, and Stanley Elkins and Eric McKitrick, "A Meaning for Turner's Frontier," *Polit-*

ical Science Quarterly, LXIX (September and December 1954), 321–353, 565–602. A work of great value in placing the influences of the frontier in perspective is Chilton Williamson, *American Suffrage from Property to Democracy, 1760–1860 (Princeton*, N.J., 1960). A basic collection of source materials is provided in Francis N. Thorpe, *The Federal and State Constitutions, Colonial Charters, and Other Organic Laws*, 7 vols. (Washington, 1909).

There is information on Vermont development in these years in Frederick F. Van de Water, *The Reluctant Republic, Vermont, 1724–1791* (New York, 1941): Charles M. Thompson, *Independent Vermont* (Boston, 1942); and Earle W. Newton, *The Vermont Story: A History of the People of the Green Mountain State, 1749–1949* (Montpelier, Vt., 1949).

There is no recent monograph on the origins of the Northwest Ordinance of 1787, although a recent article of value is Jack E. Eblen, "Origins of the United States Colonial System: The Ordinance of 1787," *Wisconsin Magazine of History*, 51 (Summer 1968), 294–314. The same author has recently written of the whole course of territorial development in *The First and Second United States Empires: Governors and Territorial Government, 1784–1912* (Pittsburgh, 1968); this came too late to influence the writing of this book. Of the old accounts Jay A. Barrett, *Evolution of the Ordinance of 1787* (New York, 1891) is perhaps the best.

Of basic importance for an understanding of the advance of government into the Ohio Valley is John D. Barnhart, *Valley of Democracy: The Frontier versus the Plantation in the Ohio Valley, 1775–1818* (Bloomington, Ind., 1953). Barnhart's conclusions support the Turner thesis, and he includes a discussion not only of the Old Northwest in these years but also Kentucky and Tennessee. Apart from the general histories of Kentucky, special studies of government and politics include E. Merton Coulter, "Early Frontier Democracy in the First Kentucky Constitution," *Political Science Quarterly*, XXXIX (December 1924) 665–677; John M. Brown, *The Political Beginnings of Kentucky* (Filson Club, "Publications," No. 6; Louisville, Ky., 1889); and Thomas Speed, *The Political Club, Danville, Kentucky, 1786–1790* (Filson Club "Publications," No. 9; Louisville, Ky., 1894). Charles G. Talbert, *Benjamin Logan: Kentucky Frontiersman* (Lexington, Ky., 1962) has information on the Kentucky conventions.

There are general comments on political development in the Old Northwest in Beverley W. Bond, Jr., "Some Political Ideals of the Colonial Period as they were Realized in the Old Northwest," *Essays in Colonial History Presented to Charles McLean Andrews by His Students* (New Haven, Conn., 1931); Elbert J. Benton, "Establishing the American Colonial System in the Old Northwest," Illinois State Historical Society, *Transactions*, XXIV (1918), 47–63; and Dwight G. McCarty, *The Territorial Governors of the Old Northwest: A Study in Territorial Administration* (Iowa City, Iowa, 1910). There is a useful compilation in Theodore C. Pease, ed., *Laws of the Northwest Territory, 1788–1800* (Illinois State Historical Society, "Collections," XVII; Springfield, Ill., 1925).

The problems of the Northwest Territory receive sound treatment in Beverley W. Bond, Jr., *The Foundations of Ohio* (Columbus, 1941) and in Randolph C. Downes, *Frontier Ohio, 1788–1803* (Columbus, 1935). There is no modern comprehensive biography of St. Clair, but William H. Smith, ed., *The St. Clair Papers: The Life and Public Services of Arthur St. Clair*, 2 vols. (Cincinnati, 1882) has much information. There is a useful interpretation in Alfred B. Sears, "The Political Philosophy of Arthur St. Clair," *Ohio Archaeological and Historical Society Quarterly*, XLIX (1940), 41–57. Alfred B. Sears, *Thomas Worthington: Father of Ohio Statehood* (Columbus, 1958) is a sound biography.

The career of Harrison in Indiana can be followed in Dorothy B. Goebel, *William Henry Harrison: A Political Biography* (Indiana Historical "Collections," vol. XIV; Indianapolis, 1926). There is an account of the early government of Illinois in Solon J. Buck, *Illinois in 1818* (Springfield, Ill., 1917) and a very useful introduction in Francis S. Philbrick, ed., *The Laws of Illinois Territory, 1809–1818* (Illinois State Historical Library, "Collections," XXV; Springfield, Ill., 1950). The career of Ninian Edwards can be followed in E. B. Washburne, ed., *The Edwards Papers* (Chicago Historical Collection, vol. III; Chicago, 1884) and in Ninian W. Edwards, *History of Illinois, from 1778 to 1833; and Life and Times of Ninian Edwards* (Springfield, Ill., 1870). There is a brief account of the early government of Detroit in Reginald Horsman, *Frontier Detroit, 1760–1812* ("Michigan in Perspective" Conference, Occasional Publication, No. 1; Detroit, 1964).

There is considerable information on the organization of government in the Tennessee region in the various writings of Thomas P. Abernethy, particularly in his *From Frontier to Plantation in Tennessee: A Study in Frontier Democracy* (Chapel Hill, N.C., 1932). The state of Franklin is dealt with in detail in Samuel C. Williams *History of the Lost State of Franklin* (New York, 1933) and there is a useful analysis in Walter F. Cannon, "Four Interpretations of the History of the State of Franklin," East Tennessee Historical Society, *Publications*, XXII (1950), 3–18. Two sound biographies of leaders of early Tennessee are Carl S. Driver, *John Sevier: Pioneer of the Old Southwest* (Chapel Hill, N.C., 1932) and William H. Masterson, *William Blount* (Baton Rouge, La., 1954).

The development of American government in Mississippi is treated in Franklin L. Riley, "Transition from Spanish to American Rule in Mississippi," Mississippi Historical Society, *Publications*, III (1900), 261–311 and Robert V. Haynes, "The Revolution of 1800 in Mississippi," *Journal of Mississippi History*, XIX (October 1957), 234–251. Also of interest is George B. Toulmin, "The Political Ideas of Winthrop Sargent: A New England Federalist on the Frontier," *ibid.*, XV (October 1953), 207–229. Legal aspects of the Mississippi frontier are dealt with in William Baskerville Hamilton, ed., *Anglo-American Law of the Frontier: Thomas Rodney and his Territorial Cases* (Durham, N.C., 1953); see also Clarence E. Carter, "The Transit of Law to the Frontier: A Review Article," *Journal of Mississippi History*, XVI (July 1954), 183–200. Garnie William McGinty, *A History of Louisiana* (New York, 1949) surveys the development of Louisiana, and Edwin C. McReynolds, *Missouri: A History of the Crossroads State* (Norman, Okla., 1962) is useful for the early government of the state.

The Development of Frontier Society

There are a number of works which have material on the general aspects of the development of western society in these years. Among these are Ray A. Billington, *America's Frontier Heritage* (Billington, ed., "Histories of the American Frontier" *series*, New York, 1966), and Louis B. Wright, *Culture on the Moving*

Frontier (Bloomington, Ind., 1955). There is also a good deal of material in John A. Krout and Dixon R. Fox, *The Completion of Independence, 1790–1830* (Arthur M. Schlesinger and Dixon R. Fox, eds., "History of American Life," vol. 5; New York, 1944).

Among the best of the works which deal with general aspects of certain regions are David M. Ludlum, *Social Ferment in Vermont, 1791–1850* (New York, 1939), Solon J. and Elizabeth H. Buck, *The Planting of Civilization in Western Pennsylvania* (Pittsburgh, 1939), and Beverley W. Bond, Jr., *The Civilization of the Old Northwest* (New York, 1935). Among many other works dealing with the Old Northwest and the Ohio Valley are Joseph Schafer, "Beginnings of Civilization in the Old Northwest," *Wisconsin Magazine of History*, XXI (December 1937), 213–236; James M. Miller, *The Genesis of Western Culture: The Upper Ohio Valley, 1800–1825* (Columbus, 1938); and Dixon R. Fox, ed., *Sources of Culture in the Middle West* (New York, 1934). Of value on the Southern frontier are Everett N. Dick, *The Dixie Frontier: A Social History of the Southern Frontier from the First Transmontane Beginnings to the Civil War* (New York, 1948); William B. Hamilton, "The Southwestern Frontier, 1795–1817: An Essay in Social History," *Journal of Southern History*, X (November 1944), 389–403; and Arthur K. Moore, *The Frontier Mind: A Cultural Analysis of the Kentucky Frontiersman* (Lexington, Ky., 1957).

The literature on frontier religion is extensive, and it is only possible to indicate some of this material here. An excellent guide to religious history is provided by Nelson R. Burr, James Ward Smith, and A. Leland Jamison, eds., *A Critical Bibliography of Religion in America*, 2 vols. (Princeton, N.J., 1961). A reasonable general history is Clinton E. Olmstead, *History of Religion in the United States* (Englewood Cliffs, N.J., 1960). Also useful are Edwin Scott Gaustad, *Historical Atlas of Religion in America* (New York, 1962) and William W. Sweet, *Religion in the Development of American Culture, 1765–1840* (New York, 1952). Two books that are valuable for particular aspects of American religion in these years are Oliver Elsbree, *The Rise of the Missionary Spirit in America, 1790–1815* (Williamsport, Pa., 1928) and Colin B. Goodykoontz, *Home Missions on the American Frontier* (Caldwell, Idaho, 1939).

Information concerning particular denominations on the frontier can be found in William W. Manross, *A History of the American Episcopal Church* (2d ed.; New York, 1950); Mary R. Mattingley, *The Catholic Church on the Kentucky Frontier, 1785–1812* (Washington, 1936); and Gaius G. Atkins and Frederick L. Fagley, *History of American Congregationalism* (Boston, 1942). The Congregationalists, Presbyterians, Methodists, and Baptists have received excellent treatment in the collection of source materials by William W. Sweet, *Religion on the American Frontier, 1783–1840*, 4 vols. (New York and Chicago, 1931–1946), and there is a sociological treatment of aspects of frontier religion in the early nineteenth century in T. Scott Miyakawa, *Protestants and Pioneers: Individualism and Conformity on the American Frontier* (Chicago, 1964). A recent study of southern religion is Walter B. Posey, *Frontier Mission. A History of Religion West of the Southern Appalachians to 1861* (Lexington, Ky., 1966). Presbyterianism on the frontier has received sound treatment in Ernest T. Thompson, *Presbyterians in the South*, vol. 1: 1607–1861 (Richmond, Va., 1963), Walter B. Posey, *The Pres-*

byterian Church in the Old Southwest, 1778–1838 (Richmond, Va., 1952), and L. C. Rudolph, *Hoosier Zion: The Presbyterians in Early Indiana* (New Haven, Conn., 1963). The Methodists on the frontier have also attracted considerable attention. Of value are the sections on the frontier in Emory S. Bucke, ed., *The History of American Methodism*, 3 vols. (New York, 1964); Wesley M. Gewehr, "Some Factors in the Expansion of Frontier Methodism, 1800–1811," *Journal of Religion*, VIII (January 1928), 98–120; Walter B. Posey, *The Development of Methodism in the Old Southwest, 1783–1824* (Tuscaloosa, Ala., 1933); and Elizabeth K. Nottingham, *Methodism and the Frontier: Indiana Proving Ground* (New York, 1941). Of value on the Baptists is Walter B. Posey, *The Baptist Church in the Lower Mississippi Valley, 1776–1845* (Lexington, Ky., 1957). Religious communal organizations in the United States are dealt with in Arthur E. Bestor, Jr., *Backwoods Utopias: The Sectarian and Owenite Phases of Communitarian Socialism in America, 1663–1829* (Philadelphia, 1950).

Frontier revivalism has an extensive literature. General histories of revivalism are William W. Sweet, *Revivalism: Its Origin, Growth, and Decline* (New York, 1945); Bernard A. Weisberger, *They Gathered at the River: The Story of the Great Revivalists and their Impact upon Religion in America* (Boston, 1958) and Peter G. Mode, *The Frontier Spirit in American Christianity* (New York, 1923). The camp meeting is discussed in detail in Charles A. Johnson, *The Frontier Camp Meeting: Religion's Harvest Time* (Dallas, 1955). Of great use for special areas are Catharine C. Cleveland, *The Great Revival in the West, 1797–1805* (Chicago, 1916) and Whitney R. Cross, *The Burned-over District: The Social and Intellectual History of Enthusiastic Religion in Western New York, 1800–1850* (Ithaca, N.Y., 1950). An interesting history of the Shakers is Edward D. Andrews, *The People Called Shakers: A Search for the Perfect Society* (New York, 1953).

A valuable pioneer work on western education is George W. Knight, "History and Management of Land Grants for Education in the Northwest Territory," American Historical Association, *Papers*, I, no. 3, pp. 79–247. Also useful is Edgar W. Knight, ed., *A Documentary History of Education in the South before 1860*, 5 vols. (Chapel Hill, N.C., 1949–1953). Much of the information on education has to be found in the books on general cultural advance in the western states, but Niels H. Sonne, *Liberal Kentucky, 1780–1828* (New York, 1939) presents an interesting analysis of some of the developments at Transylvania University.

Essential for early American newspapers is Clarence S. Brigham, *History and Bibliography of American Newspapers, 1690–1820*, 2 vols. (Worcester, Mass., 1947). Also useful is Reuben G. Thwaites, "Ohio Valley Press before the War of 1812–15," American Antiquarian Society, *Proceedings*, XIX (April 1909), 309–368. A recent work, with value beyond the region it describes, is William H. Lyon, *The Pioneer Editor in Missouri, 1808–1860* (Columbia, Mo., 1965).

Books and readings on the trans-Appalachian frontier receive attention in Ralph L. Rusk, *The Literature of the Middle Western Frontier*, 2 vols. (New York, 1925); William H. Venable, *Beginnings of Literary Culture in the Ohio Valley* (Cincinnati, 1891); Howard H. Peckham, "Books and Reading on the Ohio Valley Frontier," *Mississippi Valley Historical Review*, XLIV (March 1958), 649–663; Walter A. Agard, "Classics on the Midwest Frontier," in Walker D. Wyman and Clifton B. Kroeber, eds., *The Frontier in Perspective* (Madison, Wis., 1957); David Kaser, *Joseph Charless: Printer in the Western Country* (Philadelphia, 1963); and Walter

Sutton, *The Western Book Trade: Cincinnati as a Nineteenth-Century Publishing and Book-Trade Center* (Columbus, 1961).

The Growth of Frontier Prosperity

American economic development in the West in these years has not received as much attention as some of the other aspects of western history. Of the general works on American economic history, Curtis P. Nettels, *The Emergence of a National Economy, 1775–1815* (Henry David, *et. al.*, eds., *The Economic History of the United States*, vol. II, New York, 1962) is the most useful for the frontier in this period.

Indispensable for agricultural history in these years are Percy W. Bidwell and John I. Falconer, *History of Agriculture in the Northern United States 1620– 1860* (1925; reprinted New York, 1941), and Lewis C. Gray, *History of Agriculture in the Southern United States to 1860*, 2 vols. (1933; reprinted New York, 1941); also of general use is Oliver E. Baker, comp., *Atlas of American Agriculture* (Washington, 1936). There are also a number of regional agricultural histories. Percy W. Bidwell, "Rural Economy in New England at the Beginning of the Nineteenth Century," Connecticut Academy of Arts and Sciences, *Transactions*, X (1916), 241–399, deals with the southern New England states, but has much of value. For northern New England, there is information in Clarence A. Day, *A History of Maine Agriculture, 1604–1860* (Orono, Me., 1954), Lewis D. Stilwell, *Migration from Vermont, 1776–1860* (Montpelier, Vt., 1937), and Harold F. Wilson, *The Hill Country of Northern New England: Its Social and Economic History, 1790–1830* (New York, 1936).

Other regional agricultural histories of value are Neil A. McNall, *An Agricultural History of the Genesee Valley, 1790–1860* (Philadelphia, 1952); Ulysses P. Hedrick, *A History of Agriculture in the State of New York* (Albany, 1933); Stevenson W. Fletcher, *Pennsylvania Agriculture and Country Life, 1640–1840* (Harrisburg, Pa., 1950); J. E. Wright and Doris S. Corbet, *Pioneer Life in Western Pennsylvania* (Pittsburgh, 1940); Cornelius O. Cathey, *Agricultural Developments in North Carolina, 1783–1860* (Chapel Hill, N.C., 1956); James C. Bonner, *A History of Georgia Agriculture, 1732–1860* (Athens, Ga., 1964); and John H. Moore, *Agriculture in Ante-Bellum Mississippi* (New York, 1958).

Books on special aspects of farming development are Paul C. Henlein, *Cattle Kingdom in the Ohio Valley, 1783–1860* (Lexington, Ky., 1959); James F. Hopkins, *A History of the Hemp Industry in Kentucky* (Lexington, Ky., 1951); and J. Carlyle Sitterson, *Sugar Country: The Cane Sugar Industry in the South, 1753– 1850* (Lexington, Ky., 1953).

For manufacturing on the trans-Appalachian frontier there is information in Isaac Lippincott, *A History of Manufactures in the Ohio Valley to the Year 1860* (New York, 1914) and in Victor S. Clark, *History of Manufactures in the United States*, 3 vols. (rev. ed.; New York, 1929). Valuable for special aspects of western development are Richard C. Wade, *The Urban Frontier: The Rise of Western Cities, 1790–1830* (Cambridge, Mass., 1959), which shows the particular role of the cities in stimulating western development, and John Jay Knox, *A History of Banking in the United States* (New York, 1900) which is a useful compendium. There is also some information on western banks in this period in J. Van Fenstermaker, *The Development of American Commercial Banking, 1782–1837* (Bureau of Economic and Business Research, Printed Series No. 5; Kent, Ohio, 1965).

The whole question of trade and transportation on the early national frontier has been inadequately treated. Useful studies are Randle B. Truett, *Trade and Travel Around the Southern Appalachians before 1830* (Chapel Hill, N.C., 1935); Theodore G. Gronert, "Trade in the Blue Grass Region, 1810–1820," *Mississippi Valley Historical Review*, V (December, 1918), 313–323, and Randolph C. Downes, "Trade in Frontier Ohio," *ibid.*, XVI (March 1930), 467–494. There are a number of general histories of transportation, but they leave much to be desired. These histories include Balthasar H. Meyer, ed., *History of Transportation in the United States before 1860* (Washington, 1917) and Seymour Dunbar, *History of Travel in America*, 4 vols. (Indianapolis, 1915). Works on special areas include William J. Wilgus, *The Role of Transportation in the Development of Vermont* (Montpelier, Vt., 1945); William F. Gephart, *Transportation and Industrial Development in the Middle West* (New York, 1909); and Charles H. Ambler, *A History of Transportation in the Ohio Valley* (Glendale, Calif., 1932). George Shumway, *et. al.*, *Conestoga Wagon, 1750-1850* (York, Pa., 1964) is descriptive. A variety of routes are discussed in Archer B. Hulbert, *Historic Highways of America*, 16 vols. (Cleveland, 1902–1905); including *The Cumberland Road* (Cleveland, 1904), which is also discussed in Philip D. Jordan, *The National Road* (Indianapolis, 1948).

Western water transportation is treated effectively in Leland D. Baldwin, *The Keelboat Age on Western Waters* (Pittsburgh, 1941). Also useful are W. Wallace Carson, "Transportation and Traffic on the Ohio and Mississippi before the Steamboat," *Mississippi Valley Historical Review*, VII (June 1920), 26–38, and Grant Foreman, "River Navigation in the Early Southwest," *ibid.*, XV (June 1928), 34–55. There is an article by Archer B. Hulbert on "Western Ship Building," *American Historical Review*, XXI (July 1916), 720–733, and the coming of the steamboat is described in Louis C. Hunter, *Steamboats on the Western Rivers: An Economic and Technological History* (Cambridge, Mass., 1949).

Basic for an understanding of trade through New Orleans from 1783 to 1803 are Arthur P. Whitaker, *The Spanish-American Frontier, 1783–1795* (1927; reprinted Gloucester, Mass., 1962), and *The Mississippi Question, 1795–1803* (1934; reprinted Gloucester, Mass., 1962). Also of importance are Thomas S. Berry, *Western Prices before 1861: A Study of the Cincinnati Market* (Cambridge, Mass., 1943), and George R. Taylor, "Prices in the Mississippi Valley Preceding the War of 1812," *Journal of Economic and Business History*, III (November 1930), 148–163. There is additional information in E. Merton Coulter, "The Efforts of the Democratic Societies of the West to Open the Navigation of the Mississippi," *Mississippi Valley Historical Review*, XI (December 1924), 376–389; George R. Taylor, "Agrarian Discontent in the Mississippi Valley Preceding the War of 1812," *Journal of Political Economy*, XXXIX (August 1931), 471–505; and W. F. Galpin, "The Grain Trade of New Orleans, 1804–1814," *Mississippi Valley Historical Review*, XIV (March, 1928), 496–507.

The West and the War of 1812

There has been considerable argument concerning the causes of the War of 1812, and the part played by the West in bringing about that conflict. Julius W.

Pratt, *Expansionists of 1812* (New York, 1925) argued that one important cause of the war was the western desire to invade Canada to prevent British support of the Indians, and also the desire to capture Florida. This view has been challenged in recent years in Bradford Perkins, *Prologue to War: England and the United States, 1805–1812* (Berkeley and Los Angeles, Calif., 1961); Reginald Horsman, *The Causes of the War of 1812* (Philadelphia, 1962); Roger H. Brown, *The Republic in Peril: 1812* (New York, 1964); and Norman K. Risjord, "1812: Conservatives, War Hawks, and the Nation's Honor," *William and Mary Quarterly*, XVIII (April 1961), 196–210. A. L. Burt, *The United States, Great Britain and British North America, from the Revolution to the Establishment of Peace after the War of 1812* (New Haven, Conn., 1940) also strongly emphasized maritime factors.

The three most recent general histories of the War of 1812 are Reginald Horsman, *The War of 1812* (New York, 1969); Harry L. Coles, *The War of 1812* (Daniel J. Boorstin, ed., *Chicago History of American Civilization*; Chicago, 1965); and J. Mackay Hitsman, *The Incredible War of 1812* (Toronto, 1965). Morris Zaslow, ed., *The Defended Border: Upper Canada and the War of 1812* (Toronto, 1964) is a useful compilation. There is a collection of essays in Philip P. Mason, ed., *After Tippecanoe: Some Aspects of the War of 1812* (East Lansing, Mich., 1963). A good account of one frontier aspect is contained in George F. G. Stanley, "The Indians in the War of 1812," *Canadian Historical Review*, XXXI (June 1950), 145–165.

For the war west of Lake Michigan there is information in Louise P. Kellogg, *The British Régime in Wisconsin and the Northwest* (Madison, Wis., 1935); Reginald Horsman, "Wisconsin and the War of 1812," *Wisconsin Magazine of History*, XLVI (Autumn 1962), 3–15; Julius W. Pratt, "The Fur Trade Strategy and the American Left Flank in the War of 1812," *American Historical Review*, XL (January 1935), 246–273; and Louis A. Tohill, "Robert Dickson, British Fur Trader on the Upper Mississippi," *North Dakota Historical Quarterly*, III (1928–1929), 5–49, 83–128, 182–203.

It is only possible to include a small percentage of the many works concerning the war along the Detroit frontier. The basic work is Alec R. Gilpin, *The War of 1812 in the Old Northwest* (East Lansing, Mich., 1958), and a useful documentary compilation is Ernest A. Cruikshank, ed., *Documents Relating to the Invasion of Canada and the Surrender of Detroit, 1812* (Ottawa, 1913). A defense of Hull is provided in Milo M. Quaife, "General William Hull and His Critics," *Ohio Archaeological and Historical Quarterly*, XLVII (April 1938), 168–182, and Harrison's role is summarized in Beverley W. Bond, Jr., "William Henry Harrison in the War of 1812," *Mississippi Valley Historical Review*, XII (March 1927), 499–516. Harrison's victory at the Thames is described in Bennett H. Young, *The Battle of the Thames* (Louisville, Ky., 1903). Basic to an understanding of the war in the Niagara region is Ernest A. Cruikshank, ed., *Documentary History of the Campaign upon the Niagara Frontier in the Years 1812, 1813, 1814*, 7 vols. (Welland, 1899–1905); a sound narrative account to accompany this is Louis L. Babcock, *The War of 1812 on the Niagara Frontier* (Buffalo Historical Society, "Publications," XXIX; Buffalo, 1927).

Andrew Jackson has of course attracted the most attention on the southern frontier during the war, although there is still room for work on him. James Parton, *Life of Andrew Jackson*, 3 vols. (Boston, 1887) and John S. Bassett, *The*

Life of Andrew Jackson, 2 vols. (New York, 1911) are detailed, and Marquis James, *Andrew Jackson: The Border Captain* (Indianapolis, 1933) is colorful. Jackson's campaigns are dealt with more specifically in Henry S. Halbert and T. H. Ball, *The Creek War of 1813 and 1814* (Chicago, 1895); Eron Rowland, *Andrew Jackson's Campaigns Against the British, or the Mississippi Territory in the War of 1812* (New York, 1926); and Carson I. A. Ritchie, "The Louisiana Campaign," *Louisiana Historical Quarterly*, XLIV (January-April 1961), 13–121, together with the documentary material in *ibid.*, XLIV (July-October 1961), 1–159. Also useful on the New Orleans campaign are Charles B. Brooks, *The Siege of New Orleans* (Seattle, 1961) and Jan Lucas de Grumond, *The Baratarians and the Battle of New Orleans* (Baton Rouge, 1961).

The diplomacy leading to the peace of Ghent can be followed in Bradford Perkins, *Castlereagh and Adams: England and the United States, 1812–1823* (Berkeley and Los Angeles, Calif., 1964), and in Fred L. Engelman, *The Peace of Christmas Eve* (New York, 1962). The role of the West is discussed in Charles M. Gates, "The West in American Diplomacy, 1812–1815," *Mississippi Valley Historical Review*, XXVI (March 1940), 499–510.

INDEX

231